Voices

Behind 2 Prison Walls

"The truth, the whole truth, and nothing but the truth, so help me God."

Annie C. Woodcock

Wagtail

First Published in 2024 by Annie Woodcock with Russell-Alexander Publishing Ltd

Cover Design by Donna Laverty

Copyright © Annie Woodcock 2024

Annie Woodcock has asserted her right to be identified as the Author of this Work in accordance with the Copyright, Designs and Patent Act 1988 and Intellectual Property (Copyright and Related Rights) (EU Exit) (Amendment etc) Regulations 2019.

All rights reserved. No part of this book may be reproduced, copied, distributed, or adapted by any means, except as permitted by UK copyright law or the author. For licensing requests, please contact the publisher. The case studies shared in this book are factual, however, some names and identifying details have been changed to protect the privacy of the families involved.

ISBN: 9798345973400

Contents

Foreword 6
Dedication 10
A Word from the Author 11
Introduction 15
The Wagtail 27
Chapter 1 29
   Michael 29
Chapter 2 49
   " Do the crime; do the time" 49
Chapter 3 59
   Searching for my tribe 59
Chapter 4 75
   Jurassic Beauty 75
Chapter 5 83
   Tick Tock Tick Tock 83
Chapter 6 101
   Banged Up 101
Chapter 7 107
   Main Street 107
Chapter 8 137
   21st Century Porridge 137

Chapter 9 159
  Mr and Mrs Barrowclough 159

Chapter 10 171
  Chaplaincy 171

Chapter 11 219
  A house in not a home 219

Chapter 12 229
  Oops, I did it again 229

Chapter 13 253
  "Tails" of the Riverbank 253

Chapter 14 265
  Bromide 265

Chapter 15 283
  And Then Came COVID 283

Chapter 16 293
  Friends 293

Chapter 17 305
  Lord of the Flies 305

Chapter 18 315
  Family 315

Chapter 19 331
  Somebody's Baby 331

Chapter 21	349
Prison number P:1412131513	349
Chapter 22	353
Prison number P18381421	353
Chapter 23	357
Prison number P147234	357
Chapter 24	361
The Hardest Word	361
Chapter 25	379
Lizzie	379
Chapter 26	395
"Go free, little Wagtail"	395
Chapter 27	401
The Final Chapter	401
Biblical References	405
Bibliography	407
Useful Organisations	409
Acknowledgements	411
About the Author	415

Foreword

I first met Annie in the winter of 2015 after she had attracted the attention of a director I was working with on a documentary series for the BBC. He said he had met this amazing female vicar whose life would make a brilliant documentary and I should meet her. I was intrigued. By the time I had finished a lengthy telephone conversation with Annie, I knew he was right. When I later met Annie face to face, I was struck by her natural warmth, sense of humour and genuine compassion. Blessed with a wonderful exuberance, she was able to converse about faith in a way that gave it relevance to people's lives, whether they were religious or not. She spoke from the heart and I could see how her love and care touched people deep within.

Sadly, a documentary with Annie was not to be despite several BBC commissioning editors falling in love with her - one had even compared Annie with Sarah Lancashire's no nonsense but big-hearted TV police detective character, Catherine, in Happy Valley.

I kept in touch with Annie, always hoping that there would be some way to bring her to the television screen or radio, knowing that she could inspire so many with her wise and insightful words of support and hope. She would regularly relay her latest adventures at St Mary's Church, Hyde, and tell me about all the wonderful new people who were now attending her church. But I could sense Annie felt a calling to extend her help beyond the church walls to those deeply in need of some guidance.

One day, she emailed to say that she had just applied for the role of prison chaplain at one of the largest prisons in Northwest England. After being accepted and after some months, she would share little snippets about her new role. I again hoped to bring Annie and her work to the screen and we discussed so many ideas, but it just never seemed the right time. Sometime later, Annie advised me that she was thinking of writing a book. I immediately realised this was her chance to share her story and bring her heart-felt messages to a wider audience.

I am so pleased that Annie finally put pen to paper and relayed her many experiences during her time as prison chaplain as well as her own life journey. Her voice and caring heart shine through this book as she presents an unflinching portrayal of life inside one of Britain's toughest prisons. In amongst all the gritty sights, sounds and smells that both prisoners and staff have to endure, Annie reveals the steep learning curve she encountered as she adapted to the rigorous protocols and a very different congregation. Throughout the book, Annie's wonderful candidness and Northern humour come to the fore as she takes us on a very personal rollercoaster journey to make a difference to all those she meets.

What comes across so strongly in Annie's book is how a little human kindness goes a very long way. Many of us will never have experienced prison life nor the circumstances that led there. We cannot conceive the way in which challenges - often beginning in childhood - can distort our view of the world. When you've been abused or abandoned as a child, left to fend for yourself at a young age, or simply associated with the wrong crowd, it's all too easy to stray off society's socially acceptable pathways. When we have never been made to feel safe, loved or understood, it is understandable that we lose trust in the world around us, life in general and in ourselves. In order to survive, crime can often seem the only way.

Annie is one of those rare souls in life who sees beyond the facades, the wrongs and the crimes and attempts to see the underlying goodness in all. It's not easy, as Annie confesses, but she never gives up trying. As Annie states in her book: "We are all in this together."

Julie Davies

November 2024

Dedication

This book is lovingly dedicated to my son.

A Word from the Author

Prison is a brutal and dark abyss. It is dehumanising. The environment, the steel, the concrete, and the grime are oppressive. The vulgar, acrid smells offend all your olfactory senses. There is never a moment of quiet due to the constant repetitive banging and slamming of gates, jangling of keys and the troubling noises. The sight of downcast battered hearts and bodies, many of whom have just given up on themselves can disturb the soul of the most hardened individual. Although there were some chinks of light, this bottomless pit of sadness, trauma and brokenness had a profound effect on me, the staff and the prisoners I met.

I started working as a prison chaplain shortly after visiting a congregation member who was "doing time." My experiences and what I witnessed are my reasons to put pen to paper. It's been some time since I worked at the prison. I know there have been concerted efforts to bring about change but, overall, the system remains unchanged.

And so, here it is. I offer you, the reader, this memoir and true story. I have written this book to make a difference, however small. There may be some backlash but, like it or not, this is the truth, and the truth can really hurt. It may hold you in disbelief, but I can assure you that this is an accurate account. Throughout the book, I use stories from my life - not to compare myself to anyone, but to explain my formative years and experiences, many of which could have had a different outcome. When I consider nature versus nurture and the damage caused by prejudice and ignorance, I realise that the only person we should ever judge is the one we see in the mirror. I used to judge people; I think a small part of me still does but we all err to be human, don't we? However, my life experiences have changed me, and for the better, I hope.

Those of us who worked in the prison were told to refer to prisoners as residents. In this book, I will refer to them as prisoners. I believe that using the word "resident" distorts and minimises the context and gravity of prison life.

Before we step through the prison gates, please note that, with the exception of those who granted permission to use their real names, I have altered or abbreviated the names of the men to protect their identities. The stories that follow are genuine, accurate accounts of actual events. I've also included excerpts from letters and notes written by the prisoners themselves.

The prison was a humbling place to work, a place where I was trusted with the hearts and souls of so many. I have written this book not only for them - to tell their story - but also for you, the reader, to give you an insight and a limited understanding of life within the prison walls. However, in reality, none of us will ever fully understand unless we find ourselves in that same situation.

So, within the safety of these pages, I invite you to put on some dirty boots and walk alongside me, the staff, and the prisoners for a while. Thank you.

Rev Annie

Wagtail

Introduction

We are <u>ALL</u> capable of murder, be it premeditated or an act of passion. The likelihood is that we won't but, in reality, the probability may be out of our control.

The taking of a life is catastrophic for all those concerned; the deceased, their family and friends, the perpetrator and those who know the parties involved. It may be the outcome of a terrible accident, as part of another criminal act, or as an act of jealousy-fuelled vengeance. Whatever the reason, none of us is infallible. We could be caught up in a pub brawl or take a wrong turn. We could decide to set a trap, draw up a plan to take the life of someone who, in a single millisecond, has caused us so much pain that our innate instinct is to lash out. We have all been blessed with free will and how we use it, how we manage our reactions, is down to us and the power of self-control. Or is it? Let me illustrate this with a confession, not a murder but a much lesser offence.

In the mid-70s, probably around the tender age of twelve or thirteen, I was a plain, skinny, insecure, pubescent teenager. I had, and still have, a best friend, Jane. She lives in Australia now. Thankfully, she and her family were not deported to the Antipodes but emigrated, probably not long after the event I am going to share with you.

Jane and I were regular girls from good families. We went to church on Sundays and played outdoors for hours on end after school and at weekends. I was in love with Donny Osmond and with all the band members of the famous Scottish band "The Bay City Rollers." I was raised and nurtured in a law-abiding home, and I wasn't aware of any obvious crime, apart from Dad brewing his beer in glass demijohns which he stored in the shoe cupboard at the top of the stairs. Secretly, when Mum wasn't watching, he allowed us to syphon off the fermenting liquid into bottles. Using a rubber tube, we were allowed to suck up the beer and get a quick taste before we held the tube over a bottle neck. It was our Friday night treat! As we grew older, school holidays became painfully boring. Our time together needed some pizazz. We were a bit geeky and lanky (sorry, my dear friend, but we were). Boys (the usual pastime of teenage girls) showed little interest, despite our efforts.

And so, to another school holiday. It must have been quite cold because I remember distinctly adorning my 1970s, must-have Navy-Blue Parka with orange lining and faux fur hood. We were bored, with nothing to do; we had trawled through all the rude bits in Jackie Collins' novels and we had outgrown summer play schemes, so we had to "use our imaginations." We plotted and schemed and, like Ocean's Seven, we decided to orchestrate a shoplifting trip! This was not an out-of-the-blue or random choice; we knew exactly what we were doing. We longed to be like the girls from school who were already wearing make-up and seemed so mature (not the good girls, I might add)!

We had decided on the articles of our desire and so our day of petty crime began. At 10:00 hours, we took the bus to our local shopping town. Eyes darting, yet inconspicuous under the hoods of our Parkas, we made a beeline for the nearest cosmetics shop. We walked into a little makeup and accessory shop and, while Jane perused the Mary Quant eyeshadows, I hovered over the eyeliners. The bargain make-up was conveniently displayed in rows of clear, plastic, hand-height boxes. Jane browsed inconspicuously on the opposite side of the shop. She raised her eyebrows at me and, when the young shop assistant glanced away, I reached into a clear plastic box and grabbed two eyeliners, swiftly slipping them up the sleeve of my Parka.

Wagtail

With sweaty brows and false smiles, we left the shop. Then, faster than our usual cross-country efforts, we ran through the market, past the open fruit and veg stalls and eventually found a place of safety to inspect our ill-gotten gains. We sat on a cold brick wall, skinny legs swinging, and gazed upon our two dark brown eyeliners. We had one each and we were ecstatic. We had done it and we had gotten away with it. The high from our successful mission left us thrilled, elated, and fuelled with adrenaline.

When I asked my dear friend's permission to name her in this confession, she added to the story, as follows. That very same day, in celebration of our victory, we also stole a bottle of beer off the back of a delivery truck and drank it on the top deck of the Number 219 bus home.

I hid my eyeliner, my treasure; it never saw the light of day, let alone adorned my eyes! How could it? What would my Mum and Dad, Mary and George, do if they found out? I moved it around my room, hiding it in different places away from Mum's rooting-tooting hot spots. I have no idea what became of it, except to say that the mental imprint from the said brown eyeliner has followed me around since that day! Every time I peer into my hessian make-up tray, there it is, hidden amongst my No 7 and Revlon. Every brown eyeliner I buy (yes, I'm still wearing the same) is a small but dark reminder of that past misdemeanour; one I will never forget! I never shoplifted again. I felt tremendous guilt and, although I have forgiven my teenage self (then known as Anne Caroline), the memory stays with me.

So, what triggered me to intentionally set out, with my friend, on a shoplifting trip? Was it nature, nurture, or just teenage tomfoolery? Whatever the deep-seated reason, it was a crime - no ifs, no buts, no excuses! I wanted to be like the other girls at school but, whatever my reason, the item wasn't mine to take. Having had forty-five years to psychoanalyse myself, my leaning is to a dare of "nature" but, nonetheless, it was still wrong and risky.

Nature versus nurture is the topic of a long-standing philosophical debate. Nature is the influence of our genes in terms of our appearance and our personalities. Nurture, however, explains who we are in terms of the impact of our life experiences – our environment and how we are cared for and provided for. It influences how we form and navigate relationships, cope in all situations, and learn to deal with pain, conflict, and joy.

Wagtail

So, what does nurture say in this instance? Well, it tells me that I knew what I was doing was wrong. If my Mum and Dad had caught me, I would have been named, shamed and probably made to go back and pay for the stolen item. I would have been threatened with the Police and a potential stint in Borstal (a renowned youth offenders' prison). I would have been punished, banned from seeing my dear friend again and not allowed out of my parents' sight. Nature, however, tells me that I was high on the excitement, thrilled by the risk and the proud possession of stolen makeup.

There was little or no CCTV in the 1970s, or at least none that we were aware of. We thought it was so funny at the time. We were like the other girls at school now. We had eyeliners, even if they were stuffed under our mattresses! We didn't get caught; we were triumphant.

Fast forward another twenty years. My son, when he was about ten years old, was found in possession of a stolen, top-shelf magazine by his father, who marched him back to the shop and made him confess and apologise. I was so embarrassed. I couldn't decide if I was more disturbed that my precious child, who I thought I had nurtured so perfectly, had stolen this magazine, or if I was more distraught that he was browsing pictures of naked women's bits and the images he might have seen. It was quite upsetting that my naive young boy was growing up and becoming inquisitive. I was sad that I was losing my baby to a lude world of easily available pornography and disturbing images - my precious boy!

Some years later, I was hauled into the office of Manchester's Transport Police. Humbly seated with my head bowed, I had to apologise for my, then, pubescent son spitting on a railway station platform and refusing to clean it up at the request of a very patient Transport Officer. I was mortified. These were minor misdemeanours in terms of the bigger picture of criminal offences, but they weren't to me or his father!

To be clear, I'm not sharing these stories to be frivolous about, or applaud, criminal activity nor am I minimising the pain that crime inflicts on people and on society as a whole. Every day, lives are devastated by injury, loss and death. My youthful mistakes have long been forgotten, or rather were never discovered and, for me, that's where my life of crime ended. However, for some, such minor misdemeanours may be how a life of crime begins.

Wagtail

So, imagine, if you will, that Anne Caroline had been born into a different family; a bit of a novelty at first, a new addition to the family, and an accomplishment for somewhat under-achieving parents. However, a baby can soon become an unwanted addition, an inconvenience, a target for a jealous parent, a financial burden and an irritation. Imagine if I had been born into a culture of crime, dishonesty, violence, deception and abuse. My story may have had a very different outcome. I may well have been dragged back to the shop if I'd been found out. But what if? What if, in a much different family environment, I had failed to bring home the goods? What if I hadn't fulfilled my quota? What if I had been caught on camera? This book is heavy with stories of men whose lives are permeated with the "what ifs."

"Miss, I'm innocent. I've done nothing wrong."

"Miss, I'm guilty."

"I'm sorry, Miss, but I couldn't care less!"

What is the truth? Couldn't care less, or simply incapable of taking responsibility? The lines between guilt and indifference seemed blurred, leaving only questions.

This book is full of life, some fun and joy but mostly devastation, pain, anger, horror, indignant behaviour, violence and complete loss of dignity. It is not for the faint-hearted or the judgmental.

I have never been the victim of a serious crime, apart from an incident that happened a long time ago which I will share with you later. I don't truly understand the pain suffered by victims of serious crime – no-one can unless they have first-hand experience of it. However, as a caring human, I do empathise with those who have experienced this, and in no way want to minimise the impact of serious crime upon their lives.

I am a woman of faith, and I make no excuses for referring to my faith to underpin my narrative. I use some literature, some evidence, and some theory to strengthen my writing. This book contains some explicit descriptions and foul language – albeit partly redacted; it is not used gratuitously but as part of the reality of prison life. I would ask those who are shocked by swear words to reflect on the following story.

There was once a priest who, week after week, stood in front of his sleepy congregation. He preached tirelessly, Sunday after Sunday, about loving thy neighbour, taking in the stranger, feeding the poor and living a good, visible, faithful life. One week, looking out at his disinterested congregation, he said "Shit." The "meerkats" within the congregation stood to attention, heads swiftly moving from side to side and looking at each other in horror. Muttering, people walked out of the church in disgust.

The moral of this story is that week after week, this priest had tried to gain the attention of his flock by telling them that people were literally dying on their doorstep, not from starvation (well, some were) but dying spiritually; they were broken and lonely. The congregation had listened but no one heard his message until he said, "Shit." Instead of recognising that their priest was trying to wake them up to the plight of their fellow man, they chose to judge him for his choice of words in church. Their indignance took precedence over the meaning of the priest's message - that the world and the people in it were fractured and in pain, and that everyone had a responsibility to bring about change.

This is my first book, and in it, I write as I speak. I want to share and express my love of humanity, especially the young and broken. However, if the reader has a predisposition that all criminals should be locked up and the key thrown away, then come with me, and maybe, just maybe, I can help you understand, empathise, and look beyond the sinner to the sin. Can you go back to default in your bias and take some time to explore with me the people and stories behind the crime, whether committed by intention or accident, and consider that we are all, by omission or intent, capable of MURDER?

Wagtail

The Wagtail

The Wagtail is a common, pretty little bird; its scientific name is Motacilla alba.

It is tiny and fragile, black and white, and its name describes exactly what you see; a furiously fast, tail-pumping, frantic little bird.

It hovers over water and flies across gravel roads into concrete high rise buildings in search of sustenance, often bringing beauty to dark, grey, dry and hidden terrain.

Wagtail

The significance of the Wagtail in this book? Well, it brought life and beauty to a place where there seemed to be no hope. It was a symbol of freedom from beyond the prison walls and, although it had liberty and could choose to come and go, it chose to stay a while in the place we call "prison."

Chapter 1
Michael

"Greater love hath no man than this, that a man lay down his life for his friends."
John 15:13; King James Bible

Michael - "A bit of a pain," they said. "Not sure what to do with him," they said.

He hadn't committed an arrestable crime; the police were quite fond of him really. They tried to help him and often turned a blind eye. However, he was becoming a drain on police time and resources and was one step away from being locked up. As the kind community constabulary really didn't want that to happen, they asked me, "Can you help him?"

My friend, Michael, lived in a flat behind my church. I had been working alongside the police, local authority, and housing trust in community re-generation and supporting struggling individuals and families. Our brave and ambitious plan was to reduce crime on this inner-city social housing estate, and have less dog poo, less litter, and fewer off-road bikes. We wanted to involve the community and make the estate, that housed my huge four-bedroom detached vicarage with an acre of lawned grass and pristine laurel hedges, a better place to live. My predecessor had done some incredible work with the community, children and young people; we were like-minded and he had paved a path for me to continue with his work. He was trusted and liked, and I had been his curate (junior priest) at the church for two years. I already had a passion and love for the community we served and, when he left for pastures new, I took over as Mrs Vicar.

I spent all my formative years in search of my tribe. Although I had a caring family and a safe and nurturing environment to grow up in, I was still quite a lonely traveller. From an early age, I had a feeling of not quite fitting in. It was no one's fault; it was just the way I was. I so longed to belong - to find that place. The place where we belong isn't always a physical location but a place that lies deep within our souls.

Tribes come in many forms and guises. Many of us long to be part of something. I think I projected my desperation into my career choices. My choice to be a nurse and then a vicar partly expressed my wish to be part of a community, of something bigger than me. As a nurse, I satisfied my need to be needed and a sense of being part of the NHS tribe and then, as a vicar, drawing to the Church those who had or still were perhaps on that lonely pilgrimage. Being a super-empath, I couldn't bear to think that my neighbour, living just a stone's throw away, was lonely and isolated. If you have been in that position, you will have some element of understanding; you recognise the pain.

I had a passion for inclusion and recognised the Church as a place of sanctuary for the lonely and marginalised. I tried to encourage the Church to welcome strangers to be part of the Church family. This wasn't always easy; most of the Church flock preferred not be confronted with the reality of life outside their own bubble, wanted to shut their eyes and concentrate on church politics, finances, and the church roof repairs. The priority for them, although important, was how we were going to raise funds to fix the crumbling façade of the turrets, what colour the walls of the Church Hall should be and why we couldn't continue with the way things had been for the last fifty years or so. We failed to recall the foundations of the basic teachings of the Christian faith. We should entertain strangers, take care of widows, share our goods, and love our neighbours. We had become too comfortable and had closed our eyes and ears to the reality of a hurting world.

Wagtail

The Church should be a place of welcome, but this can be fraught with challenges and Michael, amongst others, certainly was one of those wonderful challenges.

I first met the local police team at a community meeting in a small housing office on the social housing estate where I lived. I worked closely with one very caring, compassionate community officer who was based at the local police station. He asked me if I would consider going with him to visit Michael, a man in the community who was struggling. Our local friendly constabulary repeatedly visited Michael for several minor misdemeanours. I agreed to visit Michael to see if there was any way I could help. So, on a warm summer's morning, we walked together, vicar and cop, to the flats just at the back of the church. These flats had been designed to house people in the community with "difficulties."

Now, I am a very visual person and am a super-scanner of my surroundings. My environment affects my peace, my health, and my mental well-being. I can't tolerate mess or rubbish, and I have an inherent fear of small creatures with long tails. So, as we approached the flats, my scanner was on, and I did a quick assessment for rodents. To my horror, the grounds of the flats were full of rubbish, with black bin liners ripped with teeth marks, evidence that creatures had been chewing at them to get at the leftover food inside. There were dirty nappies that had been washed with the rain, the gel spilling out onto the stumpy, unmown grass. Empty rusty cans of cheap lager, old and broken, faded plastic toys had been discarded for someone else to dispose of, and, of course, there was dog poo. Dandelions had taken root and were flourishing, their little yellow heads tipping toward the sunlight, and, in the distance, the abundant, nourished, ancient trees were swaying gently, far enough away so as not to take root in this place.

The church and its turrets could be seen from where we stood and the church graveyard was visible to those living on the first floor. The church, just a few hundred yards away, should have been a welcome sanctuary but was just an ancient foreboding structure to an uninvited community. Right here was the stark reality of the misery that existed a few hundred yards away from my church. It was not a pleasant environment. A lingering aroma of marijuana hung in the air from the flat above, the waft causing us both to roll our eyes. We hadn't come to look at the building and refuse tip, but it made my heart sink. How can people living with mental health issues and problems with antisocial behaviour ever hope to thrive in this environment? I wanted to don my cleaning gloves and make it better!

We concocted a plan of action with our safety as the priority. However, all heroic plans, positive words and good intentions can be thwarted, and I was not prepared for the broken soul I was about to meet. We knocked on the shoddy paint-peeled door. The letter box was just a hole in the door and there were scuff marks from boots on its plastic veneer. My police colleague shouted several times after his initial greeting was ignored. He peered through the open splintered letter box. Other residents were hanging over the railings above.

"He won't f*****g answer love." We peered up to the floor above. The lady took a long drag from a cigarette, the plumes making clouds above her head. "Oh, sorry love, sorry about the swearing," the dishevelled older woman shouted as she leant over the insecure steel balcony to see what was happening. She caught a glimpse of my white dog collar and felt the need to apologise. "Oh, that's okay, thank you." I replied, flashing a pious "vicar-like" smile.

My colleague shouted again through the door, "Michael, are you in? It's me. I've got someone with me who wants to meet you. Can you come to the door?" A few minutes later, a voice from inside responded, and we were greeted with, "F**k off, I'm watching telly. I don't want to meet anyone. Go away!" Undeterred, we knocked again; well, my colleague did; I wasn't touching the grimy door even with my knuckles. Then we heard a shuffling, tutting, and muttering, the rattling of the door being unlocked and there he stood, my new friend, Michael. The kindly officer announced gently, "This is the Reverend Annie. She would like to meet you. Can we come in?" Without answering, Michael turned on his bare, dirty heels, walked back into his front room, and dropped back down onto the two-seater, faux leather, black couch, which was so small that he had to curl up to fit on it. He covered himself with a cheap nylon, dirty grey, bobbled duvet.

My scanner was on again. My eyes scoured the room, trying not to be obvious as I took a mental inventory. There was a stained mattress on a bed with no sheets, brown rings stained the coverless pillows, and a few dirty clothes were thrown onto the dirty carpet tiles. The air smelled of stale cigarettes and cider. The windows were firmly shut, and grey curtains were unevenly hung on a plastic curtain rail. I trod with caution and followed Michael into the flat.

The need to be in control and obsessive-compulsive disorder often go hand in hand. My past insecurities and need to control my surroundings expressed themselves in a need for cleanliness and order. This was a very positive "thorn" when I was a nurse, when I learned and had to be in control, organised, and work with military precision. Being in control, albeit temporarily, brought me comfort and some element of peace when I found myself experiencing anxious life events. But here, in this place, I felt out of control. Observing the disarray of another person's life and living conditions was really stress-inducing. As I walked into Michael's life, my aseptic nurse brain was racing; strange things often flit through my busy mind. "Stop, stop, stop - that's not why we are here, one step at a time."

I do have an unusual habit that, when a crisis arises, I clean! I remember getting a call from my sister when my dad was critically ill in hospital. I had to get to him and from, what she told me, possibly before he died. I was so anxious and frightened that I started cleaning. I couldn't focus, I couldn't get an overnight bag ready, I couldn't leave my house. I was catatonic with fear and I was losing control. Eventually, I reversed out of my house, hoovering. Of course, this is obsessive-compulsive disorder and a coping mechanism, one that I still have; however, it is now manageable and reasonable.

Casting my keen eye over my present surroundings, I couldn't help looking at Michael's dirty quilt and thinking, "I've got just the thing for you at home; a nice floral duvet," imagining it clean and comforting. I wanted to wash his grey tracksuit bottoms, wash him, feed him, and take care of him. I wanted to don the rubber gloves and clean up, empty the "tinnies," the tin ashtrays full of cigarette dimps, and I mean dimps, smoked right down to the core, the nicotine black at the end of each tip. I wanted to clean his bathroom and kitchen and stock it full of wholesome food!

So, after my clean scan, I looked at him, making judgements and clinical observations (once a nurse...). He continued staring at the TV; then he reached out with his bare foot and pulled the half-empty litre bottle of cider near to him and covered it with the corner of his quilt. He was lonely and it appeared he had no peace. The bottle of cider was dissipation and temporary.

Wagtail

I saw his pain, his sadness and it hurt me too. I was once so lonely and strove in my own strength to fill that space. Not anymore, but I saw in him what once plagued my life: pure and utter loneliness.

We tried to keep the introductions light and friendly. I am sure we can all recall trying to talk to someone who is intoxicated. No matter how pleasant you may think you are, to the person who has addiction problems or even a one-off episode of intoxication, you become an irritating do-gooder. Beneath the patterns of addictive behaviour is a broken soul and we should tread lightly with compassion and empathy.

My shoes were sticking to the carpet. I took a sharp intake of the alcohol and stale tobacco-fumed air as Michael said, "I know what you think. What do you want?" He had read my mind! "I just want to get to know you, Michael, and see if there is anything we can do to help?" I replied. To help! What on earth did I think I could do to help him? What right did I have to intrude on a perfect stranger offering pious words, hoping that he would jump up, have a shower, brush his teeth, empty his ashtrays, and start singing the Hallelujah Chorus? Who did I think I was?

Let me tell you who I was! I was a bit of a rescuer. Not so much now, hard lessons learned; being a rescuer is exhausting. I wanted to rescue him, partly for my own benefit and the need to be needed, but mostly because I hoped that my intervention could maybe pull him from the pain he was evidently suffering. My good intentions were formed from my own life experience. I wanted him to thrive and survive just as I had; I wanted him to be healed and find peace; I wanted his life to somehow mirror my own journey with survival and restoration!

We were probably with Michael for an hour, perched on the smallest space of the settee arm, offering wonderful solutions for what we interpreted as a broken life. After a few moments of awkward and ridiculous nervous chatter, I noticed that he had some army relics and tattered photographs on his wall. At last, a talking point, a way to engage with him. I asked about the fading photos and, finally, he engaged, began to tell us his story.

Michael had joined the army after leaving school. At first, all had been well; he flourished, and the images painted a very different life to the one I saw before me now. A photograph of him in a football kit - Michael was a talented footballer, eventually gaining a scholarship in

America. Before this, he had served with the British Army in The Welsh Guards. He had been in active service in Iraq on Operation Telic. The army, for a while, had been his tribe. He showed me a photograph of himself, tanned, armed and in desert combat trousers. Physically, he didn't look any different except for the look on his face. His expressions today and back then were incomparable.

As he started talking about Iraq, he became animated; he talked a lot and kept wiping his nose with the back of his hand, and then the tears started. His conversation became erratic and confused. He launched quite aggressively and, with pain and hurt, into the story of his service in Iraq. Listening to this young veteran, possibly with Post Traumatic Stress Disorder, incoherent because of alcohol, I recognised that he was wracked with pain.

A fractured recollection is not Storytime; it is cruel and graphic. He recounted in very gory detail the story of his friend "Molly" who was shot in the head while they were seated on the ground while out on patrol. I never really got to hear the whole story in all the time I knew him. All I know is that Michael tripped in and out of the horror of Molly's death. He blamed himself; he had survivor's guilt. Later, I recognised that he sometimes used Molly's death as an excuse for drinking. This memory became a hiding place, a place that he could go to. As painful as it was, this was a place he felt familiar with. It was easier living in pain because coming back from that place was way too hard. Now, I am not a psychiatrist or psychologist; I am not an expert in post-traumatic stress and trauma, but it doesn't take an "ist" to see that in front of me, curled up under the dirty nylon duvet, lay a broken man; a broken man who had, as I later came to understand, struggled before he was in the army. His experience in the army just added to and exacerbated issues that already lay within.

All Michael's issues were important but not to share here. I would like to point out here that he had the most wonderful Mum and two sisters. I eventually met his family. Sometimes, there were funny stories and recollections about "Mikey," but more often, their pain unravelled as I listened to their sadness. They talked of their guilt and hopelessness. They had a lingering fear that he would seriously harm himself. They tried tirelessly to help him. However, sometimes, they had to keep him away from the family because his behaviour was so unpredictable. He couldn't be trusted at family events in case he turned up the worse for wear. He was abusive to those he loved when he was low, but most of the time, he was just absent. His little sister, Lisa, had Down Syndrome, and he adored her. She died quite suddenly, and I believe that the death of this beloved sister was as much as he could take.

All we could do now, and in the many times to come, was listen to him, offer him friendship and company, and sometimes laugh with him, but mostly just be there; and for me, as I got to know him, just to love him as he was, no matter how many times he told me to "do one!"

As time passed, and much to my delight, Michael started coming to church but not always in the best condition. I peered over my glasses, always watching the big, red, looming, wooden doors, hoping he would walk in as I was getting ready for the service. I watched to make sure he was greeted with kindness, and I always prayed that the words I shared would offer him some comfort. Frequently, they would have the opposite effect and he would shout out in the middle of a sermon, "What a load of shit! God doesn't love us! He killed my friend" Unlike some, I embraced these outbursts, much to the horror of some of the congregation, and they caused bottoms in pews to twitch! He made some people feel uncomfortable but, over time, most folks grew to love him and appreciate his frankness.

I loved Michael like a son and, if I'm honest, I probably spent more time with him than I should have. He was someone who fulfilled my then "need to be needed." However, one broken person in a church can drain your time and energy and this can be very difficult to navigate, as I would soon learn. I spent a lot of time consumed with his traumas. I was and still am a super-empath and I feel people's pain. It is not always an asset, and I have since learned to stop being a rescuer. For now, though, Michael had all my attention.

I received a phone call late one evening when I was already in bed. It was the police; they explained that Michael had phoned them saying he was going to take his life, but they couldn't find him. They asked for my help. I have no idea to this day how they got my number; maybe it was in a report from my police colleague. Right now, none of this mattered. Propped up in bed at the vicarage, I phoned his mobile and, eventually, he picked up. I had to talk to him for what seemed like hours and asked him to describe where he was. "Where are you, Michael? Can you tell me what you can see?" Through an incoherent, mumbled voice, he told me he was sitting on a side road and all he could see was a church spire. He told me he wanted to die; he was cold and alone and was in a dark alley. With the police in one ear and Michael in the other, we guessed where he was, and he was eventually found and taken to hospital. By this time, alcohol was destroying his body, his liver was damaged, and he needed medical attention. He had several episodes in the hospital, his health deteriorated, and his family regularly contacted me because they were desperately worried about him. I felt helpless.

Sometimes, when I walked into my churchyard, I would find Michael asleep on the grave of a young war veteran who had been killed in Afghanistan. Other times, he would sit cross-legged at the foot of the grave just talking about Molly and crying. It was so painful to watch. He told me on many occasions that he couldn't stand the torment of life and just wanted to go to be with his friend.

Over the years, Michael had lots of help with his addiction and mental health problems. There would be periods of respite, and we all had great hope that life would get better for him. On one occasion, I caught up with his Mum, who told me that he had gone to London to get some help. He had journeyed across the UK from one charitable organisation to another. I happened to be going to London on a retreat soon after and, as crazy and unwise as it sounds, I was determined to find him.

I arrived at the charity his Mum had told me about. They had been trying to help Michael and they told me that all had started well but then he had been banned from the building for drinking and being abusive. I still wanted to find him. I asked where they thought he might be, and they pointed across the road in the direction of a large city store. So, I grabbed a couple of sandwiches and drinks from a nearby shop and I walked over.

As I approached the door, there he was, with his new friends and several litre bottles of cheap cider. They were laughing and finding comfort in their commonalities. They were comrades and Michael looked happy to be with them. He was incoherent, dirty, and sitting in a nylon sleeping bag. I looked at him and, at first, I think he was confused and thought he was hallucinating. He looked at me with glazed eyes. Then, with a stark turn, he jolted up. "Annie, is that you? What are you doing here?" I leaned in and said, "I've come to find you, Michael." The image of a smiling Mrs Vicar hovering in front of him shocked him, like a little rabbit in the headlights. His cheeky grin and genuine smile were beautiful. We spent the day in the park. It was sunny. We sat on prickly grass and ate sandwiches. We talked and laughed, and then I had to leave him. I wasn't sure when I would see him again. I told him I would tell his Mum that I had seen him, and I left.

A few months passed, and I heard Michael was back in Manchester, in prison. I can't even remember how I found out; all I could think was "Prison; thank goodness he's alive!" At least I knew he was off the streets of London; he would be warm, clean, and maybe have a duvet cover. I went to visit him and found a clean-shaven, chunky young man, smiling, cracking Michael jokes and very apologetic for me having to come to visit him in prison. He was obviously enjoying Her Majesty's food and some warmth. He was off the beer. Little did he know that his spell at "Her Majesty's" would later change the direction of my life.

Michael went through many ups and downs after his spell in the Nick. He was, for a time, very happy after meeting a lovely woman in rehab. During that time, life was good; he had two dogs, a loving relationship and he reconnected with his family. I didn't hear from Michael for a while which I took as a good sign. As far as I knew, he had finally found love and had settled down, until I started receiving incoherent phone messages and abusive texts. He was back, angry and in pain, and I was the object of his anger. I had no choice but to ignore his calls and just pray he would get back up again. This never happened; he withdrew, became reclusive, and his health deteriorated. He had separated from his partner.

Then came the phone call; his brave Mum delivered the news. Michael had died alone in his flat. He had gone. It was over, no more pain in life but peace in death. His family was devastated. His younger sister had died and now Michael was gone. His Mum is one of the bravest, most dignified women I have ever met, and her courage gave me hope. She loved and lost her daughter and then her son. Although they were estranged, she prayed for and thought about Michael every day; she never gave up hope. She has become a dear friend.

This chain of events paved the way for me to write this book. If it hadn't been for Michael, I wouldn't have visited the prison; I wouldn't have walked down the grey, cold, stale and disinfectant-smelling corridors. I would have never been told about an opportunity that was coming up for a post as Resettlement Chaplain. This was to be my place of work for the next four years.

Wagtail

Because of Michael, because of his pain and suffering, because of our friendship and because of the privilege of sharing part of his time on this earth, I was prompted and led to work in the prison where he once rested his head.

Thank you, my dear friend.

Stand firm and rest in peace, Michael Lee Chapman.

10.03.1984-26.02.2020

Chapter 2
" Do the crime; do the time"

"I have walked that long road to freedom. I have tried not to falter; I have made missteps along the way."
Nelson Mandela: Long Walk to Freedom

Most of society is satisfied when a criminal has been caught, tried, and sentenced, locked up and, as we often hear, "the key thrown away." I doubt many of us understand who is in prison and what happens to them once they are incarcerated, apart from those who make the headlines. Few of us ever think about them again unless, of course, we are the unfortunate victim, or if we have been dramatically and deeply affected by offences that have had a negative impact on our lives. I don't minimise or dismiss the enormity of the price we pay when harm has been done to us or to those we care about.

After his imprisonment Nelson Mandela wrote:

"It is said that no-one knows a nation until one has been inside its jails. A nation should not be judged by how it treats its highest citizens, but its lowest ones." The Nelson Mandela Rules: The United Nations Standard Minimum Rules for the Treatment of Prisoners 2015.

If this is the case, our nation has a long way to go in recognising that, despite paying our taxes to keep prisoners behind bars, and in order to rehabilitate offenders, we are certainly not getting our money's worth.

Of course, dangerous offenders should be in prison. The truth is that many of them don't remain in prison, and they reoffend again and again. We continue to fail them and ourselves because prisons are overflowing. Where and when can we find the time to work with repeat and serious offenders to rehabilitate them? Prisons also hold men and women who are on remand, many of whom will be acquitted. Prisons are packed to the rafters and the situation is out of control.

I come from a small town in Greater Manchester with a gruesome history of heinous crime. There was Harold Shipman, a prolific and systematic murderer. He was renowned for administering lethal doses of morphine to vulnerable elderly patients. In the 1960s, the Moors Murderers, Myra Hindley and Ian Brady, both came from a local housing estate. More recently, Dale Cregan assassinated two young female police officers - shot and killed in the line of duty. I did not know these people; I have only seen images on television or read their stories online or in books. I did, however, distantly experience the impact of Harold Shipman's legacy. I had previously worked for a General Practitioner as a Practice Nurse in a GP surgery on the outskirts of Manchester. She had raised her concerns about the plethora of Shipman's death certificates.

I worked with a local funeral director who had also alerted the authorities about Dr Shipman. Some of his victims were laid to rest in the churchyard of St Mary's Church where I served as Curate and then Vicar. Prior to my arrival and under Ecclesiastical direction, some of these bodies had to be exhumed for further forensic examination and then reburied. Their graves stand as a reminder of the lasting pain and ruin that crime can have on a community.

At the time, and still today, the community was in disbelief. Not Dr Shipman! Surely not, no, never, never, never! Some of his patients talked about his kind nature and wonderful bedside manner as if he were God himself. I have also heard from families about the pain they experienced losing a loved one to Shipman's sadistic behaviour. Relatives of Shipman's victims were members of my church. The guilty and the harmed, the legacy of Shipman sadly continues to keep the community on the map. I doubt Hyde would have been on anybody's radar had it not been for these awful events.

Every day, we turn on the news and see the headlines: Murder, rape, destruction, terrorism... But just imagine for a moment if there was no criminal fraternity. If that were the case, we can assume there would be little or no headline news. There would only be good news channels and I really wonder how many of us would switch on the TV to watch good news. Crime and human pain make for interesting headlines; they sell newspapers, encourage people to go online, make money, cost money, and help form judicial policy. Crime costs; it wrecks society, makes us ultra-cautious, wary, and mistrusting, and, sometimes, causes us to live in fear. We install CCTV, alarms, doorbells that speak to intruders and so on. We are fearful that someone might break into our homes or, worse still, harm us or our loved ones.

I would suggest that some of us have a morbid fascination with crime. We want to know what happened and see the faces and names of the guilty; we cheer and jeer when people are caught and accused. There are vigilantes who take the punishment of the perpetrators of crime, such as offences against children, into their own hands. Also, many a successful acting career has flourished from films and dramas based on true crime.

Humanity has suffered the effects of crime as far back as history stretches. There are thousands upon thousands of historical accounts of murder, greed, theft, possession, and the need for control since "news" began. There is genocide, tribal crime, and atrocities between different cultures, countries, and nations. The very first crime committed in the Bible was murder. A man murdered his brother because of jealousy; a King murdered the husband of his heart's desire so he could then marry his wife, and there's more!

We often breathe a sigh of relief when the judicial system steps in to determine the future of those who break the law. Yet, the law itself is far from simple. It's rarely just a matter of guilty or not guilty. In the courtroom, barristers draw upon precedents - previous crimes that serve as guides - while individuals are often judged on points of law. These points reflect past situations and their outcomes. The history of crime, in turn, plays a key role in determining the length of a sentence. A jury must decide, beyond reasonable doubt, that the accused person is guilty. Who on earth decided that a group of lay people could make that decision? I have never quite fathomed this. Also, why do people who rob banks often get longer sentences than those who are found guilty of a sexual offence? I have so many pressing questions.

The final decision is made and we are satisfied when the gates open, the guilty are stripped of all dignity and the gates locked behind them. Out of sight, out of mind. Very few of us give the slightest consideration to what happens to that person, the guilty one. Very few recognise that most of the people (not all) were born into a prison; into a life of misery and torment, a life where there is little or no discipline, no love, no hope, and no way out!

In all honesty, I was with the "throw away the key" brigade. I didn't want dangerous psychopaths wandering the streets where I lived. I wanted them to pay for the decisions they had made. Throw away the key, out of sight, out of mind and leave them to receive their due punishment. I was ignorant of the possibility of another way, a way of compassionate justice and reparation. It takes tremendous empathy and compassion to look beyond the sin to the sinner. I have experienced this difficult journey and transformation. Why and how should we even consider the perpetrator, especially when they have caused harm?

Back in 1965, a lady called Phoebe Willets, a godly woman, married to a Vicar, was arrested for participating in the campaign for nuclear disarmament. She experienced a stretch in Holloway women's prison, and wrote:

"We have to decide if the prisoner is someone to be punished and get out of the way because he or she has offended us, or if each prisoner is a personality important in himself or herself or whom it is our responsibility to offer the most favourable conditions for reform." Phoebe Willetts: Invisible Bars: 1965

Almost sixty years later, we are still battling with the concept of reform.

Prisoners' lives are often chaotic; they are the product of abusive family lives and have witnessed violence and crime from their early years. Many will have struggled with education and will have behavioural problems and mental health issues. Newly released statistics from the Prison Reform Trust give a reflection of the extent of this problem:

"Nearly two in five prisoners (39%), said they had been diagnosed with depression, 29% had been diagnosed with anxiety/panic disorders and 11% with Post Traumatic Stress Disorder." Bromley Briefings Prisons Fact file: 2024

The most common presentations are anxiety and depression, personality disorders and psychosis. Only 10% were found to be receiving help whilst in custody.

Many of the men I met had addiction issues and an inability to form positive relationships or hold down jobs. As young people, both men and women were a drain on the social care system and were often passed from pillar to post. They were given a life sentence from the time of their conception. Of course, this is not always the case. I met lots of prisoners who had simply made silly mistakes; speeding tickets, unpaid fines, tax evasion, returning to a girlfriend's house (mostly invited) when an injunction was in place, to name but a few. Is prison really the most suitable place for those who make a one-off poor choice? Is prison the best environment for people with severe learning disabilities and for those with mental ill health?

Where is the compassion? Most of the prisoners I met had difficult and sad lives. They often had absent fathers or, if fathers were present, they were not ideal role models, often far from it. A large proportion of the prisoners had never experienced loving discipline, only the negative abuse of power. From my experience, there is usually, but not always, the love of a mother who is often struggling to bring up children alone, in poverty and chaos. There were parents with addictions, parents who used their children for financial gain through exploitation, sometimes sexual, sometimes as drug mules, sometimes because life had never shown any other options but that of crime. To protect themselves, the prisoners build fortresses to protect their hearts. They have been in survival mode since they were children. In prison, this is triggered and unleashed, by the power and punishment of the judicial system. They are being admonished again by another authoritarian.

And so, it begins...

Wagtail

Chapter 3
Searching for my tribe
"Alone we can do so little; together we can do so much."
Helen Keller

From the age of 17 years and 9 months, I have been a nurse. School years left no rosy memories for me. My Mum had high hopes of me getting into grammar school, but I failed her, and she was disappointed. Back in the 70s, career options for girls were within a limited sphere. We could be a secretary, a hairdresser or maybe even a nurse!

I couldn't wait and, after leaving school with only three GCSEs (O Levels in the 1970s), I applied to take a pre-nursing course at college. I changed stale flower water, gave out tea and Horlicks, talked to patients, and lovingly admired the nurses in their smart uniforms and starched caps. After a year, I had two Advanced Subsidiarys (AS levels), and I was ready at 17 years and 9 months to enrol as a Cadet Nurse.

Earlier that year, my parents had told me that they were thinking about moving to the South of England as my dad had been offered a good job there. I didn't think it would ever really come to fruition, but it did. Although I craved independence, I felt a foreboding fear of abandonment. I wanted to forge a career as a nurse, yet I felt pain at the thought of my family moving away. As a teenager, as much as I loved them, my parents drove me mad, (not unusual, I suspect). I thought I was mature enough to live independently but I wasn't ready. Although on the outside I appeared strong and vivacious (Mum's words), inside I was hurting and lonely. I hoped, maybe subconsciously, that being a nurse and being needed would heal some of the brokenness. It did to a degree and nursing was formative, but it was also a very hard career to follow, especially for a vulnerable 17-year-old who didn't really like herself and had a very poor self-image.

My family moved to the South of England in November 1980; they did try to persuade me to go with them, but I had made up my mind to become a nurse.

In October 1980, I started work and nursing was now my vocation. I couldn't wait to put on that recognisable National Health Service green uniform for the Manchester Royal Eye Hospital. Two years later, when I was training as a then State Registered Nurse, I proudly wore the recognisable pale blue check. I was fastidious about the folds in my cap and adored my swirling red cape. I was a good nurse; caring for people was second nature. Nursing was in my blood, and I enjoyed many wonderful years in the profession. Albeit a wonderful profession, and as much as I adored being a nurse, I was initially still the same hurting girl inside. As much as I felt needed by the patients, and as much as I poured my very soul into my work, it didn't heal my heart. When you are in a profession that demands so much, there isn't time to dwell on your own feelings. You are taught to carry on regardless; you can't cry or show emotion unless you take yourself off to the sluice and sit amongst the bedpans to shed your tears. You see things, sometimes horrible, gruesome things that most people never encounter. These experiences can harden you on the outside, but inside they exacerbate hidden fears and pain.

I remember seeing my first dead body. My only previous experience of death was when my uncle died. I certainly didn't see him after he had died. We didn't attend the funeral as was commonplace for children then. My uncle was a formidable character; he had a large moustache and had been a keen rugby player. I didn't know him very well, but I remember watching him sitting in his armchair and being quite in awe of him.

Wagtail

The pale-yellow phone on the sideboard rang one day. My Dad picked it up and then passed the phone to my Mum. She listened, quietly spoke a few words, and then walked out of the room. All I heard from Dad was that Mum was upset because my uncle had died. That was it, no more conversation, no visible tears and his death was never mentioned again. I didn't quite understand what was happening, only that we had to behave because Mum was sad.

I can picture the ward that I worked on at the Eye Hospital. The washed-out, faded floral curtains drawn around the bed were a sign to staff and patients that someone had passed away. There was a hush that came with death; as an act of respect, patients whispered about what was happening. Death wasn't common in the Eye Hospital. Patients were admitted for cataract operations or ophthalmic emergency care and were expected to be safely discharged home. However, here I was a few weeks into my training, looking on at the rare occasion, the end of someone's life.

The Sister in charge was formidable and feared yet I had a deep respect for her. I wanted to be like her one day. Although this was over 50 years ago, the memory stays with me as she pulled back the curtains and asked with a broken Chinese accent, "Have you ever seen a dead body?" The Sister had a beautiful, starched white cap and navy-blue uniform with a silver buckled belt around her waist. She asked me to help her. I breathed deeply as we slipped sideways through the curtain. She pulled down the white starched sheets that covered the elderly woman. We removed the pillow wedged under her chin to keep her mouth closed and her head flopped back on the bed. Sister systematically guided me through the process of preparing a body after death. The naked, elderly, wax-faced woman lay before me; I didn't know anything about her, her family, what she had achieved in life, or what her experience of life had been. We talked to her while we washed her body, which I found most unnerving. We put her false teeth back in her gaping mouth, tied her toes together with a bandage, put a label on her toes and wrapped her in a shroud. Then a label with her name and date of birth was placed on her chest.

This was my first encounter with death and a lifeless naked body. The Sister taught me and, in the hush of my first encounter with death, she was kind to me, and I learned about respect for human beings in life and in death.

Wagtail

After the deceased had been taken to the Mortuary in a steel box, we washed down the bed, flipped the plastic-covered mattress, and made it up with crisp white starched sheets. The patient's death and my feelings were never discussed.

At the end of the day, I just wanted to run home and cry with my Mum, but I couldn't because they had gone too. I sat alone in my little room in the nurse's home, with its linoleum floor and pastel-flowered wallpaper and I cried. I was so alone and trying to deal with this sad event. My young nurse colleagues drifted in one by one and sat on my single bed, which was covered with a starched, pale green, hospital counterpane. They asked about my experience with gruesome youthful interest, but none of them could console my first encounter with the fragility of life mixed with the pain of loss and feelings of abandonment. I was left to deal with it. After all, as Mum would say, "things will always get better."

Now, my life as a nurse wasn't all about loss and sadness. We had a fabulous time in nurse training and, as our tribe formed, we developed lifelong friendships. The Social Club was our go-to place three to four nights a week. There were young men there who kept our attention, courted many of us and then, when a new intake of nurses arrived, tossed us aside. There were traumas, tears, and tantrums. There were parties, late nights out to Manchester clubs and way too much alcohol consumed. At the time, it was great fun and quite the norm for a cohort of 17-year-old nurses. After working as an eye nurse, I started training for my General Nursing qualification. Another social club, more parties, more tears, and more dramas. I look back with amusement at the scrapes we got into.

Eventually, I qualified as a Registered General Nurse; Staff Nurse Woodcock, proudly donning my silver nurse's buckle around my then-tiny waist! For a while, I worked in a hospital on an arterial surgery ward, then in orthopaedics. I also worked in a GP Practice and then in Accident and Emergency. Then, I bravely moved to America and worked as a Registered Nurse in Los Angeles, California. At first, the novelty of Venice Beach and living in "La La Land" was great. However, after some time, I realised that no matter where you go, you have to take yourself with you and this escape did nothing but exacerbate my lonely heart.

I returned to nursing in the UK after 18 months in America.

Wagtail

Over the subsequent decades, I noticed a tangible shift in the presentation of patients in A&E departments and in hospitals generally. Ill health, particularly mental ill health, was escalating at an alarming rate. My last permanent nursing post was in 2010 in a very busy inner-city Primary Care Centre. People could walk in without an appointment. Patients were triaged and would present with anything from minor wounds, infections, rashes, minor injuries, the need for emergency contraception, to chest pain. My experience evidenced that many of the patients presenting with physical ill health had underlying histories of mental health ill health and emotional problems which, in turn, led to poor physical health and sometimes addiction or self-harm.

So many people were traumatised, suffering the effects of broken lives. I found myself in consultations, listening to people's psychological pain and fragility, now manifesting as physical disease. I remember once dressing the festering wounds of an addict who had injected heroin into every available part of his body. All that was untouched were his feet and he had weeping sores all over his legs. He clearly had mental health problems, and his behaviour was quite disconcerting. As he cornered me in the consultation room, his story was one of rejection, pain, and anger. The abuse, pain and rejection had manifested as a life of misery, addiction and eventually homelessness. I was alarmed but not afraid when he told me that he wanted to kill a woman and smash her head with a brick. I fearlessly took a step back, inhaled deeply and listened. I was rescued shortly afterward, and he was seen by the Mental Health team.

I was always willing to see the broken and sad. My colleagues would shout, "Here's one for you!" I had a reputation for wanting to see the "heart sink" patients. I listened well and offered my advice with well-chosen words. But still, they came back week after week; it was relentless. There would be a waiting room full of dishevelled, broken men and women and I would race to see them, sometimes being gently admonished for spending too much time listening and talking to these people to the detriment of those who were still waiting. I was looking for some way to reach out to these broken people and I was feeling a pull, a call, to do more for the lost and marginalised.

I was 40 years of age or thereabouts when I made the big announcement to my closest friends. When I tipped my head slightly to the side and declared that I was considering the calling to ordination, they just smiled, nodded, and said, "Right then, are we getting a taxi to the club or the bus?" They weren't dismissing this dramatic life-changing announcement; they were simply acknowledging it; taking it in their stride as they had done with all the other interesting life events I had pronounced. I don't think it came as a huge shock to them. After all, I hadn't told them I was going to disappear to a convent or take a vow of silence.

I had been studying for a master's degree in theology at The University of Manchester and this had validated my path. I wanted to know more about faith and about the Bible. I had listened to preachers and sermons, but I wanted to explore more. For a long time, I had been committed to my faith and my belief in God. As a child, I had always attended church and, in my early teens, I had been dragged reluctantly to my mum's Methodist Church. Despite my objections, a small seed was planted, one which would eventually start to germinate later in my life. For now, thanks to my Mum's persistence, I had the grounding of my Christian faith, and it was to carry me through some very difficult years to come. For my close friends, there may have been some comfort in the fact that their dear best mate now had a hotline to God!

And so, there we were on our way into Manchester to a nightclub and I doubt we got home before 4.00 am. Oh no! A potential woman of the cloth going out on the tiles, having a few glasses of wine and dancing! What is the world coming to? Well, the world is coming to this. In decades past, it was the norm to go to church. If we look back at episodes of Little House on the Prairie or the Waltons, we see idyllic families trotting off to church in their bonnets and Sunday best frocks. I have a box full of photographs of generations of my own ancestors who were staunch Methodists; that Is my lineage. They had Sobriety Society certificates, went for Whitsuntide walks and had a habitual Sunday routine. But society, religion, and a belief in something other than self, has changed.

So, what is so terribly wrong with a vicar who loves to dance to 70s classics? Where is the sin in going out, in moderation, dressing up, socialising with dear friends, and generally being a normal human being? It is my experience that we (the Church and leaders of the Church) try to paint a picture-perfect image of holiness. We rarely share our weaknesses, our vulnerabilities, and our pain, just in case we are judged or seen as weak. How will crushed people with chaotic lives be comfortable with our supposed perfection and the persona we present? Our own vulnerability should be an invitation of welcome.

This is my calling; it was then and it is now. Broken souls are my love because I, too, am a broken soul. The world is such a challenging place and life's journey can be tumultuous. Even if we have been raised in a good home with caring parents, it is still far from easy. I yearned to make a difference. And so, my goal as an Anglican Vicar was to help restore people and rebuild lives and what better place to do this than in the Church - the way _we_ do church, no more habitual routine but a new and welcoming church community. My intention was to create a place of invitation, something that is integral to all clergy, something we are all supposed to be called to. We are to serve and love our neighbour, warts, and all.

Churches are places of worship where people can gather in fellowship. Although many of the buildings are beautiful, traditional, and part of our history, they are only bricks and mortar; they are not people. The foundations of churches stand on solid ground as they have done for hundreds of years but, unless _we_ stand on solid ground, unless our lives have been influenced and nurtured by solid families, friends, and teachers who have shaped and loved us, we will inevitably be broken in some way.

I try not to think of myself as religious. The very connotation brings about images of control, conflict, and division. I would rather think of myself as a Christian spiritual woman. I totally agree with biblical teaching, but I don't always see the Church or, indeed, myself emulating the true meaning of the Christian faith. A member of my congregation once asked me why I invited poor people to come to church. Why didn't they put anything on the collection plate? On one spectacular occasion, somebody put their hand into the plate and stole £10. A lovely, well-meaning lady saw the perpetrator, followed them home and asked for it back! Tradition and religious thinking are hard nuts to crack, especially when a large cohort of your congregation has been attending the same church, sitting in the same pews and doing the same thing for years.

Church should be about looking outwardly, not inwardly. Our priority should be to meet our neighbours, seek out places where we can make a difference, and be kind to the lost. We should be kind and generous to those who are poor – financially and in spirit. After all, we are all susceptible, and life is fragile.

Wagtail

Are we confident that <u>we</u> will always be, okay? Are we confident that <u>we</u> are far from the prison of life whatever that may be? Life can throw a curve ball when we least expect it. Financial instability, family breakdown, mental ill health, and crime are some of the cracks in the road that can cause <u>any of us</u> to trip and fall.

I must say here that, as my congregation increased in numbers, many of us were transformed; we changed and grew. However, many of the traditionalists struggled but many embraced it, and we started to look outwardly, welcome new members, and take care of the vulnerable. But you know what a minority can do if they set out to destroy, and they did.

I have quite a fearless spirit and I can stand up for myself. I will fight for righteous justice but, when confronted with an oppressor, I crumble. There were one or two people who set out to hinder me, to stop me in my tracks. I tried to implement change, to welcome the stranger. I wanted to open a food bank, to invest in the hurting community, but they did their utmost to stop my endeavours and hurt me. And there again I heard Mum, "Things will always work out for the best."

As a child, after being bullied at school, she would pinch my tear-sodden cheeks on and tell me, "Just get on; everything will be alright." But these people did stop me; they stopped my endeavours and caused me pain. They pushed me until I was at breaking point but, at the same time, they did me the greatest favour and now I can forgive them.

It was and is my conviction to move out of my own comfort zone and the realisation that perhaps I wasn't the best person to lead this church, that shaped my decision. I moved away from a building, a place of comfort and tradition, to don dirty boots and march toward this precious, yet challenging, new community. Prisons are hidden communities, but they are still very much part of our society; and, if they can't come to us then we must go to them.

I have a small tattoo on the inner part of my right wrist which is inked in Hebrew. It says the word "להתיר אותם," which translated means ``unbind them." There is another that reads "ליברטי" meaning "liberty." They remind me that this is my calling as a priest, to set the prisoners free; not free in the literal sense of opening gates and letting them out but rather setting them free from the chains and weight of their pain. These tattoos triggered many conversations, and still do, albeit appearing quite unusual for a vicar to have a tattoo which, for some, is a theological no-no!

So many people have been born into a prison, and for many, even after they are physically free, they are still prisoners of their past, present and maybe their future.

So, after seven years of managing a church and balancing all its complexities, I decided to make a significant career move. I had to make the difficult decision to leave the church and those who had my back and walked with me; my tribe, those dear and faithful friends who had tried to stand up to the opposition, and were sad that I was leaving.

Visiting Michael in a Manchester prison had thrown open the gates to a new future; to go out, to seek out and to minister to people in a place that was locked away, hidden and dark. It is an ugly, huge, foreboding grey fortress, off-road, and just out of sight; a place that is home to almost 1,500 male prisoners and a place that was then to become my second home for the next four years.

Chapter 4
Jurassic Beauty
"I go to nature to be soothed and healed, and to have my senses put in order."
John Burroughs

This Category B prison, a new millennium build, opened in 2000 and has the capacity to hold 1,460 male remand and sentenced prisoners.

This monstrosity of a building was purpose built using the finest grey concrete and steel. Just outside the city, it sits off an urban main road, opposite a large cemetery. The cemetery is lined with uniform rows of graves, some adorned with flowers, some plastic and fading, and the odd pink or blue deflating balloon. Soggy, tattered toys often signify the final resting place of a child. Some graves are ancient, some brand new with recent mounds of clay and a basic wooden cross to identify the person's final resting place. Some are tended beautifully but others are abandoned and forgotten, left to the mercy of the elements, weeds and wildlife.

I walked amongst the graves at lunchtime when I needed some space and air. Sounds morbid, doesn't it?

I find cemeteries to be places of great peace, occasionally, tragic sadness but more often places of tranquillity. I sometimes saw my namesake's headstone entangled in wild ivy, forgotten. Pulling back the ivy to expose the name again reminded me of how precious, short and unpredictable life can be. I talked to God in this place, prayed for the prisoners or just chatted with Him about my day.

Ironically, this black-painted, steel-fenced graveyard is one of the last places prisoners catch a glimpse of as they sit in the big white van, "the Sweatbox", bringing them into the prison or transporting them to and from court. Peering out of the steamy windows in the claustrophobic transport cell, they can see row upon row of graves, another irony just as they turn into their place of incarceration.

As I pulled into the car park every morning, I gazed at the foreboding building. Green moss falls like tears down its grey concrete walls, trying to blend the ugly building into its green surroundings. Barbed wire rolls across its turret and walls, and birds perch in between the sharp knotted spikes but they take off and land without injury. Why would anyone inside ever attempt an escape? It would be so dangerous and impossible.

The walls are so very high, but their rounded, smooth tops may be a temptation to risk a roll or slip down onto the grassy verges beneath.

Even taller, in the distance, is the local church spire. The steeple towers are above the height of the walls with a cross perched right on top and reaches up to the sky, up to the heavens.

Most of the prisons I have visited are conveniently tucked away, often hidden in the vast countryside in places that are difficult to travel to and even more difficult to escape from. They are hidden in the "sticks," perhaps to ensure that we don't, and are not tempted to, give a second thought to the people inside.

Apart from the distinct notice board outside, a passerby wouldn't know they were outside a prison, and would never have to give a second thought to the lives of the people safely locked away inside.

On the other side of the cemetery is a lush green forest, mature and abundant with huge Jurassic plants and wildflowers. Giant deadly hogweed inhabits the paths along the side of the river. The ugly hidden fortress has life all around. Baby rabbits sit on the grassy verges in the early morning mist, feeding and scurrying away at the sound of car engines approaching. The birds sing and the heron's fly. Early in the morning, families of timid deer can be seen wandering in the low settled mist, peering through the trees in the gravel car park.

At night, at the end of a shift, I could sometimes hear the gentle hoot of owls amongst the shouts and jeers of the prison residents. On the way in, the trees and wildlife may be a small gift of life and grace for some before pulling up outside the immense secure electric gates.

There are pathways carved through the forest, teaming with dog walkers who are oblivious to the chaos that is confined within the walls just beyond the wild umbrella plants. There is a small lake with lily pads and dragonflies, nesting ducks, and peahens amongst the reeds. A pretty duck's nest is on the lakeside, sheltering from the looming heron that is scouting the water for baby chicks to pounce on! Nature can seem so cruel. Critters kill to survive, foxes root through the rubbish left by walkers in overflowing bins, and birds peck on and devour dead mice or rats on the riverside. Nature and nurture in the animal kingdom! The nature here in the forest is untouched, raw, and so beautiful.

The forest was a place of escape at lunchtime. I went there to think, to be at one with nature and to observe the behaviour and survival tactics of the little creatures, not so different to many of the prisoners I came to know over the years. I went outside to walk when I needed air, and to reflect on the day's traumas; to get away from the sometimes-awful smells inside the prison walls. I sat by the pond, breathed deeply, unwound, and said hello to dog walkers passing by.

Occasionally, I saw or heard rustling in the bushes, and, on a few occasions, I caught glimpses and fleeting shadows of tracksuits dashing back and forth, causing me to retreat quickly back inside the prison. There had been sightings of people in the evergreens before, armed with machetes; a shout over into the prison from someone hiding in the woods and scurrying footsteps through the bushes; then a quick dash, only to learn later that a parcel had come over the wall into one of the yards. It is an ideal launching pad, with no security cameras and is in direct line with some of the prison yards. Flurries of parcels come over the walls, laden with drugs, tobacco, and mobile phones. Sometimes, the contraband is stuffed inside burning tennis balls for a grand slam. The balls burn their way through the protective nets that hang over the yards. Parcels coming over the walls is a perpetual problem. There are so many new and ingenious methods for getting this contraband into the prison, yet it is causing serious issues, and fuelling addiction and crime within the prison walls.

Going further into the forest's depths, huge umbrella plants with concave leaves provide food and shelter for forest dwellers. Even the weeds are glorious, the colour, the smells, the life, the growth. This place is so near yet so very far from the prison environment in. I often wished I could walk here with some of my friends inside the prison so that they could feel the breeze and remember what freedom feels like; to have conversations about life and experience nature's healing. Just a stone's throw away, a little oasis but, for some, just a mirage.

Unlike humanity, nature is so kind and gracious; it hasn't forgotten us. The birds sing within earshot of the prison cells, the tall trees sway and creak, giving a glimpse of hope, no matter how guilty the listener may be.

I used to suffer from anxiety due to years of being a nurse, feeling lonely and alone, and being far from my family. The madness of the world we live in can have such a negative impact on our mental health. Nature is a wonderful remedy and should be on prescription. Over the years, I have learned to deal with my anxious thoughts; in fact, I rarely have negative intrusions. I go for a walk, watch nature, smell nature, breathe in the wonders of creation and regain my peace.

Nature makes its way beyond the gates and into the prison. It is graced by visiting birds amongst other less-welcome creatures. The prisoners have the company of hundreds of wagtails and sometimes the odd pigeon. The pigeons are often seen swooping down the main corridor, known as Main Street, flying up to try to escape through the small gaps in the steel. Sadly, some of the larger birds swoop in unknowingly and can't get back out. They become victims of the ferocious steel bars and the elements. On the landing of one of the floors, a pigeon had died after becoming trapped in wire. It hung there for the entirety of my time working in the prison. It was a plump dead bird when I arrived and, every time I climbed the steel staircase, I saw its poor body decaying. Seasons came and went, and still it was there - trapped. Its feathers fell one by one until it was nothing more than a dry, hanging carcass. Poor sweet bird, too far away to rescue, too far away to remove from sight.

Wagtail

Pigeons really struggle to get out once they have flown beyond the barbed wire and steel gates. However, the little wagtails always manage to make an escape. They are so nifty and swift. They fly at the speed of sound, so fast that you can't really get a good look at them. They don't become entangled; they are small enough and clever enough to go back the way they came or find a different escape and the freedom to soar until one day… but that story can wait.

Chapter 5
Tick Tock Tick Tock

"There is a time for everything and a season for every activity under heaven."
Ecclesiastes 3:1-11 King James Bible

In life, time is such a precious commodity and one that, perhaps, we all take for granted. No matter the quality or even existence of the relationship with our biological parents, if nothing else, they gave us the gifts of life and time. I used to share this thought with the men in prison, trying to help them appreciate the time they had, albeit inside, and use it wisely and to their advantage.

When we are young, time doesn't seem to be an issue. We think we will be forever young! Then, in the blink of an eye, we are 20, 30 then 40. When we get to 50 or 60, time speeds up, believe me! We can't control time; we can't stop it; we can't zoom forward or go back in time. Even the most incredible scientists have yet to discover time travel. And so, we only have this present minute, this hour, this day.

Take what you will from the following story. In the tale of *Peter Pan*, Tick Tock is a fearsome, green crocodile that first emerges on the shores of Never Land.

Wagtail

After accidentally swallowing an alarm clock, he earns his famous name. When Peter Pan cuts off Captain Hook's hand and feeds it to the croc, Tick Tock develops a taste for more. Eager to devour the rest of Captain Hook, Tick Tock lurks near his ship, sending the terrified crew fleeing from Never Land to escape his razor-sharp teeth. What an enchanting story! As the saying goes, "Never smile at a crocodile." With each ominous "Tick, Tock," time was running out for the captain.

I often thought that many of the prisoners I worked with were forever Peter Pans, afraid to grow up and take responsibility for their own lives, let alone the lives of their families or children, the Tick Tock of time resounding in their ears.

Do you and I flee from time when we hear the resounding chimes? Do we ignore time? Do we serve it well? Time takes us all captive; but when spent without wisdom, it will chew the hours up and swallow them. Gone!

There are few clocks in prison. One was in the Chaplaincy office. I was always a few minutes late by the time I had parked, made my way through security, and waited for keys. My gracious boss always glimpsed up at the clock! It was always 08:05, no matter how I scrambled to be on time. Time is something we all watch. It rules our days and nights, helps us plan, and looms ominously when life seems to be passing by too quickly. Time seems to pass quickly in the summertime, yet in the cold, bleak winter, it seems to go on and on while we wait for the change of season.

In prison, everything revolves around time. From the moment a prisoner arrives, time takes on a new significance. Life accelerates and decelerates simultaneously - moving too quickly to grasp, yet dragging on endlessly. Time cannot be rewound, nor can it be hurried. It simply *is*.

The ticking begins the instant prisoners cross the threshold. It continues relentlessly - through sentencing, imprisonment, and even release. Occasionally, it stops abruptly and tragically, as it does when a prisoner succumbs to a drug overdose or to injuries inflicted by themselves or others.

Time becomes the axis around which prison life turns. It brings structure and routine, but it also magnifies pain and frustration. For some, it is indefinite, an unyielding stretch of uncertainty; for others, it is fixed, yet just as daunting. Time can be fruitful and hopeful, offering the chance for change, or it can feel devastating and oppressive, dragging the prisoner into despair.

Beyond prison walls, time remains the most precious currency. How we spend it shapes our future. Squandering time - on ruminating over regrets, harbouring negative thoughts, speaking hurtful words, hesitating to act - only leads to missed opportunities. We waste it waiting - for courage to apply for jobs, for the "right" moment to speak up, or for circumstances to change themselves.

Yet, even as we feel captured by time, it moves forward relentlessly. We age, we lose chances, and the blur of passing days leaves us wondering where it all went. Distractions, procrastination, and meaningless busyness devour our hours, leaving behind a hollow sense of fruitlessness. Time is the one thing we cannot afford to waste. It is both fleeting and immeasurably valuable; a force that holds the potential to transform or to trap us, depending on how we choose to spend it.

Time consumed by negative thoughts often leads to regrettable decisions. How much of our precious time do we waste in anger when someone hurts us? Instead of choosing forgiveness and redirecting our energy toward positive actions, we dwell. We plot, plan, and obsess, pouring hours into thoughts of revenge, squandering both time and energy in the process.

The speed at which time seems to pass is closely tied to how we use it. Too often, we spend it yearning for what we lack, neglecting to appreciate the blessings we already have. When we're fortunate enough to possess good things in life, how often do we truly pause to enjoy them?

Time is fleeting, and how we choose to fill it shapes the quality of our lives.

It is not my intention to diminish the struggles of those who grapple with choice. Some people require support to manage their time, and others have time stolen from them by physical or emotional illness. Yet, while we still have time, there is always hope. As long as we are breathing, we are alive and that means we have purpose.

I have witnessed families cherishing the final moments with their dying loved ones, moments when those individuals, despite their frailty, remain present and able to give and receive love. Even in the twilight of life, our presence holds profound meaning. In those precious last hours, we can offer comfort and connection, leaving a lasting impact on those we leave behind.

Sadly, I have also sat at the bedside with people at the end of their lives who, due to misspent time, unforgiveness, isolation, pain, and disagreement, die without loved ones by their side. When they have passed, there is nothing to write, and their eulogy is blank except for the day they were born and the day they died because there is no one to remember them. There are no funny anecdotes about family holidays, no accounts of their hobbies, or how everyone loved them. There is no one to share stories about their time on this earth.

And so, the clock starts to tick as the prisoners arrive together in a big white security van, usually straight from police custody or from court. The time of day they arrive differs depending on how busy the courts have been. If a man is deemed to be unwell and must go to hospital, time can be delayed, but not for long and the delay is frequently a failed attempt at stalling the inevitable.

Once the prisoners have been processed, convicted or detained, they begin their journey to the prison gates. They pass the church with its steeple touching heaven, the graveyard, and the forest. From this point, time takes on a whole new meaning for them. Peering through grey tinted glass, they arrive. The van's doors open, and the prisoners are led inside one by one. They are now a statistic, a number, an inmate, a prisoner. They then enter the Reception; a reasonably pleasant environment with electric blue and white walls which, at first glance, resemble a hospital or the Manchester City players' tunnel with bright neon lighting.

Depending on the day and the luck of the draw, prisoners may have a friendly, fair officer welcoming them for the first, second or maybe the umpteenth time. Some staff have worked here for years and are accustomed to the revolving door. Reoffending prisoners return month after month. For many, this is home; a familiar place where they know they will be reasonably safe and warm and get three squares (meals) a day. Some have nothing and no one on the outside and being in prison is a temporary reprieve from begging, robbing, or just being a general nuisance to get by. Here in prison, they have people to talk to, people who understand and maybe someone who shows an interest in them and in their future.

Reception is also staffed by a few prisoners who have progressed and have good reports. They are blessed with having the luxury of cheese on toast or a bacon sandwich for breakfast, a staple for the officers and staff in Reception. It is a reasonably peaceful environment, located a short distance from the rest of the prison, and a welcome reprieve from the chaos therein. I always thought it a little bit cruel to have the new arrivals, who may be battered, bruised, anxious and confused, experience the olfactory delights of warm cooked food that they wouldn't get to sample. They certainly wouldn't be smelling sizzling bacon again for a while.

The Reception area is a long corridor with rooms on either side. There are individual rooms with scratched Perspex windows. Vulnerable Prisoners and those On Protection are segregated and wait to be processed. The general population (not Vulnerable or On Protection) are taken to a holding room, a large square room with an old, battered TV on the wall and grey metal bench seats. Belongings in clear plastic bags are thrown onto the benches. They pace and stand about, waiting to be processed, with nothing on offer except tepid water in a polystyrene cup. Sometimes, they banter about why they are in this situation, laughing and swearing, which is a big macho defence mechanism. Some sit, head in hands, exhausted and bewildered as their time in prison begins.

Prisoners arrive with documentation. Some of the files are fresh and new, with just a few slim pages. Others contain volumes of thick, tattered documents, each with the stamps of different prisons on the outer covers. However, new or old, these files detail the prisoners' history of offences, prison terms, behaviour, length of sentence, and family contacts.

Occasionally, there is a single arrival. A man dressed in a yellow and green jumpsuit alerts staff to the fact that this man is a genuine Houdini who has attempted or successfully managed to escape custody. You can't really miss them, and they are watched like hawks. Those with a history of self-harm have orange Assessment, Care and Custody books tucked into their biographies with page upon page of hourly observations. The documents tell a sad story of years of self-abuse, of cutting up, and of the numerous suicide attempts.

Wagtail

They wait together or alone, depending on individual circumstances. Their personal items, if any, are bagged up for safekeeping. They are permitted to keep some items, but everything is scrutinised. Their mobile phones and many personal belongings may have been taken already. What remains are clothes, books, shoes and, occasionally, canteen - food and snacks that can be purchased in prison. These meagre belongings are taken and put into large, clear plastic bags.

The prisoners are briefly reminded or informed of the basic rules, questions are answered about their belongings, and they are told what will happen in the next few hours and days. Sometimes prisoners arrive together from another prison and may know each other. They talk about their experiences in the last prison and their disappointment that they have ended up in this "shit hole." I suspect these conversations and banter are similar wherever they end up.

If they have been arrested and taken straight from police custody to court, the likelihood is that they will be dirty, unwashed, hungry, cold, and frightened. If they have been in a brawl, they may be covered in dried blood, have bruised eyes, broken glasses, or be disorientated. If they have an addiction, there may already be signs of withdrawal. Prisoners may be aggressive, confused, paranoid, angry, and/or violent. The only contact numbers they have are on a mobile phone which is now on a shelf in Reception with the rest of their belongings, and the tiny scrap of paper with mum's landline on it is screwed into a ball in the pocket of their confiscated jeans, and they can't remember it.

Each man is seen by a member of the Healthcare team. At this point, a short health check is carried out, including an assessment of any addiction problems, history of any chronic illness such as asthma or diabetes and current medication. Prisoners are encouraged to be honest about their feelings, fears and anxieties. A rapid mental health assessment determines their state of mind, and, for the moment, a decision is made about which prison wing they will be going to, depending on capacity. If there is any likelihood of self-harm or attempted suicide, they are immediately commenced on a self-harm assessment and care file.

Body scanners detect concealed drugs or mobile phones. If it is suspected that bottoms are holding in these items, the prisoner is taken to Segregation to await their confession, a further scan, a bowel movement and an interview. Prisoners lie, protest, argue and shout but, one way or another, those items are coming out before they take another step into the general prison population.

These introductions to the prison are the same for all prisoners. They are stripped of their liberty, their only precious belongings are removed and bagged up and their only means of contacting the outside world is confiscated. They are now a number, a statistic, and a member of one of the most difficult communities they may have ever encountered. They are escorted from the Reception wing, with permitted belongings in clear plastic bags slung over their shoulders. Theoretically, this process sounds organised and fair. It is necessary for the institution's systems and the safe management of prisoners yet denotes the removal of liberty from the men.

The first few days can be overwhelming for prisoners. If they are old school and familiar with prison life, they know the routine and what to expect. Some of the kindest actions I witnessed were by experienced prisoners toward those new to prison life. No matter what crime prisoners have or have allegedly committed, they are all in it together.

The "Wing Mentors" help new prisoners to settle in. They explain the regimes, how to get contact details for loved ones, and how to navigate the Kiosk for ordering weekly canteen (biscuits, crisps, shampoo).

"Listeners" are volunteers; carefully vetted prisoners who are trained by the Samaritans and can be called on to listen to prisoners who are struggling, and they do a fantastic job. They are useful for those prisoners who are dazed by finding themselves banged up.

Prisoners have a very small income if they work, or a meagre amount of money sent in from outside. Money never exchanges hands and is limited to avoid further corruption once inside. In prison, there is an entirely new system for a prisoner to get what they need. This is a currency only of any value inside. The prison tries but fails to manage it. In the days when smoking was allowed, tobacco was a great bargaining tool and was worth a small fortune. Goods can be exchanged for other goods, including drugs. Here, everyone is supposed to be equal, and no one has access to a significant amount of money or luxuries, or so it appears.

Induction happens after the first night and, for those who are awake and well enough, this is the time to get to grips with the routine of prison life. The Reception wings hold all the new arrivals until an appropriate place is allocated for them. Those who have, or allegedly have, committed sexual offences or those who are "infamous" are kept separate from the general community. Eventually, they are housed with other Vulnerable Prisoners. Often a man who is On Protection for debt or has a price on his head must go to an On Protection wing.

There is a social caste system within the prison community, the worst being child sex offenders, child murderers or "kiddy killers" as they are known, followed by other sex-related offenders. Prisoners who are On Protection are angry to find themselves housed with "paedos or nonces." A prisoner may be On Protection because of gang-related crime or the murder of a local who is known to the prison population. Convicted police officers or notorious offenders are On Protection to keep them safe.

To the general prison population, focussing on a sex offender is a deflection away from thinking about themselves and their own guilt. Many prisoners see themselves as higher up the ladder and; unlike sex offenders, they are accepted by the prison population and they fit in. No matter the brutality of the crime, there is no way they want to be housed anywhere near the worst of the worst. It is an alarming phenomenon that a man who may have murdered his wife, chopped up her body and put it in the boot of his car holds a sex offender in such contempt. Prisons house a mixture of characters. Many have serious mental health issues; some are petty criminals and some genuinely dangerous people. It shocks me that they are all thrown in together.

If prisoners are violent, aggressive, or threatening, they may go straight to the Segregation Unit. If they are unwell or have serious health needs, they go straight to Healthcare, that is, if there is an available bed. Some prisoners arrive in wheelchairs; some elderly and chronically ill prisoners need special care which must be provided to the best of the institution's ability. If there are no beds, these prisoners, including those with acute physical or mental health problems, must be accommodated on general wings. I once heard an officer respond to a prisoner who had diabetes who rang his bell several times, saying he was feeling unwell, needed medical attention, and was frightened. The officer said he would have to wait! Officers are not medically trained, and this sort of situation is commonplace.

On arrival, repeat offenders plead and beg to return to the wings they were previously on. They know the staff and the regimes. But this is prison - not an all-inclusive vacation. Unless there is a genuine reason for not housing prisoners together, they will go where they are allocated, no questions asked. Rival gang members, victims' family members, current girlfriends, and ex-partners are all reasons that need to be considered in this complicated process. Several prisoners can arrive together making Reception and Induction a very stressful and busy time for officers and staff.

The nurses, a doctor, and the chaplain see the new arrivals again on Day One. An all-out scramble happens. At first light, it is utter chaos. The staff from various disciplines rugby tackle each other to see the new arrivals, and cell doors open and shut, as they try to get a look in before anyone else. It can be exhausting, running up and down metal staircases with confusing lists of people's locations, trying to identify the Catholics from the Methodists, the Nonbelievers, the Atheists, the

Agnostics, the Buddhists, the Muslims, the imaginary and the extraordinary. There are many declarations of Judaism, not because of the prisoner's in-depth knowledge of the Torah, but because the food is tastier and prepared away from the enormous pans of bland chicken curry!

Access to a person of faith is the right of each prisoner, and it often gave us cause for jovial conversations back in the Chaplaincy Office. The Rabbi would patiently go to see a potential convert and, within minutes, be back at the Chaplaincy to tell us that they didn't know their Kosher from their best bacon!

Day One of this chaotic period is not the best time for anyone. If they have never been in prison, prisoners are confused and in a state of shock. They may have just received a very long sentence; they may forget what they are told or be way too out of it, or under the influence. Some may declare if they have faith quite openly at the induction talk, many will laugh or jeer with macho embarrassment, and some will welcome the help of the Chaplaincy. The "old hats" know and have a familiar quote that, "The vicar gets it quicker." They are aware that we have more time and our main concern is their welfare. They know that if they ask to see us, we will be able to see them quickly, be it for a complaint, a request to be moved, problems with regimes, queries about church services or services to lost dogs (I will explain later).

I never had a clue what time it was. I didn't have my phone with me and my broken watches were left at home. I had to squint at the neon timer on the wing call box in the office or ask if someone knew the time. Time rushed by in the morning as there was so much to do. I could be asked to attend an Assessment Care and Custody meeting or run between compulsory daily visits to Healthcare or Segregation.

So, the process begins and time starts to tick away. Lives have been shattered, children abandoned, families devastated, and, in this peculiar environment, an entirely new experience lies ahead for those "doing time" for the first time. The prisoners are removed from society, removed from the carnage they have caused, and away from loved ones, if indeed they have any. This is the result of nature and nurture, mistakes made, history unravelling. Strict prison regimes are followed, yet the military operation is fraught with pain, and so the journey, and time, begins for all of us.

Chapter 6
Banged Up
"An eye for an eye only makes the whole world blind."
Gandhi

Most of the time, I am a peaceful, non-confrontational being. But, on occasion, I just can't keep my mouth shut. I know I'm a woman of the cloth, but some things really drive me crazy, and I find myself reacting, swearing (never the "f" word), and cursing in the most irreverent manner.

One day, I was driving to my Diocese for a training day, and someone cut me off on a main road. My dog collar was in full view, made more obvious by my black shirt which emphasised the white of the plastic band tucked around my neck. The car cut me up, causing me to swerve. I was so shocked and angry that I stuck one finger (not two) up at the driver. I couldn't believe it was a woman; how rude! What had happened to the girl code? A few moments later, I pulled into a church car park, only to see the same woman walking toward me, quite oblivious and going to the same meeting. Oh no, please! I wanted to make a flighty getaway, run back to my car, and do a Hamilton-style screech out of the car park. I was so embarrassed; caught out again! She just threw me a crooked smile; I wanted the earth to open and take me into oblivion. I don't know to this day that she recognised me or even registered that she had caused me to sin. For my part, this was really purely a reactive act of fight-or-flight.

These situations cause many of us to react; we are human, after all, and our instincts cause knee-jerk reactions. I can be righteously angry at situations which have caused me to blurt out and put myself in jeopardy. I can't help it, sorry world, sorry people, sorry God!

So, I went for a lovely swim early one morning with my dear friend, Sue. We swam for an hour and then made our way, slipping and sliding to the sauna. In full costume, we went into the less-than-hygienic sauna and plonked ourselves onto the sweaty tiles of the hot, misty room. Not long afterward, came the blurred image of an older chap opening the steamy glass door. I could just about catch a glimpse of his rotund belly and short briefs. He splodged his bottom on the tiles on the other side of the room and started chatting to his pal. I lay on the tiles thinking about how many sweaty bottoms had been sitting on these tiles and we started to giggle, earwigging at the pair of middle-aged posh men. Their conversation soon turned to "the world we live in." They were moaning about youth and kids, and about cars speeding up and down their roads. Then one of them declared that "they" should all be locked up, and the old familiar chestnut, "the key thrown away." Then his pal responded with another banal statement. "Well, I think they should be made to do national service – blah, blah, blah.," Then the squidgy bottom said, "Prison isn't a deterrent. They get nice food, and the cells are like hotels these days. They get televisions and spend all day on Play stations!"

Fuel to fire, I was raging. I was very still, and my friend wriggled about, knowing me well and anticipating, due to my under the breath cursing, what was about to come.

"Hello," I said through the sweaty mist. "Have you ever been inside a prison?" Squidgy bottom shift, a clearing of the throat and then silence.

"Well," I launched in, "I work in a prison, and let me tell you..." I then corrected these men and quickly educated them with a swift reality check. I responded with information about the battered plastic televisions that the prisoners may get if they are lucky, the reality of the mass-produced grey food, the dirty cells, rancid toilets, and plastic torn mattresses. I talked, or rather raised my voice, about our collective responsibility to make a difference. I concluded my speech with a suggestion they might visit my workplace. I could arrange a visit and would be more than delighted to show them around. There was complete and utter silence until my friend, Sue, whispered.

"Anne (my naughty name), I think we need to leave, we have been in here long enough." We gingerly slipped across the floor, disappeared in the mist and left them to ponder as we took shelter in the female changing rooms.

On another occasion, there was an illuminated and flashing comment on social media about those with a criminal leaning. They were described eloquently in a comment from a female as all being "scrotes" (spelled "scrotts"). After shamefully correcting the spelling, I commented on her beautiful description of all known criminals and then proceeded to invite her to the Carol service at the prison. The service was open to the public and she would have the opportunity to meet these "scrotts" and then form an opinion. I suggested that we all are criminals to a larger or lesser degree, and many of us have been dishonest by intention or omission. She didn't take me up on my offer or reply! Then, to my horror, I realised I was in full view, and she would be aware, looking at my social media account, that I lived around the corner and was indeed a Vicar!

I never understood why the entire population of young people and those with unacceptable behaviour causes them to be compared to part of the male anatomy! Never quite got that visual! Why don't we refer to those who irritate us as arms, ears, or eyes? Why always the abbreviation of the male anatomy, namely the scrotum?

I can't keep a lid on it! Not because I condone crime or the pain it causes. Moreover, there is ignorance and a lack of education about our judicial system and the institutions that strive to manage a chaotic community. It is a thankless task day in and day out to be faced with stories of utter sadness and tangible pain. Added to the trauma of human life is the institution that houses them. The idea of locking up someone with serious mental health issues or dangerous behaviour is never going to rehabilitate and reform them.

I cannot comment on all prisons, only those in which I have worked or visited. I have worked in other

Northwest prisons as an agency nurse and, from my experience, they are all pretty much of a muchness. It is commonly known that prisons are overpopulated and understaffed, with little incentive for recruiting enthusiastic and promising men and women who want to make a difference. The environment is oppressive, gloomy, smelly, and forgotten. I am sure there are some very good prisons, but I can only comment on those I have experienced.

So, I now invite you to come with me for a walk through the prison; a journey from the front door to the cells and everything in between.

Come with me as I share with you, the sights, sounds and smells of my place of work, the reality of prison.

Chapter 7
Main Street

"If you want total security, go to prison. There you're fed, clothed, given medical care and so on. The only thing lacking is freedom."
Dwight D. Eisenhower

The staff arrive in droves. Some hover in the car park having one last cigarette before the day begins. Then we, not unlike the prisoners, are herded like cattle and searched in the reception. The glass security doors close behind us, and we stand in a Tardis-like room. We huddle in groups of four or five, making pleasantries about the weekend, football, or snippets of the latest gossip.

There is a neon sign in view as we wait for the security gate to open, sometimes with encouraging words but occasionally a mugshot of a convicted ex-colleague caught bringing in contraband or another misdemeanour. We gasp at the bedraggled image of a former officer, "jail pale," in prison-issued clothes with pimples and greasy matted hair. It serves as a gentle reminder of what will happen if you decide to take such a risk! Our belongings are scanned, our bodies are patted down from head to toe, and then we wait to pick up the keys. The staff line up while the security gate is opened, and we are in. Dashing across the small courtyard in the rain or strolling and chatting, we make banal jokes.

Through two sets of steel gates and fences, we are now entering the long corridor, or "Main Street", as it is known, walking together and never quite sure what the day will hold.

Main Street is a long corridor that runs through the main part of the prison. On either side of the metal road are Industry, the Gym, the Staff Canteen, the Library, the Chapel, the Probation and Offender Management Unit, the Segregation Unit and Healthcare wings. All the doors are brightly colour-coordinated doors to help prisoners who can't read to recognise the department they are going to. A prisoner with an appointment is given a slip with the colour of the door and appointment time written on it. It proves that the prisoner is in the right place at the right time. The roughly painted doors with layer upon layer of paint brighten up the somewhat grim metallic corridor.

The entrance to the main corridor is a double steel gate that is always locked. There is no access except with a worn steel key. The bars of the gate are white with a coating of grey, greasy matter made up of years of human hands opening and closing it. It is disgusting; the dirt is solidified, and I imagined years full of dead skin cells, E. coli and grime. Every time I opened a gate, I pushed against the bars higher than the grease plaques to avoid contamination.

Once the gate is unlocked and relocked behind you and your bunch of keys are safely back in the pouch, you make your way to Main Street. This is your first glimpse of the stretch where staff spend the next long day or night. The steel, off-white bars open it to the elements. In winter, it is freezing, and in summer, roasting heat cooks the familiar stale smell. When rain falls, it pelts down on the metal roof. The acoustics exaggerate the reality of what is really falling from the sky.

Main Street smells of disinfectant on good days but, more often, it reeks of a mingling of cabbage and curry - a stifling blend that clings to the air. The grey concrete floor is peppered with spots of spittle, visible if you arrive before the floors have been cleaned with buffers. Underfoot, discarded e-cigarette ends and crumpled movement slips are scattered like fallen leaves. When I started work at the prison, I wore sensible Clarkes' shoes but soon swapped them for prison-issue boots to avoid transporting the residue spit home on my feet.

The visual reality hits us all, staff and prisoners. Recognition of the familiar or, for newbies, the great unknown.

During "movement" the corridors are bustling with men. Movement happens at the same time every day when the prisoners move from their wings to places of work, Education, Chapel or the Gym. The vulnerable population, namely sex offenders, gang members, ex-police officers and known killers of other well-known criminals, move at different times and during lockdown, to avoid fracas, abuse or violence. The Vulnerable Prisoners are always somewhat subdued compared to the general population; they march quietly, heads down, some chatting with each other, but mostly heads down as they head to their destinations.

During this time, Main Street is alive with streams of prison-issue grey tracksuits or grey and black Under Armour tracksuits, some with friends, some on their own. There is a steady movement back and forth to the Gym, the workshops, to Probation or to the chapel.

During the day, I walked side by side with crowds of prisoners bustling down the corridors, smiling, saying hello, and watching the extremes of personalities; the high-fiving friends going in opposite directions, the sad and withdrawn, the unkempt and dishevelled, the unshaven, the young and trendy with top knots or long hair tied back with bobbles.

The prisoners are generally escorted by officers but, occasionally, they are alone if they are deemed trustworthy, clutching a colour-corresponding movement slip in their hand. If they are attending an appointment, they stand outside the purple, blue, red or yellow door and bang repeatedly through the bars and on thick painted wood. Often, they are ignored or not heard and violently and repeatedly bang and rattle the door until someone takes notice.

Staff walk up and down the corridor, sometimes escorting prisoners to an appointment with their solicitors, video link to court, sometimes to healthcare, and sometimes with prisoners to collect belongings from Reception. Staff move freely, with keys jangling from their black key pouches and belts, personal radios, and fish knives which are used to cut ligatures. All staff are required to wear a body camera attached to their upper torso to provide evidence of any kind of aggressive incident.

Occasionally, when the prisoners are on Main Street, they try a sneaky visit to the chapel. They take a chance and bang on the door hoping one of the Chaplaincy Team will let them in without a slip. Often the absence of a movement slip is overlooked, so prisoners use this to their advantage. "They let me out, Miss."

On a couple of occasions, an inopportune visit to the Chaplaincy ended up in a crisis stand-off. If you allowed someone in, there was always a possibility that they would refuse to leave. This happened to me on a couple of occasions. I opened the door, responding to the repeated banging. My heart sank, my empathy rose. Once inside, a young, vulnerable man sat in the chapel in tears. He was absolutely terrified of returning to his wing, in fear for his life.

Such incidents were taken seriously and were usually dealt with promptly. Senior prison officers were summoned, and a had long-drawn-out discussion with the prisoner. If his concern was deemed to be genuine, the prisoner would be moved to a different wing.

On another occasion, a young man came pleading for help because his ex-girlfriend's ex was on the same wing and might recognise him. He was terrified. Manoeuvres were made and the situation was resolved. A few weeks later when ex number two was leaving chapel, they bumped into each other on Main Street. After an initial exchange of choice pleasantries, they were separated and moved on. However, just weeks later, meeting again and recognising they both had children with the same "baby mama," the men became best pals! They compared notes and laughed it off, with the girl becoming the common enemy. They were letting on to each other as if nothing had ever happened.

Many took advantage of slipping into the chapel with bleeding hearts; they saw it as a place of sanctuary. Here wisdom and discernment were key skills to sort the genuine from the wingers!

The Segregation Wing (Seg) is off the main corridor. Behind the big double doors and the greasy white bars, the segregation unit houses some very dangerous, violent, and unpredictable individuals. Frequently, shouting and screaming can be heard from behind the locked doors. From inside the chapel, which is next door, Chaplaincy staff can hear the thud of prisoners kicking their cell door repeatedly or banging the windows. These sounds become the norm. I would be sitting at my desk, my conversations with prisoners drowned out with a throbbing, repetitive bang, bang, bang. The excruciating thuds would inhabit the air, sometimes all day and night, causing unrest for everyone on the wing. The constant shouting and jeering became an invitation for everyone else to join in. Finally, absolute exhaustion and anger would cause other residents to retaliate and shout. "Shut the f**k up!" The guilty ignore the threats and so the banging continues.

Carl Cattermole writes in his "*Prison Survival Guide*":

"*Kicking the door is a nationwide prison tradition. Prisoners bang the door when something noteworthy happens…The yearly pinnacle of door banging is New Years Eve: every single person in jail up and down the country absolutely kicks the shit out of their door.*"

Fortunately, I was never resident on New Year's Eve to witness this.

When a prisoner is being escorted to Segregation, the entire prison must be locked down. The prisoner walks if willing. I once witnessed a prisoner being restrained and carried naked, everything on show, with shielded riot officers on either side. He was carried in the air; he looked like a crowd surfer, his arms showing evidence of bruises and scratches from his attempts at resisting the brute force he encountered.

Sadly, brute force is the only apparent way to move a resisting prisoner to the Segregation wing. If a prisoner is violent or in danger of harming himself or others and, at the same time, resistant to orders, it is a necessary evil! It seems that no amount of prison reform or welfare is enough to stop this from happening, and the solution to handling resistant prisoners without causing harm appears to continue despite welfare objections and media horror stories.

Chaplains' statutory duties involve visiting Segregation every day. As you open the doors and then the double steel gates, you can quickly assess the mood. The officers here are patient and tolerant. They must deal with some of the most difficult men in the prison. The prisoners shout and scream at each other. Often, there is a dirty protest, and the stench of stale urine and faeces causes everyone to gag. Stashes of incense sticks are a Godsend from the chaplains to mask the stink. The prisoners are quite ingenious on Segregation. There is a slick trick of sending vape e-cig batteries or fluid from one cell across the width of the linoleum floor to the opposite cell. The e-cig refill is attached to a length of cotton unravelled from a bed sheet. I could be walking down the unit and a piece of cotton with a tiny weight attached would slide along the floor at great speed. All sorts of tiny items make their way between the cells, often ignored by the officers, as this is the least of their worries.

I had to brace myself for the rounds, being advised who to see and who to avoid. Sometimes, I stood a metre or so away from the doors to avoid the swell of urine or watered-down poo. Chaplains have to make sure every prisoner is alive and have to ask if they are okay - such a banal question in the circumstances.

I was always alarmed by the mood and the volume of the prisoners shouting and jeering. It's difficult to describe. As I walked down the corridor, I listened to shouting and profane language, from men with deep gruff voices. Then, when I arrived at a cell door and peered through the battered and scraped Perspex window, the tone would change. The presence of a chaplain suddenly caused the baritone to yell and give tough responses and raise his pitch to a more pleasant higher note. "Hello Miss." From a baritone to a soprano, it made me smile. It was often bravado.

The Gym is popular with those who want to stay fit. It is an opportunity to try something different, an opportunity to release their pent-up anger and sexual frustration, and to be in a positive environment. At allotted times of day, a catwalk of handsome muscular bodies makes its way to the gym.

The gym instructors, who are also officers, are respected, maybe due to the common interest in fitness. Being "hench" in prison is an advantage and I guess you are less likely to be threatened or attacked if you are six feet tall with "guns" - big biceps.

A football academy offers football coaching and training. It is fantastic and very well attended. It is so encouraging to see the prisoners and the coaches running around the outdoor pitch in all weathers. The faithful trainers, who work for a Christian charity, have been coming into the prison for over ten years, week after week, in the hope that the love of football and the discipline it fostered will offer some hope for the future.

The Staff Canteen is just off Main Street where staff experience the culinary delights of mass-produced chicken curry, and salads that have been stored in the fridge overnight and are delectably soggy. The best is the daily offering of chips with everything or a jacket potato. The food is prepared by supervised prisoners, and there are suggestions that the prisoners slip extra ingredients, courtesy of their own body fluids, into the curry! You can ignore the thought or not bother eating canteen food.

At lunch time, the canteen bustles with staff lining up to inspect the delights of the prison menu. Newbies line up looking smart in their new uniforms and make for an interesting and alternative topic of conversation with comments on how young they are, how long they will last, how much make-up the girls are wearing and how they all look. Staff sit in their teams and shamefully make the same joke every day about the food, how many carbs they have consumed and how they might start bringing our own food in, but when it is free and convenient, everyone just opts for the free stuff!

When I worked at the prison, some staff members joined the God Squad, some looked terrified at the team of religious folk while eating our obligatory chicken curry and chatting. Over lunch, staff eating lunch in the canteen swore under their breath, within earshot. Sometimes, they swore loudly and aggressively; I think it was intended to unnerve and shock us. It didn't cause a flinch. Lunchtime was an opportunity for me to catch and trap someone who had been ignoring my call or who was genuinely just too busy to respond! It was an opportunity to crouch down next to an officer and briefly discuss a prisoner, to say, "I'll come up to the wing later and I'll see what I can do." The officers sometimes shouted as I was leaving, "Are you free for an assessment review later? 2 pm ok?"

There were several romances during my time at the prison, made evident at lunchtime by who was sitting with whom. We giggled and took bets on who was in a relationship, who was sitting on the love couch, who was having an affair, and who was having whose baby! It was dark humour, but understandable when we were all working in such a dark place.

The Healthcare wing is also just off Main Street, and the Chaplains are daily visitors. Through two sets of gates, past the doctor's office, the dentist and nurses' office, and to what I suppose can be described as a ward - a short corridor with individual cells on the right side and the same heavily enforced steel doors. Little dreary pale faces appear at the windows, or the Chaplain has to peer through the window to make sure they can see a chest rising. Sometimes the windows have faeces, urine or food thrown at them, so distance is key.

The mental health team has an office here. I want to mention this incredible team. The mental health nursing team certainly had their work well and truly cut out. If we consider that 75% of prisoners have mental health problems, you can only imagine the demand. They are very astute, firm but fair. They can spot those trying to self-diagnose from those who have a genuine illness. One conversation with a prisoner and these professional men and women can triage and decipher those who are at most risk. They have to listen day after day to the saddest stories and accounts of years of abuse, hospitalisation, failed suicide attempts, self-harm, and hopelessness. They are also adept at recognising manipulation and risk. They deserved a COVID pan clap every day.

The Healthcare unit can be a very distressing place. Prisoners with serious mental health problems can often be naked, unaware of their indignity. Sometimes walls are smeared with their own excrement or blood. Some prisoners lift a curtain made of loo roll or green paper towels and talk through the tiny window and tell the most extraordinary tales; who is after them, who is conspiring to murder them or who is sending them signals through the plug sockets? I recall one older man who had dementia and used to express delight that we had come to visit; however, could we possibly open his cell door and take him to his office to have a chat? He was elderly, incontinent and confused, and none of us was equipped with the required knowledge or skills to engage in therapeutic conversation, so we often just went along with his stories. He asked us to post letters (an absolute no-no), gave us his drawings and told us that he shouldn't really be there and that it was all a terrible mistake.

Another young man was a permanent resident in healthcare. He had swallowed so many dangerous things on umpteen occasions and had several admissions to the hospital. He self-harmed regularly by opening the wound on his abdomen. This had happened so many times that his wound was impossible to close. His bowels were visible, and he picked and poked at them causing further damage and infection. I was surprised he was still alive; I don't know if he still is.

There was also a young Asian man in healthcare for months on end. He lay face down on his bed for hours. Sometimes, he stared out of the grilled windows day and night. He often slept for days and days. He refused food, drink and medication and his body began to shut down. None of us could get through to him. His mother phoned every day and, to be honest, we told "white lies" to reassure her that he was okay. The Healthcare team had to wait for a hospital bed and, eventually, after months, he was transferred to a secure mental health hospital. I don't know what became of him.

A side ward just off the Association area is the bay for prisoners with chronic or serious illnesses; and those who have a terminal diagnosis and are just waiting for God. They receive daily care to meet basic hygiene needs. At one time, three offenders were in the side ward, one in a wheelchair and the other two in bed. I tried to cheer them up with my visits; I brought them books and tried to make them laugh with my terrible jokes. They were old and helpless but offenders, nonetheless. They were at the very bottom of the pile, so it was safer for them to be there than anywhere else, where they would die with little or minimal end-of-life care. They were visited by the nurses for medication, dressings and a shower and then left to sleep waiting for the inevitable.

The Healthcare wing is basic, clean-ish and clinical. The prison staff are overworked and disillusioned, are not medically trained and have little or no knowledge of mental health illness, let alone chronic or acute diseases.

There is a team of highly qualified nurses, but they are based away from the main ward. Their time is consumed with regularly running to emergencies, including self-harm, heart attacks, drug overdoses and acute illness. They also hand out medication several times a day. The nursing team is dedicated yet weary, having to face day after day of trauma and abuse from dissatisfied prisoners. The nurses have daily routines of first visits, routine health checks and meds. Controlled meds are distributed in secure hubs. The nurses are often run off their feet and are overwhelmed by the constant demand for urgent medical assistance.

A code red or blue indicates that a man has been cut up or has collapsed and is in a very serious condition. The nurses run past with grab bags and run with several other members of staff to an incident. A cell on fire, a suicide, a drug overdose, or an unsuspected death behind locked doors are all in a day's work and something everyone grows accustomed to witnessing.

There is an observation room that means a very unwell patient, usually due to mental illness or prolific self-harm, can be observed. Officers take turns sitting outside the observation cell recording hourly observations in the familiar orange self-harm and assessment books. Makeshift curtains hang over the outside windows to offer some dignity to naked bodies.

There was a man in healthcare for over a year. I'm not sure what his offence was. He had been on the general wings but his mental health deteriorated. As his hair and beard grew longer, so did his health. He once sewed his lips together. I think he used wire and cotton thread, I can't recall everything, but he couldn't eat or drink and was quite unwell. The Chaplaincy team had supported him throughout his stay, but we were helpless in this situation. He eventually pulled out the stitches from his lips and made some progress with his health. He left the prison eventually. I have no idea what happened to him.

Like Segregation, the smell of blood, urine and faeces often lingers on the Healthcare wing, making staff heave as they have to check on the prisoners in the cells. Sometimes, a patient is so unwell, yet so unpredictable and dangerous, that they live and lie in their own excrement for days on end. Eventually, they are forcibly restrained and moved out so that the cell can be hosed down. This thankless job is offered to the prisoners working on the Healthcare wing as an incentive to add a few more pounds to their meagre income. The volunteers or staff don white Bio-Hazmat suits, gloves, and masks to scrape the walls of encrusted blood, puke and poo; sometimes messages are written on the blue fading walls, often religious depictions of a crucifix are drawn in blood, or the opposite symbol of an inverted cross! Taps are turned on and cells flooded, water mixed in with urine seeping under the cell doors that are padded up at the base with old sheets and towels to stop it coming out onto the corridor.

When the Synthetic Cannabis, (K2/SPICE) made its way into the prison, we were in chaos. The drugs came in through various means and, as one method was detected, another was invented. Through visitors passing in family meetings, in babies' nappies, over the walls in burning tennis balls, sometimes from prison staff, you name it, it happened.

This mind-altering, synthetic drug is a mixture of herbs and lab-made chemicals. The substance elevates the heart rate and causes extreme confusion, violent behaviour, vomiting, hallucinations, and catatonic symptoms. The drug can lead to cardiac arrest and sometimes death. The medical teams and wing staff resuscitated prisoners or monitored them as they recovered from ingestion. Initially, it was frightening to witness a SPICE collapse. After hundreds of these events, however, we all became desensitised; nurses didn't run as fast, prisoners were left to come around after initial checks, and, sadly, it became part of the daily routine. There are many stories to tell about these and other critical incidents, but these are best shared later in the context of the individuals I knew.

The other departments on Main Street are the OMU, Industry, Stores, and Education.

OMU, the Offender Management Unit, is the busy hub that houses admin and probation staff. On occasion, I visited to speak with a social worker or the OMU manager if I was trying to contact a relative or meet with probation officers. This unit has a plethora of frustrated tired staff trying to manage the intricacies of sentence planning, behaviours, and outcomes.

Industry is like a factory, and it was one of my favourite places to visit. The officers were all friendly and helpful. If a prisoner had asked to see a chaplain, we often had to go and find them at work. There are several workshops on either side of what looks like a factory corridor. The corridor is full of huge containers, re-modelled and recycled office chairs, sealed crates full of newly cased DVDs, and computer hardware from local businesses. This is a good place. The officers experience a different side to the men. They are occupied and productive. They learn new skills and sometimes get the opportunity to be supported by the companies on release. There are a lot of men, heads down, packing DVDs, tearing up old hotel sheets or taking redundant PCs apart for recycling.

When I jangled my keys and opened the huge doors, everyone looked over and the place went silent. It usually meant I was checking up on a prisoner with an Assessment book or delivering a requested bible. I always shouted, "It's okay, I'm not bringing bad news." With that, the prisoners breathed a sigh of relief and carried on with their work and muffled chatter. The prisoners worked on long benches and looked up and spoke to me. "Morning Miss, how are you?" They usually welcomed a chat, and breathed a sigh of relief that the news wasn't bad or being told something about their loved ones on the outside. I liked visiting here.

Sadly, on occasion, I had to deliver bad news. A loved one on the outside had died or was critically unwell! If this was the case, boots on steel-grate steps, I would climb the stairs to the officer's watch tower. The unfortunate soul would be pointed out to me. To prevent unrest and try to minimise risk, we then escorted the man back to the wing to tell them.

Walking back up the stony grey corridor was like walking the Green Mile. They would know it was bad news and would beg me to tell them all the way back. It was an unbearable and painful journey back to the cell to announce that a parent or sibling had died. I was the grim reaper; it wasn't a pleasant job.

The Stores have wall to wall shelves full of shampoo, biscuits, toothpaste, all things that we take for granted. These items can be bought by those prisoners who work or have small amounts of money lodged into their prison accounts. Known as "canteen," weekly orders are restricted and basic but are so valuable. They are valuable as treats and rewards for a prisoner's week's work but are also used as currency. These small luxuries are the highlight of the week. That is, of course, if the prisoner's order hasn't gone missing or hasn't been stolen in transit.

The Education wing with its sunburst yellow walls, is another encouraging place in the prison. There is a library that houses fiction and non-fiction books, educational books and all sorts of other literature. There are stands with colouring sheets and sudoku, lots of things to help pass the time. There are opportunities to learn to read, to learn basic English and maths skills. Art adorns the display boards with positive messages about learning and continuing education courses. The teachers are kind and patient. Maybe they are so patient because the prisoners show an interest in education and have a desire to better themselves. They have a hope and maybe a future.

There are very few scuffles here and it is generally a peaceful environment. Classrooms are comforting to Illegal immigrants and asylum seekers. Here they can learn English to better communicate their needs and concerns. With basic English skills, they can get to grips with prison etiquette. They can use the wing kiosks, which are essential for requesting canteen (basic food, snacks and essentials), booking visits, telephone numbers, and booking attendance at the chapel and the gym. The library also hosts the job centre, where prisoners can talk about future aspirations for work, or get help understanding the benefits system. It is a hopeful place for many and is a gateway for understanding and opportunity. With some education and work experience, there may be a slim chance that they can turn their lives around. They have the possibility of a new beginning.

Recovery: Turn around and back down Main Street to the junction leading to the Recovery Wings. Go through the gate again, through another gate, and then onto another long-curved corridor. There are often queues of grey-clad, bleary-eyed prisoners waiting at the second gate to be escorted to work. They are always polite but often try a crafty request to be allowed through the gates without an officer.

Battling the elements, clipboard in hand, I used to dash down the corridor on the way to the wings that were at the end of the corridor. If prisoners were in the exercise yard, they called me over and talked through the steel grate. "Hey, miss, did you manage to get me a bible?" "Hey Miss, I'm out on Friday. Will you come and see me? I've got nowhere to go." I wrote their name and wing on the already long list and then hurried off to do the day's urgent referrals, hoping I would have the time to get back to them.

Recovery houses some general prisoners but mostly those who are known to have serious addiction issues. These wings are close to the Recovery staff officers, Shelter and Through the Gate teams. One of the main issues of release is the lack of suitable housing and supported accommodation. Part of my role was to try to get the men some help on release and so I was a regular visitor here. As you enter the building, there are often queues of bedraggled prisoners with drawn faces, their skin dry, tired, and grey, the result of years of abuse. They queue to wait for medication, antidepressants, methadone, and antipsychotic drugs. The nurses stand behind a secure door and call them one by one. If a prisoner doesn't wake up in time or misses the call for meds, it's tough. Everything here is about schedule and time. There is no compassion for late risers or those who miss the call for whatever reason.

Safer Custody Officers are based in the Chaplaincy. Their role is to monitor and manage the safe custody of prisoners and work relentlessly to reduce harm and assess risk. Prisoners who are at high risk to themselves and others are interviewed, placed on assessment and care books, and generally observed for increased activity, such as self-harm and increased violent behaviour.

The Chaplaincy is also situated on Main Street. There is a large, tattered Perspex notice board outside highlighting upcoming events, church service times and encouraging displays offering hope. The work and experiences of the Chaplaincy team will be shared later.

The Security and Admin building is away from the main prison. When you walk down the corridor toward Security, from behind the locked door, there is often a very potent aroma of weed - trophies from wing raids. There may be stashes of tiny mobile phones (often recovered from orifices) in plastic bags and other illegal and confiscated items.

If a prisoner's relative dies, it is also the decision of the Security team to risk assess and decide if it is safe for a man to attend the funeral. Standing outside the door, knocking, the Chaplaincy team humbly delivers requests. However, the final decision lies with Security. Attending funerals does not appear to be a priority and is often knocked back. If there are enough staff and if it is deemed a low security risk, the man may have an opportunity to attend but only if it is the death of a parent or a sibling who has died. If a grandparent has died, the Chaplaincy team must prove that they had been the man's main carer throughout his life and only then, if it is 100% evident, is the prisoner allowed to attend. During Covid, this became impossible.

In the main administration hub, staff busy themselves dealing with updating prisoner information, staff HR details, finance and all the other essential tasks necessary to maintain and manage the system. Desks are clad with family photos, sweets and stained coffee cups. Piles and piles of hard copy files hold the stories of almost 1,500 human beings: War and Peace bundles of sad lives, each one a script for a potential horror movie or tragic documentary. Huge bundles of notes are boxed up to be archived, some ready to go with an unsuspecting prisoner preparing for a night ship out. One office holds the Family Liaison records, records of prisoners who have died in custody, records for court cases, and records for the coroner. The pleasant, light, and airy Governor's and Senior Manager's offices, with carpet and unstained office chairs, are also in this building.

The prison is a huge community, a small village; it is another world, another life. Basic, and I mean basic, human needs are organised and monitored within these walls; it is non-stop. Day and night, there are officers, admin staff, and security all trying to make this place a safe environment. Big Brother cameras monitor activity 24/7; cameras watch the prisoners as they go about their prescribed activities, watch staff making errors, slipping contraband, or even opening gates when they shouldn't - oops!

The persevering officers work tirelessly and unrecognised, never mentioned in gratitude like other first-line services, yet probably undertaking the most difficult career. It's a thankless job and one that I thought I could never do. Officers are the main object of abuse and hatred. They represent the law, loss of liberty, rules and incarceration. The officers with body cameras and keys control and manage these men. They are a constant reminder that their ability to make decisions, their common sense and their freedom are no longer their own.

I was in a privileged position with access to all areas and to everyone, from those who had committed the most horrendous crimes to the Governor who held overall responsibility for the smooth running of the institution. Behind all these doors were hard-working staff, people with other lives, families, children, secrets, hopes and dreams, sadness, and joy. In this respect, they were not unlike the 1,500 prisoners they were observing, educating, feeding, disciplining, and enduring. This is the reality of prison life, and we are all in it together.

Wagtail

Chapter 8
21st Century Porridge

"The best way to keep a prisoner from escaping is to make sure he never knows he's in prison."
Fyodor Dostoevsky

I was born in the 60s. I remember in the 70s watching generally wholesome television dramas such as Peyton Place and the Love Boat (It's a Plane); some will get it! My sisters and I would sit together in the front room with Mum and Dad on a Sunday evening and watch the sometimes inappropriate and not-so-wholesome Morecambe and Wise show, and The Two Ronnies. My Mum and Dad would cough and start inquisitive conversations at the rude bits. I also remember us watching the Onedin Line, with its haunting but beautiful theme with echoes of ships bells and seagulls.

Another family favourite was the prison comedy-drama, Porridge. This was a popular series made between 1974 and 1979. The main characters were Fletcher (Fletch), Lennie and the prison officer, Mr Barrowclough. The senior officer was Mr McKay who lords it over the sometimes naïve and inexperienced officers. The sitcom portrays the funny and perhaps more caring side of prison life. The character Fletch, played by Ronnie Barker, is serving five years for attempted burglary. He has a fatherly nature and takes care of Lennie with whom he shares a cell.

Compassion was sometimes, but not always, evident in prison and the prisoners did, on occasion, demonstrate their kind and caring nature. When you're trying to keep your head above water and manage each difficult day, survival becomes very much about I, me, and the means to get by.

Porridge was made in the era of such crimes as the Great Train Robbery and of the infamous Kray twins, looming large in the East End of London; long enough ago for films and dramas to be shown on television, the impact somewhat softened with time. These infamous criminals are remembered for their audacity, their scheming, and their sociopathic personalities. I guess the setting for Porridge gave us a rather romantic image of the reality of prison life in that generation. The hysterical Ronnie Barker drama was always set in a grey oppressive cell with bunk beds, stone walls, and a rough cotton prison uniform. The doors were often open, and comical conversations were exchanged between Mr Mackay, Mr Barrowclough, Fletch, and Lennie.

Porridge is a nickname given to doing time because yes, porridge is a main staple. Porridge is also known as gruel as depicted in the musical Oliver. The staple of these Institutions is bowls of thick, tasteless cement-like offerings.

Time, society, diverse culture, materialism, media, and poverty, to list just a few, have had an impact on the prison population as we now see it. Some of the Victorian buildings are long gone, but a few remain in our cities.

An Old Victorian prison stands in the centre of Manchester and looms over the city, its tall turrets a reminder of the rooftop protests and riots in April 1990. This ancient and eerie building has secrets and was witness to the last execution in England in 1964.

Noel Proctor was the chaplain at Strangeways Prison in Manchester in 1990, which became famous for the 25-day rooftop siege. There were hostage situations, prisoners turned on staff and other prisoners, and fires burned throughout the prison. The chapel, where the riots started, was desecrated. The prisoners plotted the riots in protest at the conditions they were living in and, sadly, the protest became a painful stand-off. Staff were injured and there were fatalities. What initially was a protest about prison conditions became international headlines. The prison, now known as Manchester Prison, still stands, looming over the city centre, still drab, still in a poor condition, still Porridge.

We are no longer dealing with the same calibre of criminal. Yes, some are still of the same ilk, sadistic, sociopathic murderers, prolific extortionists and fraudsters, rapists, and dangerous sex offenders. For them, prison is the only option. There are also severely mentally ill people who have committed terrible atrocities. There are those who continue to be a danger to society and to themselves. There are some who display simply pure evil behaviour, who have taken lives by intent for their own gratification.

However, today a large percentage of those in prison are living a very different drama on a very different stage. Yes, some have committed similar crimes and, yes, some have an affinity with some of the most dangerous men and women in history.

There are still a lot of "old bins," as they are nicknamed. The institutions are saturated with the spirit of prisoners. If the walls could speak, they could tell many a sad tale and they hold some horrifying stories. Sights and smells seeped into the brickwork, smells of disinfectant, blood, urine, and the spirits of the evil and not-so-evil. The walls hold secrets; they hold photographs of loved ones, semi-naked photos of men and women, artwork, letters, certificates, and calendars to tick off the months as they drag by.

The prison I worked in was quite a contrast from the red brick bins. The brick walls were replaced with insipid grey and blue painted plaster walls. In an anonymous book *"The Secret Prisoner",* the writer who had been in custody gives a perfect description and his cell as a public toilet. Most cells have double bunks, but there are also single cells. There is a small desk and a plastic chair in the cell. A plastic television might be propped up, usually with Bibles. Bibles really do have their use in prison. There are photographs and artwork on the walls, profanities such as: "F**k the screws," pictures torn from newspapers of naked women and football pictures. Mostly, officers ignore these additions to the plain blue walls unless they are particularly personal or offensive. On the odd occasion, names of staff or threatening messages have to be removed. The prisoners themselves are made to clean them off. Some of the men, especially those with serious mental health issues, adorn the walls with profane religious statements, images of the cross or biblical references. Some of the pictures are quite disturbing and give an insight into the minds of these troubled men.

Some cells are immaculately clean. Sometimes, when I opened the cell door, I saw rows and rows of perfectly measured bottles of shampoo and conditioner. Clothes on hangers were hung with the exact same distance between each hanger. Clothes were set out with great accuracy, colour coded and very clean. The floors of these cells were so immaculate that you could eat off the floor! They were, of course, symptoms of obsessive-compulsive disorder, and the desperate need to be in control of surroundings. I always praised the cleanliness of the cells, but also asked if they had an issue with obsessive cleanliness, at which the prisoners laughed and said, "Yes Miss, I've got a problem with dirt." Obsessive cleaning can cause ructions if a man with this mental health problem shares a cell with a problem at the other end of the spectrum, being called "scruffy bastards." Sharing a cell is down to the fine art of patience and grace.

The cell door is made of steel with a small window at head height. The dirty window ledges capture layers of dead skin cells, old bits of tissue paper, and bits of old J-cloths. Some of the Perspex has been scraped to a misty haze to keep out prying eyes. Some of the windows have burnt edges where the Perspex has melted in cell fires. The windows always have it bad. They are used to throw urine and faeces through, but they are windows just big enough to peer through, and to communicate through.

The same keys open every cell door and mastery of the keys is a skill. Once the doors are pushed open, you get a glimpse of home. The beds, with chipped and peeled painted frames, are on one side. The blue mattresses are ripped and worn. Sometimes, the prisoners sleep on what is left of a damaged mattress. The exposed grey foam must do until a new mattress can be found. Occasionally, a man is seen sleeping under a bed, curled up, hiding away from reality. They are often quite unwell or just refusing to conform. Laundry takes place at specific times, but often prisoners can't be bothered, so sheets smell of impregnated grease and testosterone. There is an exposed toilet with years and years of urine- and poo-stained rings around the plastic bowl. Sometimes, the toilets don't work for days or are intentionally or unintentionally blocked with tissue paper or torn up cloth. If they need to use the toilet for a poo, the prisoners have to sit doing their ablutions in full view of their cell mate. Some prisoners make curtains across the toilet out of bed sheets to create some privacy. Modesty curtains are great for concealing a crouching body but are not good at dissipating the aromas. On occasion, I have put my key in a cell door, and opened it to be greeted with, "I'm having a shit, Miss. Can you come back later?" There is very little dignity.

The external windows in the cells have bars across them with Perspex slotted into the frames. The Perspex is often smashed or cracked, creating some ventilation and relief from the heat in summer but freezing with the adverse winter wind and rain. If you look up at the cell windows from the outside, you can see rubbish pushed through the windows, bits of old bread, food wrappers, old socks and used loo roll blowing in the wind. A lot of the rubbish ends up on the yards below the wings, encouraging rats to scurry during the night and sometimes during the day, to devour the welcomed detritus. The yards smell like refuse tips in the summer, and, in the winter, the rubbish mixed in with human waste and food disintegrates in the rain. The exercise yards are a perpetual problem. With broken windows and gaping holes, the temptation is to throw rubbish out of the tiny cell into the grounds outside for someone else to clean up.

At the height of Covid, when the prisoners were locked up 23.5 hours a day, this became a huge problem. Because of isolation, rubbish bins were left in cells for days and began to smell. Maybe the only way they could protest this inhumane treatment was to discard their rubbish outside, a sure treat for the visiting forest vermin.

The yards are also a perfect landing strip for drug parcels. The nets that are in place to stop the drug parcels have holes in them due to burning tennis balls that melt the net and drop down. Guards patrol the yards during exercise.

Once I was running up the steel staircase to the second landing. The dead pigeon in his usual spot flapping in the wind. There was a lot of commotion and a couple of prisoners and staff were watching over the yard. Drug parcels had come over and we all stood and watched the farce that unfolded. The parcels landed on the nets. The guards were all flustered. They were mostly junior staff but one or two experienced guards. Instead of first moving the men inside, they panicked.

They started to poke at the parcels with long poles, much to the delight of the men. The parcels dropped and there was an all-out scuffle. Punches were thrown, prisoners rugby tackled the officers, and the goods were seized by the prisoners and stuffed through dilapidated gaping windows. There was so much confusion. The prisoners were running laps holding parcels as trophies until they were caught. There was cheering as prisoners peered through the grates to watch the spectacle. The alarms were sounded and soon the yard was descended upon by twenty or so officers. It was quite a sight and, rightly or wrongly, we looked on and giggled, officers and prisoners together huddled to watch the madness of the moment with the dead pigeon.

The wings house 90 + prisoners on the ground and upper landing. All the prisoners are accounted for, well most of the time. Headcount happens after every movement and return. After one afternoon movement, we were all confined to barracks as the numbers were down. Occasionally, officers got the numbers wrong, panic broke out, a recount happened, and then we all breathed. If the headcount was incorrect the prison went into lockdown. If this happened at the end of the shift, everyone was held back until there was another count. On one occasion, the headcount happened three times, and it was still one prisoner down who was later found hiding in the laundry room on his wing!

The two floors on each wing are connected by steel staircases. Foot flow is loud and consistent day and night. Walking or running up the stairs, if you are fit, creates a resounding thud and echo.

The second floor creates the opportunity for "over the bars." The prisoners sometimes go over the bars for the most mundane reasons, but sometimes with quite serious intent. They hang over the bars and cling on making threats and demands. Over the bars causes pandemonium. Sometimes, looking down at the pool table triggers images of someone falling headfirst onto the wooden tabletop and breaking limbs or fracturing skulls. Others hang there for hours. The big red inflatable mattress is dragged in, and the negotiators arrive to try to talk the man down. Sometimes, I heard the air blowing into the huge bouncy mattress as soon as I opened the door of a wing, only to be ushered away. The officer dismissed me when I could have been of use. "Nothing to be seen here, Miss!" Once talked down, the man is hauled off to Segregation as a punishment, and he either walks or is carried by the shielded warriors. Whatever the reason for this attention, it is dangerous and yet such an easy option. There are no safety nets, just a blink and they could die or be critically injured.

Cell fires are another common occurrence. Ingenious and determined prisoners poke at electrical sockets and use anything they can get their hands on to start fires. There are no matches in prison and cigarette lighters are locked away. However, they manage it – the fire starters. As smoke puffs under the doors, the alarms ring out. Sometimes the smoke alarms are tampered with, and they don't work, but the evidence of fire in a confined space is alarming. The wing officers are tasked with dealing with the fire and they must act quickly.

An incident happened when I was visiting a wing. A man set his mattress on fire. The room was filled with smoke and the melting mattress caused burns to his legs. The extinguisher was pushed through the fire hose hatch, and it was soon dampened down. The man was dragged out, skin peeling from his legs and dealt with harshly and with little compassion. Fire causes time to stand still as everyone's attention is on the potential of a disaster. Officers are seen running, some strolling if they have a bit of excess weight, down Main Street to the scene of the fire. The medical team, armed with emergency equipment, follows the senior officers on duty. Fire out, prisoner is removed and sent out to hospital. The cell is now out of use; it is just a huge inconvenience, and there is no compassion for the arsonist.

At the end of each wing landing is a large window, through which you can glimpse beyond the walls and catch sight of the local church spire and the swaying treetops. There is a set of stairs at each end of the wing. Depending on the whereabouts of the person you are visiting, you have to climb the steep stairwells and work out at which end the cell is situated.

In lockdown, wandering around the wings was easy, straight to the cell to meet a prisoner. However, before Covid, and in association or mealtime, it was usually havoc. Trying to find someone who had requested to see you entails wandering around with slips of paper and lists, a bag full of reading material, plastic rosary beads, crosswords, and pencils. It takes hours sometimes to navigate around the wings and it's quite overwhelming and sometimes intimidating. I soon learned to avoid the pool table and dodge waving pool cues and flying balls. I always hesitated, imagining the harm that could be done to my head if I was at the receiving end of a missed shot.

During Association (relaxation time), the prisoners play cards, chat, and plot, and make games out of anything they can utilise, quite brilliant really. Barbers' plastic chairs are set up, and clippers are loaned out by staff to the trustworthy prisoners. There's a bit of bonding over homemade weights and barely clad young men doing pull-ups on the bars of the stairwells. It is a hive of activity. If you are foolish enough to leave your cell door open and leave your cell during Association, your TV, maybe precious belongings, packets of biscuits or other meagre essentials can be stolen by other prisoners.

Over 90 prisoners are on each wing so you can just imagine the potential for lumbar - trouble. And lumbar there is. There are fights and arguments and the ability to shift quickly is an art. Sometimes prisoners collapse due to an overdose or an intake of the dreaded SPICE. This gives other prisoners a distraction as they look on and laugh, which eventually turns into terror as they see their comrade being resuscitated by the ever-busy Response team.

At mealtimes, the servery hatches are opened, and food prepared by the prisoners who assumed this very sought-after position is served. Huge plastic bags of anaemic apples sit on the tables whilst the servery staff butter piles of white plastic bread. Apples are the only fruit allowed in the prison; this reduces the possibility of prisoners brewing "Hooch." I soon learned the intrepid skills of keeping bread and fruit in plastic bottles to ferment, producing disgusting potent concoctions to help numb and pass the time.

Mealtimes are a welcome distraction. Grey food, white bread, and bruised apples were the staples. The prisoners hardly ever saw the light of day, outdoor exercise happened for a very short period, and so their vitamin D intake was limited. The prison diet is unhealthy and unappetising. Vitamin D and sun deficiency gave the prisoners a recognisable "jail pale!"

All the prisoners were issued with individual green plastic cutlery, plates, and plastic cups and were expected to wash them and keep them in their cells. One lunchtime, I visited a new resident who hadn't quite caught on to the regime. He was eating hot food on his plate with his hands. I asked him where his cutlery was. He was anxious and embarrassed to say that he had thrown it away. He didn't realise this was his to keep for the entirety of his stay. He told me that he had asked for some more but was told there wasn't any, so he would have to make do, and so he used his fingers! Like a mad woman, I marched to the office and, with some restraint, asked why this had happened. The rolling of eyes and a blasé response that was less than helpful. "We haven't got any." And so, I took it upon myself to search. I let myself into the locked kitchen on the landing and rooted through the sparse crumb-filled drawers to find him a plastic knife, fork, and spoon. Such a simple task but too much for officers to be bothered with. I was astounded and made my feelings known, much to the disdain of the officers.

There is a kiosk in each wing. They look very much like cash machines and, for those who have the skills to use them, they are an essential lifeline. The kiosk is activated by entering the name, prison number and fingerprint of the individual. They are used to book visits or appointments with any number of staff. The Chaplaincy visits are booked on here, requests for courses, requests to see Education and the list goes on. These little machines are great, that is if you can read and write, and are a saving grace for communicating with essential services.

Every so often there is a wing search, evident by mattresses and sheets thrown out on the landings. The prisoners are locked down and the cells of the targeted prisoners emptied and searched with a fine-tooth comb. It is during these searches that illegal items are confiscated and taken to the already pungent security offices. If items are found, then the prisoners are dealt with accordingly. Time may be added to sentences or a spell in Segregation if creative weapons are found. Sometimes, lists of debtors are discovered, which causes an even more extensive investigation.

If prisoners are at risk of self-harm anything and everything that can be used to cut or hang themselves is removed. Vulnerable prisoners will have to sleep on bare mattresses and have no access to plastic, metal or anything else that might be used as an instrument of harm. However, when you are in prison for a long time there are ways and means to create, conjure, and invent ways to harm yourself or others. Sometimes there would be smouldering bits of paper thrown out of windows, fires started through plug sockets and more inventively smoke alarms. Everything is possible when you are determined.

There are education and meeting rooms on each wing. They were forlorn places. Graveyards of old broken furniture, tattered, Christmas battered decorations and anything else thrown in there because demoralised staff couldn't be bothered to dispose of it. Old fading paintings and drawings that had probably been made with patience and pride are now discarded around the room. I would go onto a wing to see a prisoner who had requested a visit and sit amongst the rubbish rocking on an unstable plastic chair. Sitting in a cell is not advisable because of personal safety. Finding an empty steel bench on the wings in social time would not be beneficial for a private conversation.

A request to see a chaplain could be for a million reasons. They may want a Bible, to come to a class or for "rosemary beads" as they were affectionately known. Once I was asked to track down a dog that had been left in a flat alone. The prisoner had been arrested and was beside himself with worry, and so was I. The search for the dog eventually involved the police and RSPCA only to find that the dog had been taken in by a friend. I also spent a full day tracking down a dog that had been taken by the police and put into a shelter with the promise it would be looked after until the man was released.

What can start off as a simple visit can also soon escalate into something much deeper and more worrying. I would sit at a table near the staff office, and a conversation that began with "Have you got a Bible, please, Miss?" could end in flurries of tears. Tears are not something you see very often, especially when there are other prisoners around, but occasionally it did happen. Amidst the shouting and the pool balls darting, prisoners may want to tell you the most shocking stories. A few will want to go to a private area, but lives can be so desperate they don't care where they sit. Missing family members, access to children, bullying, lack of clothes, lost phone numbers, bereavement, grief, mental health, and the hopelessness of life. Occasionally they may want to confess or say sorry. Not all but some of the prisoners never could think about what they have done, the harm caused. An opportunity to talk and say sorry can be a huge relief. We can help with the powerful suggestion of reparation and forgiveness, but this is another chapter. Trying to make eye contact and listen was difficult because prison eyes were always dancing. Deep in conversation, the prisoners were eyeballing and watching, looking over their shoulders to see if anyone was listening.

During prison craft training, we were advised never to touch a prisoner, never to hug them or make any physical contact. I broke this rule so many times and, so many times, officers turned away because they could see how distraught a prisoner was. I would reach out over the table and hold their often-tattooed forearm and reassure them they could come and talk to me again and I would find the right help. Sometimes, I found it hard to hold back the tears listening to young men who had never known their biological family, they had just been moved from one foster care placement to another.

One young man's story reduced me to tears. We were sitting on a wing; he had been let out of his cell to talk to me privately. On this occasion, we sat together after the association was over. He began to talk. He had been in care all his life. Several different families and places. He talked about one placement that had been quite successful for a time. He told me about this one family that was great. He had a lovely bedroom and lots of toys, and they took him to nice places. Then came the blow. "They were nice. They sexually abused me, but they were nice."

No, no, no! I was so sad for him and couldn't hold back my tears. No, they weren't nice to you, they abused you. My stomach wrenched as I composed myself and held his forearm. Let's get you some help! Both of us sat face to face on a plastic chair at a sticky table with the remnants of tomato ketchup and a few dried chips, and away from earshot, he poured out his heart. I listened until I couldn't listen anymore. This was too big for me; all I could do was seek help and pray!

There are so many stories like this. It would fill volumes. But for now, just imagine being locked in a tiny cell, with a urine-stained stinky toilet. Nothing else to do but think about your life, what you have done to others and what has been done to you. Trying to distract yourself with a game of pool or a good book. Imagine listening into the night, to the shouts and jeers, the pain of other prisoners. Feeling threatened or being a threat. Imagine hoarding drugs for another prisoner or being a mule for the wing boss! Imagine you are one of the 75% of the population of the prison estate with mental health problems. Please imagine because this is the reality. This is 21st century Porridge.

Wagtail

Chapter 9
Mr and Mrs Barrowclough
"Only those with the highest character and integrity should be entrusted as a correctional officer."
Rollin Cook, Utah Department of Corrections

Prison is one of the dreariest environments. Everything is the same. Same colours, same cells, same smells, same clothes, same food, and the same routine. For some, this can offer a sense of rest and relief, a long-awaited sense of stability and discipline, something they have subconsciously waited their whole lives for; but, for some, it is a discipline they just can't come to terms with. Those who don't adapt to the prison regime spend their entire sentence kicking against it. The anger and pain are transferred to us, the officers and the system that holds them. For those who embrace prison, it can be a respite from their chaotic lifestyle on the out.

The prisoners must live in this environment for the entirety of their sentence, but so do the staff, particularly the officers working day in and day out. There are two sides to every story. The officers had an awful lot to deal with and I don't know how they managed to stay and work in this environment. Turnover of staff was a problem and remains so. Carl Cattermole states that prisoners hated the system and were treated like dirt; similarly, the officers who tried to be loyal to the system were treated the same way. The shortage of staff is a constant issue. The salary is poor in comparison to other frontline professions and there is very little chance of progression. Some staff joined the team with the intention of using prison experience to gain access to the police force. Some of the best and younger officers successfully left to start a new career with the police, and who can blame them?

The Governor and senior staff rarely set foot on the wings. They were housed in decent offices away from the proletariat. Occasionally, they graced the staff and prisoners with their presence, but this was only once in a blue moon.

Staff frustration about the working environment and the pressure was voiced but the reality was rarely witnessed. If there was an inspection, the staff would have to clean up and clear out everything that was detrimental to a good report. Even though many of the managers had worked their way up the ranks, it appeared they had forgotten the reality of being on the shop floor. Senior staff rarely visited the staff canteen (understandable). The famous Christmas dinner was an annual occasion when the senior staff would don kitchen whites and serve the staff dry turkey, overdone potatoes, and soggy sprouts. An annual treat and a welcome change from chicken curry, but not enough to lift the spirits of the overworked and overwhelmed staff.

The heroes of the prison workforce are very rarely mentioned in awards; they miss out on the praises of the public and, although they are very much frontline workers, they were not recognised along with the other 999 services during the very trying Covid 19 Pandemic. The Chaplains tried very hard to encourage and look out for the staff. We offered our support to deal with distressed or difficult prisoners, which provided some relief. The staff welcomed the odd packet of sweets and treats, they appreciated someone to talk to about their own issues, and there were plenty of those. If staff had a good relationship with one or more of the chaplains, they were welcome to come to the Chaplaincy offices and have a private conversation or just to have half an hour's peace away from the madness. If there had been a particularly traumatic situation, we tried to offer comfort. Most of the time, however, the staff just had to buckle down, take it on the chin and get on. What choice did they have, except to leave and seek employment elsewhere?

There were marriage breakups, affairs, staff assaults, tearful male and female officers, criminal activity, disciplinary action, and other sad situations amongst staff. These situations often called for our support. One young female officer came to me in tears. She had broken up with her partner and she came to my office and just cried through rolls of prison issue loo roll. Her partner still worked in the prison and it was heartbreaking for her to see him every day. Eventually, after a good strong cup of prison tea, she felt better. I spoke with her manager, and she went home for the day. I later supported her decision to leave and pursue a career in nursing.

Staff were also vulnerable and could be unwell. Physical injuries were often sustained during the restraint of a prisoner or from an attack; burns were commonplace from hot water being thrown at officers. Sometimes, the daily grind just got to staff; some suffered from stress, resulting in self-harm in all its guises and mental ill health. Just as with any other large organisation, there were accusations of bullying by other staff, and of inappropriate sexual conduct; you name it, it happened in prison.

The staff was made up of all ages and experience. There were the older, calmer ex-forces gentlemen. I always found the ex-servicemen very professional and a delight to work with. They had seen it all, and life had given them an inner calm, something that many of the younger members of staff had yet to master.

There were regular intakes of fresh-faced, young recruits. Some of them became excellent officers, but some didn't. Many had to leave before they completed basic training because of undeclared offences or misdemeanours.

The officers had tattoo sleeves, and some of the female officers had huge false eyelashes, fake bake tans, talon-long false nails, and plump lip enhancements. This caused no issues on the outside, and I am not judging them, but the "old hats" would often comment about their appearance, and how some of the girls could cause the male testosterone-fuelled prisoners to struggle.

There were a few occasions when staff had been sacked for their inappropriate discussions or even relationships, (female staff with prisoners.) Such relationships, even if genuine and rooted in love, are unhealthy in this environment. The prisoners could be very persuasive, leading to coercive behaviour. There were some very handsome and charming men in prison and female staff could be taken in by their chiselled features and vivacious personalities.

On occasion, staff would bring in illicit substances and contraband. Not always because they were in a relationship, sometimes because a friendship had overstepped boundaries, or sometimes for their own gain or because of threats. Officers have been caught bringing in mobile phones, tobacco, and drugs. Thankfully, most were caught as we were reminded daily by the neon news flash at the entrance to the prison where the dreary greasy-haired images of ex-officers, now with a number and dressed in prison attire flashed before us. Caught in the act! A reminder but not always a strong enough deterrent for some.

We all had lives outside of work. We all had stories of broken relationships, difficult family lives and even experiences of abuse and unhealthy childhoods. Working in prison can be mental torture when you are suffering from the damage and pain life has thrown at you. This was often demonstrated in bullying behaviour, the need to control, lack of compassion and empathy and just plain cruelty. This, on top of the daily drudgery and conflict, resulted in officers bringing their own issues into the workplace.

It was easy to recognise the bullies and the controllers. I had several occasions to question officers' behaviours. I am rarely confrontational but some of the situations I witnessed demanded righteous justice and for me to stand up for the prisoners.

On one occasion, a newbie officer was screaming at a cell door. The prisoner was someone I had been spending time with. He (the prisoner) had Asperger's syndrome, and he really struggled with regimes, taking orders and communication in general. The man had long red hair and a beard. He wouldn't allow anyone to touch his hair, and so it had grown long and untamed. You can imagine the mocking and jeering he had to tolerate from the other prisoners and staff. This difficult situation caused me to get to know and support him.

I had latterly spent time with him trying to arrange for one of his grandparents to be exhumed from a cemetery to be laid to rest elsewhere. An unusual, maybe yet difficult task while you are in prison. The request was, after hours of research, quite genuine for his own reasons and he had the legal right to request it.

However, I gained his trust, and we got on well. If all this wasn't enough, he became the target of a young arrogant officer. He was pointing his finger and swearing, calling the prisoner a "F**king C**t." I don't like bad language, and I only use it here to relay the horrible exchange. I detested bullying and I was angry and defensive. I intervened and shouted at the officer to stop. I then took it upon myself to shout back at him. Yes, it was wrong, but my reaction stemmed from righteous anger, and I couldn't contain it. The officer said, "But you don't know what he has done." This was referring to his crime. I can't recall the crime and, at that time, or indeed any time, it wasn't a factor here.

This was dangerous, provoking, inappropriate, and unprofessional behaviour. This sort of bullying and threatening can only cause unrest and can put everyone at risk. Other residents cheered and shouted as I asked the officer to come away from the door and speak to me in private. When I spoke to him, his bottom lip quivered, and he looked terrified. I later apologised for my outcry, and he accepted my apology. After this occasion he was offered further training and support, a rare but satisfactory outcome. Later the prisoners on the wing expressed thanks that I had stood up for them. I did concede with humility that my behaviour hadn't been the best. I had gone up in their estimation, I spoke on their behalf, I was almost human.

There were a few more, not that many but a few occasions when I felt the need to intervene and one particular incident stays with me.

An offender was having a self-harm assessment, care and custody review. The purpose of a review is to establish how the resident is dealing with thoughts of self-harm. It is not an invitation for an officer to interrogate him about his offence. The officer who was working on the Vulnerable Prisoner wing led the discussion and took the opportunity to ask how the man felt about his offence. I was appalled as the officer questioned him about what he had done and how bad he felt about his crime. Did he feel guilty? Was he sorry? The meeting was stopped abruptly, and I had to remind the team that was not the purpose of the review. The officer was angry and defensive. He never looked at me in the same light, but I didn't care. This wasn't about me or him; it was about a man who was living with the consequences of a terrible crime but whose well-being and rehabilitation were a priority. This sort of conversation can just trigger more self-harm and further conflict. No matter what our own opinions, we were employed and trusted to manage the well-being of this community.

In hindsight, I should have reported this officer, but I didn't. I should have stood up for the man who was already struggling with what he had done, but I didn't. To be honest, if I had reported every incident that was unprofessional or harmful, I think I would have been known as a "grass," and I was too cowardly to cause any ructions. I must live with this, and I am sorry I didn't pursue this situation. Although you can understand the frustration, exhaustion, and hopelessness many of the officers experienced, we cannot let our own issues shape the way we interact with some very damaged personalities.

We come to work with our own stories, and we leave with our own stories. What happens at home, in our personal lives, or with our families must not shape our conduct at work. We think we have the solutions and the morality to judge. Yes, we can empathise with staff, but this is not a place to laud our power, or ideology, about how others should live their lives. All of us struggled, but the behaviour of staff sometimes added fuel to the fire.

By the grace of God, we can all leave at the end of the day; we have a choice. Sometimes, however, we can and do become prisoners of our own unresolved issues and pain.

Wagtail

Chapter 10
Chaplaincy
"The Spirit of the Lord is on me, to proclaim Freedom for the prisoners and to set the oppressed free."
Luke 4:18 New International Bible

I could write another book solely on the work of the multi-faith Chaplaincy team. It was an honour to work with my "friends." This is the longest chapter in this book because it draws directly from my experience and that of the team.

Most of the prisoners and staff appreciated the Chaplaincy team. The work of the chaplain is very different from other staff. Sometimes, we were seen as a "soft touch"; mostly, we were viewed as different from the officers, and we presented an alternative approach. A lot of the staff were unsure of our role in the prison. Many had never encountered a person of faith and we had mixed responses. A lot of the support and conversations we had were in private. The very nature of what we did, the conversations we had and the support we offered appeared to be a great mystery for some. The ethos of prison is mainly punitive, but the chaplains explored redemption. The prison experience is often negative, and we offer hope and positivity. The prisoners were broken, and we tried to offer a road to healing and light in a very dark place.

With access to all areas, we can swiftly move from the kitchen to the wings, through industry and education. We could be seen standing through the gate on release, in Seg or in healthcare. We were the modern-day Mr Benn (if you are over 50 you will get this). Mr Benn was a character from a children's television programme in the 1970s. He worked behind the counter of a fabric shop. Mr Benn was a polite character yet with a formidable presence and an amazing talent for time travel. In his recognisable bowler hat, he would transport himself to places and situations that needed some intervention from wise Mr Benn.

The Chaplaincy team were the Mr Benn's of the 21st century. We didn't don bowler hats but were recognisable in the prison. The Christian team often stood out because of the white dog collar or, in the case of my Muslim colleagues, because of their traditional robes. Some of the team wore civvies but they were still well known to staff and prisoners. My work attire transformed over time, swapping my sensible Clarkes Nurses shoes for a more substantial prison-issue boot. The boot I found soaked up less urine-soaked loo paper,

SPICE or yellow spit that attached underfoot on the metallic staircases. My sensible Marks and Spencer bootcut trousers were replaced with prison-issue black industrial work pants with handy side pockets.

One moment, we could be kneeling next to a collapsed SPICE overdose, attending a senior meeting the next, not imposters but welcoming contributors or bystanders ready to act. We tried to be ambassadors for the prisoners and for staff, taking a step back in violent or critical incidents, yet at the same time visible enough for a supportive and empathetic response.

Some staff were happy to see us. Some were encouraging, some offered gentle mockery, some belittled us about our attempts to bring hope, and some were obstructive and resentful. Some were dismissive, while others were so angry with their own lives that they refused to consider that faith could make the slightest difference.

The officers would sometimes do rounds with us. They would go ahead of us and open the cell doors, saying, "Chaplaincy. Do you want anything?" They would shut the door before the prisoner, or I had time to speak. I caught on to this quickly and would try to jump in front of the officer before they had a chance to shut the door on my wedged foot.

We held to our own beliefs without judging others. We worked tirelessly and thanklessly. We supported one another, shared our fears, talked about our own lives. I hold them all in high esteem; they are all still there doing what they can, restricted with clipped wings. All the Chaplaincy team no matter what faith had a common goal, to care, love, support, and guide and to serve this unique community of souls.

I was always late, no matter how hard I tried—and I really did try, boss. I didn't arrive at all one day, and I was on the missing list thanks to the salivating officer who comprehended me at the gate with an accidental phone in my bag drama!

The daily routine.

08:05: Tip up, out of breath after quickly marching down Main Street, boots pounding past the prisoners dodging circulating industrial cleaning machines. Through the liturgical purple doors and into the office. The doors of the Chaplaincy were a mixed wishy-washy shade of purple. Years of overpainting left tear-shaped drips of paint on the doors. Ironically, in the Christian faith, the colour purple symbolises royalty; it does, however, also symbolise death! Now there's a dichotomy if ever there was one!

08:10: Sign into HMP Gov red book (I always wrote 08:00), grab a cuppa. We sit down to start our day.

08:15: Prayer. We prayed together for staff and residents, and then it was the report of the day. A review of what events had taken place overnight. The management team issued a report every day, including who was on an Assessment Care and Custody book or Challenge, Support, and Intervention plan (CSIP), how many self-harm, how many violent situations and anyone that had been sent out to hospital and bedsits. Any wing raids and who was the Commanding Officer for the day.

The orderly had a barrage of recycled jokes. Today was National App (Kiosk Applications) Day, Used Underpants Donation Week, or National Chicken Curry Week. Then he would offer us an account of the usual suspects and revolving door prisoners that had returned for the umpteenth time. The usual football banter, zzz, then down to business. One chaplain to Segregation, one to healthcare, one to Reception and one to Assessment and Care visits. These were the staples. Then we would look over the list of Kiosk Applications. Triage the Application, staring down at the overwhelming list of 20+ kiosk and telephone requests from families and friends outside. Anything from 'wants a Quran', to toilet broken and all the plethora of requests in between. Sometimes, we were requested individually or by faith and tradition. The list sizes varied and grew larger as the day progressed.

08:30: And we are off, leaving the chapel, heading in all directions.

10:00: Back for a quick prison coffee, say hello to the Chaplaincy orderly. The orderlies (prisoners) were a great addition to the team. The orderly job was highly sought after. Well-trained, they had my coffee ready as soon as those keys turned in the door. They switched on the fresh coffee machine and reached for the cinnamon topping (only kidding). Another look at the Application list that has doubled since we left. There are several new requests: a family member is ill, Nan died, wants to see a Rabbi, a lost dog, needs glasses, no undies.

Our admin officer always gives a full breakdown of the menu, which is always the highlight of our morning and a great source of amusement.

Is it sausage Tuesday or chicken curry Wednesday?

10:30: Off out again to visit and to attend Assessment and Care reviews on various wings.

12:00: Lunch...oh goody another chicken curry with additives!

12:15: Compulsory quiz, hosted by the Chaplaincy admin officer. I lost every day.

13:00: Paperwork, input information onto the HMP IT system.

14:00: Prison movement and courses start in the chapel. Rapping, Bible study, Islamic studies, Sycamore Tree, resettlement meetings, meetings with Offender management, Shelter, and Through the Gate.

15:00: Off out again to finish off the afternoon Applications form the kiosks.

16:00: Home, usually on time but occasionally locked down! This only happened once during my time. Headcount: One missing, hidden in the laundry!

We took turns covering the statutory and urgent calls on Saturday, and on Sunday, there were church services. The morning would see a flow of prisoners to the Roman Catholic service for the general population, followed by two services for the Church of England/Free Church. The services were split: one for the main and one for Vulnerable prisoners. For some, the chapel was a place of sanctuary and peace but, for many, it was just another space, indifferent to the respect that sacred spaces invite on the outside.

The Chaplaincy department has several offices and a larger multi faith room. People of all faiths were invited to use this chapel space for prayers, activities, and reflection. We tried to discourage bad language, usually from officers, ask for respectful behaviour, and just offer an alternative to the sometimes chaotic and unnerving atmosphere on the wings.

I had a small office to meet with prisoners of all faiths and none, those who were looking for resettlement options or rehab in faith charities. The prisoners would book an appointment, and if it was deemed safe, they could come along to the Chaplaincy for a chat, or alternatively, I would go to them. We always had officers present in the Chaplaincy, so there was always someone around for our safety.

The air in the office was pungent, with marijuana fumes drifting in via the ventilation shaft from Segregation; no wonder I ate so much! The office was back-to-back with the Segregation unit, and day after day, we could hear the methodical thud of the feet on cell doors for hours on end. The thuds on doors were heard day in and day out, and it became commonplace.

The shelves were packed to the rafters with books, testimonies, literature, and study books. There was a stock of donated clothes, used socks and undies, and donations from the most fabulous Mothers Union; they were spectacular and their generosity and compassion were in another league. They supported us with every festivity. The donations of clean socks, glasses, and Christmas gifts made such a huge difference. The Diocese of Manchester also donated toys and gifts for the children of prisoners, and they supported the Chaplaincy team in many ways.

Other kind-hearted people with the best intentions would donate new and used clothes for prisoners who had no belongings. I still struggle to imagine what impressions those kind souls had of the prisoners who had nothing. Even though they had nothing, they did have some pride. Prison-issue underwear is sparse, and it is hard to imagine, but faded stained underpants and socks were sometimes a blessing when you had none. I once rummaged through a bin liner of used garments. When I opened the black bag to peer inside the smell was revolting. It was full of sweaty poo-stained old jeans, mothball shirts, ties, yellowing baggy necked t-shirts and wee-stained briefs! How could anyone possibly use these? The shoes were classic. There were rows of brown leather shoes for the older gent, obviously from a deceased chap lucky enough to own a collection of beautiful stylish brogues, each with their own shoe shaper, but not much use here in prison.

The stinky clothes were all chucked out after our admin officer had jokingly tried on and modelled some of the garments! I soon became aware of well-intentioned donors and when these kind folks would ring up and ask to drop donations, I would explain that our shelf space was overflowing but thank them for their kind offer.

The Chaplaincy Team was multi-faith. There was a Buddhist chaplain, Muslim, Hindu, and Roman Catholic chaplains, Pagan and Jehovah's Witness, Free Church, and Church of England. The Jewish Chaplain would visit on request. There was a visiting Yoga teacher and the most amazing Alcoholics Anonymous (AA) chaplain. My friend, Tommy, facilitated AA groups and went out of his way to support prisoners with addiction. Being in recovery himself meant he could identify with the struggle and pain caused by addiction; he was amazing and continues to go out of his way to love and support others with the same struggles.

The main faith groups that most of the prisoners identified with were the Church of England/Free Church, Roman Catholic, and Muslim. There were occasional Sheikh prisoners and very rarely Jewish. Despite having an O-level Grade A in religious studies, my time with the team was the best spiritual education. I learned so much about other faiths. We supported one another and my own ideologies were often corrected with love! My dear

Muslim colleagues were run off their feet, delivering Qurans, prayer mats, beads and other purchased religious items requested from the Kiosk. Holding well-attended Friday prayers and supporting the families of the men. Endless phone calls from faithful parents of Muslim men. Sometimes Muslim prisoners declined visits from an Imam. I asked why this was when a chaplain was requested, (but don't send the Imam). Shame and guilt deterred the man from seeing someone from his own faith community.

My boss struggled and worked tirelessly with the catering staff to ensure that the prisoners had access to correctly prepared Halal food. The provision of food for people of faith was an uphill battle. Kosher food was available, but only if the Rabbi was satisfied that the occasional Jewish prisoner was genuine.

Parents and partners of prisoners with faith or none could be quite demanding. We soon recognised the telephone numbers that flashed on the screen, and we would wave and dodge and promise tongue in cheek to return the calls. There were so many phone calls, usually from partners and Mums. Often distressed tearful Mums whose sons were feeding information, stories of being bullied and threatened by other prisoners. In the pandemic we would be getting relayed messages about the symptoms their loved ones had recounted. The panic this caused was tangible. Your boy is coughing, has a high temperature, is locked up, has no shower, no social time, no movement, and no Mum to take care of him. When you have tried every department in the prison to get attention, the chaplains are often the last call. Those families and prisoners who knew the system were wise to the fact that "The Vicar gets it quicker."

Mums and partners have a space of their own in this book. I could only try to imagine the pain caused by their incarcerated son or partner! They were frustrated, helpless and hopeless.

It wasn't unusual for family members to ring us then to sob, to scream, to threaten. The abuse was commonplace. Families shouting and swearing, threatening us with all sorts of actions. If we couldn't answer questions, they would say we were all "f*****g useless," just like the rest of the prison staff! We became used to the abuse and adept and mostly patient enough to empathise or simply to pass the receiver to the boss! Sometimes phone calls gave us no end of amusement, usually due to utter disbelief at some of the requests.

Missing dogs, as I already mentioned, were the speciality of The One! If a man had left a dog at home, they would be frantic with worry. You could spend a whole day, if not more, trying to track down a lost or abandoned dog. The RSPCA, housing, and police force all rallied to save the doggies. Not one dog was unaccounted for on my watch.

Telephone calls to housing teams to retrieve belongings, demanding parents' faith leaders, people calling us with learning difficulties or mental health issues. It was a standing joke for the office administrator who used to say, "She (meaning me) is off again trying to save the world." A prisoner once asked if I could find his girlfriend who was also homeless. After hours of phoning the homeless charities, all I could tell him was that she had been seen at a shelter a few nights previously.

The saddest and most regular phone calls were from family members telling us that a prisoner's Mum, Dad, child or sibling had died. Death of a loved one is extremely distressing at any time, let alone when you are locked up, locked in and unable to contact family members. Unfortunately, this is the high price paid when you are in prison. I doubt the potential or implications of natural, accidental or expected loss of family members ever cross the minds of prisoners when they are entrenched in criminal activity. Freedom and choice are shelved when you are working a stretch, and so is the final goodbye!

The chaplains verify the death of loved ones with the mortuary, the hospitals, or funeral directors, and then the boot-clad Grim Reaper makes the journey from the chapel to break the news.

Telling a man that his child, Mum, Dad, sibling, partner, or Nan had died was heart-wrenching for all of us. Even the toughest hardest nut to crack officers recognised that this was a difficult conversation. At this point we are all reminded of our mortality, the fragility of life and that any one of us could be at the receiving end of this news. It is the predictable beginning of life and the end that none of us, no matter how wise, how tough, or how hench can ever escape.

After the Chaplaincy team receives information about a death, serious illness, or accident, it becomes a race to deliver the news before rumours spread throughout the prison. If a death is gang-related, maybe revenge killing the news will be out. In the Northwest, as

I guess anywhere else, there are communities of rival gangs and families; they knew what had happened, often before we did. It is a difficult but known fact that the prisoners had contacts on the inside and the outside. The timer was on as we tried to speak to them before they had the Chinese whisper echo its way down the wing.

Once the prisoner was located hopefully on the wing, we knocked uninvited. The unexpected visit from a person of the cloth usually only meant one thing, the death of a loved one. The news is shared, using succinct and clear language. I never used words like "passed away" or "gone" or "not with us." The stark reality here is as stark and hard as the reality of prison. After asking them to sit and explaining that I had some bad news it was a straight and clear message. Their mother, father, child, partner, or sibling has died. Sometimes, the man would already be aware; sometimes, the death had happened a few days before, and we were not the first to tell them.

The reactions and expressions of grief were sometimes overwhelming. On the odd occasion, a reaction may be, "good riddance," but then followed by a scream or a cry as we walked away; the pain from complex grief about a father or mother that had physically or sexually abused you, or simply not been there for that once young, innocent boy! Prisoners holding their hands and sobbing from the heart, so sad it pulls on your guts. The non-touch rule would fly out of the broken windows, and I would sit on the blue smelly mattress whilst tears and snot soaked through my clerical shirt. Because they are in prison and out of touch grief is exacerbated and confusing. Locked in a cell alone left to grieve with only strangers to comfort you. The Chaplaincy team prioritised those in grief, offering time in the chapel, time to reflect, time to talk, time to shout and swear, and time to talk about the abuse their loved one may have inflicted on them. The love never experienced, the love that will never be.

The self-harm and assessment process is considered for prisoners who receive bad news. The chaplains could open an Assessment and Care book if they had concerns for their well-being. After loss, this was quite common. Maybe for the first few days, with heightened pain, the risk of harm or suicide was high. The Chaplaincy team and all the officers were trained in identifying those at risk of suicide or self-harm. There was a protocol in place to make sure that prisoners were checked on hourly, two-hourly or more throughout the night and day. There were regular cut-ups, drug overdoses, and suicide attempts.

The death of a prisoner was rare, but when it happened, it had a huge impact on the community.

There were deaths behind doors, lives taken on purpose, and accidental overdoses when young, fit men were often found slumped or wedged behind doors at unlock. Hangings and attempted hangings were often done with intent and were carefully planned. Those who threatened to string themselves up had everything removed from their possession such as shoelaces and sheets that could be torn and tied into a ligature. The prisoners who hung themselves successfully did so without any fuss. Bed sheets were ripped and tied together unnoticed in the quiet of the night. Officers carried fish knives to cut down the ligatures holding hanging bodies.

After a death in custody, the cell became a crime scene. We had to pray last rites outside the door, not allowed near the deceased. The tomb doors closed and locked, the ticker tape, the blood congealed, the body lay alone, a shocking silent death, no fuss and painfully, painfully sad.

Sometimes, we were asked to accompany prisoners to challenge, support and intervention plan meetings to talk about plans for activities and how to enhance their progression during their stay. These meetings would be fraught with anger and denial. Some would welcome the chance to change but more often not. These prisoners are the most difficult to engage with and have special regimes. They have plans made and remade and are quite soul-destroying. Just as you think someone has a chink of hope it is dashed by a drug misdemeanour or act of violence. These prisoners are self-destructive, damaged, and broken and it takes commitment and time to intervene. Often there is no change, but we carry on regardless.

Before COVID, we would host several weekly events in the Chaplaincy. The Sunday services were held in the chapel and at different times for the vulnerable, those who were On Protection and regular prisoners. This was probably the part of my job I really enjoyed. The prisoners would line up, bleary-eyed, be checked at the door and march in. It was down to the wing officers to alert the prisoners that it was time for chapel. However, this was another issue. Officers with no faith or those who lacked 'joie de vie', couldn't be bothered. They would make a half-hearted shout-out over the speaker.

Wagtail

This was 08:30, 09:30 and then 10:00 and 11:00 am on a Sunday morning. The message that the church service was starting shortly was rarely delivered with joy, it was slightly muffled or intentionally omitted. It was not a priority for most staff to have to release the prisoners for church. Most did eventually make it down albeit weary and unwashed. If nothing else this was a welcomed and short relief from the wing. Some came searching in hope of answers, some to socialise, some to pass drugs, some to experience a private poo. It always intrigued me how many times the prisoners would go to the loo. I would always check the toilets but never found anything except unflushed remains of white, bland food and bits of tattered loo roll on the floor, soaking up the poorly aimed wee.

The Christian chapel services were light and hopeful. The Catholic services were first, then the Church of England Free Church. My dear volunteer friends would give up their Sundays to play the keyboard with great gusto. Out-of-tune and testosterone-fuelled loud, gruff voices would sing the prison rendition of "How Great Thou Art." Nothing gave me more pleasure than listening to Matt Redman's 10,000 Reasons and My Lighthouse, both popular requests from the Church's top ten.

I encouraged questions and we would have conversations about hope, love, joy, peace, and forgiveness. I loved how prisoners would put their hands up or shout out questions, it was so much more encouraging than a sea of blank faces, and I never had to say shit once! On the odd occasion, the attending officers would catch a sneaky pass under a church chair. The prisoners were searched at the door supposedly but sometimes a quick movement from around the testicles or down a sock, articles passed to another man would be seen from hawk eyes. They would be marched out and banned for a few weeks or permanently.

We sang, we talked, we laughed. The prisoners hung on every word, no blank faces, they remembered previous talks and would have a multitude of questions.

Guest speakers from Christian recovery organisations, other church leaders and some of my friends visited. I invited my dear friends Les and Debbie along one Sunday to talk about forgiveness. Les had lost a brother, he was murdered. For years and years, Les waited for his revenge. He had a plan. The time came but God intervened. Les found the strength to forgive him. He found faith and was released from the terrible bitterness that he had suffered. He had been halted in his tracks, he thought of his beautiful family, and he didn't join the ranks!

At the end of each service, the prisoners lined up for Holy Communion. I was honoured and humbled to place the wafer on dirty, unwashed hands. I prayed for them and loved them. Most services flew by without a hitch until one day, the day the Bishop came to visit!

My dear friend, the Bishop, used to visit the prison throughout the year. I knew he would have a profound effect on the men. Not only would they feel special and loved because of his visit, but he was a man of wisdom and a gentle reflection of God's love for all humanity.

Church was full. All the rows of chairs were occupied. The prisoners often sat with their friends, sometimes using this time to catch up with pals who were on other wings. We started well, with good renditions as usual, a prayer and a few questions asked. Halfway through the hour-long service, there was a lot of chatter and laughter. The Bishop, dressed in his fine liturgical purple, was preaching and some of the prisoners were unsettled. The prisoners on the right side of the chapel were quiet and intent. However, the back few rows of prisoners were talking and becoming disruptive. I did my motherly "Gents, please," which usually worked. They are not in school, and usually, a passive-aggressive word will work. They settled for a moment then it started again. This time, I said nothing. I didn't get a chance.

One of the very faithful men, a big, tattooed hench and not to be argued with, turned and said politely. "Bit of respect, lads." Another request, then another and then all fury broke loose. The lads on the left told the others in no uncertain terms to "Shut the f**k up!"

Church or no church, the war began. Alarms were triggered and chairs were flying in the air, with metal legs prone to attack. I rugby tackled the Bishop and threw him behind the altar just like any 50+ years menopausal vicar should do! It was undignified but I was in automatic pilot.

The officers waded in. The prisoners were twisted up (tackled) and thrown to the floor. Punches were thrown, threats made, and then, just like that, a top-class northern scream from "Miss", and it stopped. The perpetrators were carried off, and the Bishop scrambled back to the lectern, straightening his purple robes. We all sat down and caught our breath. The ethereal presence of the Bishop brought us all back to focus. A quick rendition of "How Great Thou Art", Praise the Lord, peace was restored.

Sundays were mostly fabulous, and so were our weekly meetings and group sessions with the men. We would sit and chat with freedom, no prying eyes, no uninvited shell likes (ears), and time. This precious time was spent encouraging, teaching, and loving these souls. One young man told me that this was the only place he felt safe and valued. He felt here he was with friends.

All the seasons and festivals were celebrated, (before COVID). These occasions were like a double-edged sword. Easter service was popular because it meant a chocolate gift, usually a chocolate egg, but more importantly, it was a time to gather, celebrate and reflect on life and new beginnings. Christmas often amplified feelings of loneliness. We did what we could to make the season as enjoyable as possible. On the wings, old, battered, plastic Christmas trees would be dragged out of storerooms and adorned with broken lights and a few tattered decorations. A solitary tree, bent and broken, would be set in the middle of this steel-grated, cold, and harsh place.

Christmas for the team was an epic undertaking. Being a bit of a bar humbug and since discovering Santa wasn't real, it has always overwhelmed me. The stress and the smashing of shopping trolleys, the race for the last sprout and the ridiculous pressure on finances. The adverts that start in September, promising 40% off a new settee, delivered in time for Christmas, drive me crazy. In prison, however, my colleagues and I tried to make this a special time of year. In prison, the festive season looked different; it felt different, and it was distant yet present. Prison ironically resembled a similar story, one of poverty, oppression, and struggling to find shelter. A cold, sparse cell yet a distant light and hope.

Despite the sadness, the year of the Christmas RAP was one of the most joyous times. There was a RAP group led by my dear friend and Christian colleague Nick. Nick had a way with the men, he was young and trendy and wore the most ridiculous baggy Jeans with a dropped gusset! I used to threaten to buy a pair of drop gusset jeans to fit in! We used to laugh a lot; I really admired his commitment to changing the lives of the young prisoners he worked with. I would sometimes listen through the door of the chapel to the conversations that were going on. Sometimes I would go in because I didn't want to miss out, but Nick would admonish me quietly and tell me off for distracting the men. Sports and music are key to building relationships. Most of us love music, maybe not RAP but here the prisoners were comfortable making music and rapping with a shoosh down the microphone. They would often RAP about their lives; it was a good release.

Close to Christmas Eve, I wandered into the chapel to chat with the men! They were packing up after their session. I was downhearted because I was leading the Christmas Day services, and I had no musicians. Now I can do quite a lot of things well, but I cannot sing! My sister Liz told me that I was the most confident terrible singer she had ever heard.

One year I went on holiday to Egypt with my three girlfriends. We arrived late to the hotel and were off to bed. However, distracted by luminous green cocktails we were lured into the hotel bar. The poor DJ was struggling to get anyone up to dance or volunteer for the Karaoke. Still dressed in the clothes we had travelled in we ventured to the disco room. My friends always made a point of telling everyone I could sing and that was a vicar, not sure why! Anyhow, after a couple more radium green cocktails, I volunteered to get up and treat everyone with my rendition of Amy Winehouse's

"Valerie." Well, that was it, my awful confident singing drew in the crowds. The dance floor filled up and I spent my first evening dominating the microphone, singing Waterloo and other ABBA greats. I think we finally retired at 2am. The disco Karaoke night was to be on the following Wednesday and Friday and the DJ begged me to come back, and so I did! A few years later I was walking my dog on the reservoir when a couple approached me and said they recognised the singing vicar from Egypt! My claim to fame, the most confident terrible singer!

On another occasion, my shocking singing helped me bond with the prisoners. I had gone onto a wing to track down some men. Sometimes, the prisoners would respond if you shouted their name but sometimes, for whatever reason, they would totally ignore the bellowing. On this occasion, I was fed up with trawling around the wing, ducking and diving to avoid the pool cues. Eventually, and about to give up, I climbed the metal stairs, stood on the top landing and at full pelt sang "I Will Follow Him" from Sister Act, followed by Stormzy's "Blinded by Your Grace." After getting the attention of the whole wing and rapturous applause from the men, I found who I was looking for and it was a job well done.

Wagtail

I would just have to lead the Carols on Christmas day, I wasn't hopeful! A couple of my 'friends' asked me if I was ok; I was perched on the edge of the altar with a couple of CDs, looking at the festive selection. This was my only option; I would have to print the words, play the CD, and we would have to manage.

The two men looked at each other, feeling sorry for me and concocting a plan to avoid me having to sing! "We'll help you, Miss," they volunteered. The two men, who I will call Mr C and Mr D, came up with a plan. Now Mr C was a delightful young man. He had a calm and steady personality, and he was always willing to help. He had a very mature and caring nature and would often help men who were struggling with his words of wisdom. He didn't profess to having a particular faith, but his time in prison had caused him to dig deep to find his peace. He would come to church regularly and he attended a lot of the courses and events we held. He was also a great poet, and I had listened to a few of his cleverly worded and posed descriptions about life. He offered to write a poem about Christmas. Mr D also volunteered. Mr D was a famous rapper, he had made a million or more. Mr D had the pearliest veneers I had ever seen. I always used to joke that I could see him coming from a mile away. However talented he was and however much money he had made he found himself on the wrong side of the law. This time he was doing a lengthy stretch.

The next day, after lunch, we pulled up three chairs around the chapel audio system; we only had a few hours to prepare. Mr D had written a RAP overnight and assured me that the service on Christmas day would be packed because his team and his fans were all going to come and support him. I was, of course, delighted at having a chance to share the joy of Christmas! So, we decided to use the I song "O Holy Night." I wasn't really prepared for the perfectionist that Mr D was and, as the RAP unfolded, I was a little taken aback. We rehearsed all afternoon. The song would start "O Holy Night the Stars are brightly shining….," and pause, press hold. Mr D would then come in with the RAP. The beauty of the song started, the beauty and fantasy of a perfect Christmas, stars shining, baby Jesus being born, Heavenly Angels descending, then stopping.

I was his techy, I oversaw the pause and listened carefully to the boss to make sure he had enough time to bring in the words he had written. I pressed pause to listen and I couldn't quite believe what I heard. The expression of grief and sadness in the RAP was moving yet quite shocking. I don't remember all the well-rehearsed words that flowed from his heart and into his vocal cords. It was about his chaotic life, his childhood and his father who had taken his own life whilst he too was in prison. The description of the blood coming under the cell door was vivid and shocking. I pondered and tried to consider if I dared even criticise his motives or his reason for wanting to interject this beautiful song with such a traumatic story. Then I had a realisation, and I understood the meaning from an entirely different perspective. This was *his* Christmas! It wasn't mine to intervene, although I did ask for a few of the expletives to be removed. "O Holy Night" was interspersed with tragedy and pain, not unlike the real Christmas story of rejection and poverty yet with the joy of a baby being born. After hours of rehearsing, we were ready.

And so, when it arrived, I welcomed my friends; the chapel was full. Mr D walked in with his entourage clad in Gucci tracksuits. His was black with a gold Gucci pattern design, and his wingman was the same, yet in blue and red. I tried hard not to stare at the expensive gilded tracksuits. They stood out and they were a statement of power and ill-guided success. They were also an indication of a long sentence because personal clothing can only be sent in after sentencing. We managed to squeak and grunt a few popular carols, I shared a message of hope, Mr C read his poem, rounds of cheers and applause, and then came time for the showstopper. The RAP! And it was amazing! The joy of Christmas was interspersed with the raw pain of this young man's life. Mr D was not on stage, he was in church. He didn't have his usual possie, he was on his own, sharing his vulnerability with an audience of fellow hurting men. He told us after the performance that it was the most nervous, he had ever been! An uproar of appreciation and clapping set us all in tears and Christmas was complete! For me, it was the best gift ever. Mr C and Mr D pulled it off and the service was the talk of the prison for many months after.

Now this next story should really be in the Oops chapter! Before COVID, we planned the annual community service. We could invite friends and family to come, and this was a special event for the staff, management, and the men. I dressed as a mad old lady with straw and feathers in my hair and made a complete fool of myself. I used awful tacky singing birds and other homemade props and sang the 12 Days of Christmas. The guest list included senior managers and some charity partners, Oh and Andy Burnham, Mayor of Manchester and this is where the Oops comes in. Three months prior, I had written to dignitaries including Andy.

Wagtail

No response from the mayor's office so I presumed he wasn't attending. Then the day before a response, he was coming along, delighted to get the invite. I dashed around happily with my efforts to mix with the higher echelons. I told my boss. I expected a brownie point. Oh no, here we go again. Little did I know the pandemonium this would cause. Word got through to the head of security and I was hauled in again. How was I supposed to know that this was a high-security visit? For me, he was just the mayor. My poor boss, who by this time referred to me as unpredictable, was kind and he supported me.

We didn't have to cancel the visit; we didn't have time for red carpets, but we covered it! Mr Burnham arrived much to the delight of the men and, to be honest, the managers schmoozed around him after the service. I sang with wellies on and straw coming out of my hair, and there were readings from staff, and the men really appreciated this time. They were visible, the centre of attention and of great fascination and intrigue for my guests. Everything went off swimmingly, thank you very much! Another lesson learned on the hoof!

There were other faith events throughout the year. Ramadan proved to be an ongoing struggle for my

Muslim colleagues. The battle to make sure the food was correctly prepared and delivered caused no end of problems. The catering manager and my boss spent hours trying to organise and meet the needs of the Muslim community. The water flasks, the distribution of prayer times, food being available after fasting, it was a tumultuous task, one I guess my dear friend is still losing sleep over.

Meeting the faith needs of prisoners is a human right. Sadly, however, for those staff with little or no faith, it seemed a drudgery; some were helpful, but most just saw these times, understandably with extreme staff shortages, as another demand. We did what we could with what we had.

Pagan and Buddhist festivals were also celebrated. Before lockdown, a side room in the chapel was used as a gathering place for short meditations and recitation of Pagan readings. The Sikh community was supported by the most wonderful, kind, and gentle leader; he visited weekly. He was amazing and just overflowed with peace and tranquillity.

Our Rabbi visited on High days and Holy days within the Jewish calendar. There were very few Jewish prisoners. I only ever met one Jewish prisoner. The Rabbi visited him and made sure he had his Holy books and that he had access to Kosher food. This Hasidic Jewish man looked so out of place in prison. It was hard to comprehend what he was doing there, but there was no other option after he had been arrested for what seemed a very minor offence. He sat in his cell, unable to speak English, in his holy robes, looking like a terrified deer in the headlights. There were one or two others, but I didn't meet them. I never came across Jewish characters, the likes of Fagin, portrayed by Ron Moody in Oliver, and Alfie Solomon, played by Tom Hardy in Peaky Blinders. Sadly, Tom Hardy never crossed my path, and Fagin must be long gone.

It is my observation that Jewish communities look out for one another. Crime within this community is almost non-existent. If they haven't got it, they don't take it! If they struggle the community will come together to provide.

There was a community of travellers, in the prison. I really enjoyed their company; they were funny and very respectful to the folk of the cloth. They did struggle with the possibility that a female could be a priest, (But not in the Roman Catholic tradition.) It took some explanation.

I have always been fascinated and interested in the travelling community. They often have an inherent fear of God. The travelling fraternity would sometimes boast about their crimes. I wouldn't listen to their stories and would receive honest and tough talk from me.

In 2011, a study was published to inform the prison estate about the culture and needs of travellers. The study: *"Voices Unheard"* shares this MORI pole from 2001 that states:

"The life of an Irish Traveller is often short, framed by exclusion and discrimination. In Britain and Ireland, opinion polls frequently identify Travellers as the most disliked group in society."

Outside Ireland where the Nomadic community originate from, the UK has the largest travelling population. There has been a historical resistance to the rights of the Irish travelling community from land legislation and the resistance from settled people. Unfortunately, the negative social factors that face travellers, sometimes extend to prison. They, too, have needs that may be different from the general population. They live in a community, and being incarcerated and isolated can perhaps have a more serious and detrimental effect. The study identified that travellers are most likely to be Roman Catholic, and they identify the chaplain as the one person they could trust.

I had a great fondness for the travelling boys and men, but I could never quite marry up their fear of God with the arrogance of committing a crime without addressing the consequences. This is God-fearing culture, with at the same time a nonchalant attitude to crime. I am not suggesting all travellers are criminals, far from it. However, maybe here, crime is underpinned by culture, survival, the need to impress, youthful tomfoolery or plain greed to get what you haven't got.

Donald Stoesz gives an explanation in his book, Glimpses of Grace. He suggests that *"...the intentions of our heart are sometimes evident to other people while remaining hidden from ourselves." I recognised this on occasion. Maybe the dare-devil attitude was inherited from a chaotic childhood."* Donald Stoesz: Glimpses of Grace: 2010

It is interesting to observe different cultures. We all do things because of our culture; it defines us to some degree. Nature and nurture again play a part in our behaviours and decision-making. We can try to influence the detrimental actions of others, but when they are intrinsic, it is difficult. Some things we should try to change, but sometimes we have no right to.

A Roman Catholic Priest, Vincent Donavon, was a missionary to the Masai Warriors in Africa. European Christians had previously made their way into Africa and had attempted to convert these strong individuals. In a bid to do so, they attempted to westernise the men, dressing them in suits and educating them in scholarly institutions. This attempt to evangelise and bring people to the Christian faith failed miserably. Although one or two remained faithful to the faith, they were few and far between. The priest worked in Africa amongst the Maasai years after the initial venture. He soon recognised that to reach people you must understand and respect their culture. Living incarnate with these people had a greater effect than taking them away from their cultures and embracing Western influences. He faced many challenges and recalled stories. At one time after witnessing such a challenge, when a warrior had been banished and cast out from the community. Donovan suggested they might consider forgiveness and reconciliation. He didn't force it, but it was a welcome alternative. There are so many fascinating stories in his book *"Christianity Rediscovered."* He lived with them, worked with them, and hunted with them whilst showing love and respect for their traditions.

Often, the prisoners from the travelling community in prison couldn't read or write, and we would help them navigate the Kiosk to make appointments and be an advocate for them. Sometimes we just used to chat. I have a terrible habit of impersonating accents, when I engage in conversation with someone with a different accent, I adopt it. It's embarrassing sometimes but I really can't help it! I have done it in meetings, at funerals and in other inappropriate situations. In this case, however, my Dublin accent worked wonders. I added the best-rolled "Rs" to my Dublin accent, which always went down a storm. The prisoners would always ask me where I was from and at this point, I had to confess, I was a Mancunian through and through.

These prisoners were very territorial and always hung around together. Entire families could be in prison at the same time. There could be cousins, brothers, and once a father and son sharing a cell. I liked the travelling folks, mischievous as they were. In this terrain, I learned so much from them about their beliefs; they brightened my day.

Apart from regular Chaplaincy duties, we were sometimes asked to volunteer and hold other responsibilities. Many of us had other skills and experience and the prison welcomed this. I was part of the "Dying Well in Custody" team. As the prison population continues to grow and age, the number of older prisoners is inevitably increasing. In addition to accidental deaths, suicides, and acute illnesses, natural deaths from age-related causes are becoming more common.

With an aging prisoner population, prisons are facing a rise in chronic illnesses, disabilities, and other age-related conditions, which require additional care and attention. No matter how unwell or how near to the end of life, prisoners are expected to stay in prison until their life ends. There are some facilities available for end-of-life care which involve transferring prisoners out of the prison. End-of-life policies were written to make sure prisoners died with dignity and care.

Working in the Chaplaincy was hard, every day presented difficulties and trauma of one description or another. There were, however, many funny times. Dark humour kept us going. There are so many stories to tell but a couple really come to mind.

Wagtail

I had been called out to Healthcare to see a prisoner/patient. Just as I was about to leave, another man was carried in and dropped on the floor face-first. I recognised him; I had spoken to him several times. He was face down and then turned onto his side whilst he riled around with the effects of SPICE. The staff looked on at his catatonic body as it stiffened. They were rough with him, and I objected. They then laid him on his side. I knelt beside him, and he threw up on the floor and on my knees. My pen that was hanging off the lanyard dropped into his vomit. It was a decent pen! Disgusting, I know, but I picked it out of the vomit and wiped it. I put it back on my lanyard. Later in the day, as we all do, I chewed on the end of the pen! In a sheer state of panic, I realised that I had probably ingested SPICE! I hadn't cleaned it with sterile wipes as was my intention and so I spent all day with psychosomatic symptoms of SPICE ingestion, much to the amusement of the team.

My friend, Joe, and I had concerns about a man in Segregation who we were convinced was possessed. I was nearing the end of my time at the prison, so I was extra bold. Together we snook through a gate that led to the outer walls of Segregation and crouched outside the cell of the man who was screaming and quoting the Bible with a demonic screeching voice. He was causing no end of disruption. We didn't think we could get near enough to him on the wing, so instead, we knelt under his window. Knees on gravel, we started praying and throwing holy water into his cell. Through the grated window, he saw us and started cursing louder than ever. We turned and dashed, not quite sure if we had done the right thing. Hours later he calmed down. Say what you will, but desperate times often call for desperate measures, and we both believed that there was a need for spiritual intervention. We giggled at the madness and kept it to ourselves.

Ironically, when I started my new Chaplaincy post at a Manchester hospital, this unbelievable thing happened. I was walking into my place of work. It was my first day. Sitting in the smoking shed outside was a man, head down, wearing a cloth hat, looking unkempt and dishevelled. I didn't recognise him. He shouted out as I walked past, "Hey Miss!" That recognition and familiar address stopped me in my tracks. I turned, he removed his hat, and there he was the same man who was screaming out religious profanities in a gruff, frightening voice, sitting in the smoking shelter. "What are you doing here?" I asked with some confusion. "Nowhere to go, thought I'd come and sit here for a bit. I've been up all night." He returned the question. "What are you doing here?" We chatted while I made him a cuppa. I asked him if he had remembered the episode that resembled an action shot from "The Exorcist." "Yes, I remember everything," he laughed, "Your nutters throwing holy water through the bars. I was better after that." We chatted a bit more and I told him to come back. I found some clothes and food for him. He didn't come back, and I never saw him again!

Boredom was a huge problem for the men. The team tried to help alleviate the boredom by delivering books, colouring pencils, paper, and craft materials. This was really the job of education and other departments, but they were overwhelmed, so we tried to help. Apart from a tambourine episode that I will explain later, we would always check that materials were permitted and safe to use.

Some of the prisoners were fantastic artists. We had a collection of unflattering portraits on the Chaplaincy notice board. This was a great way of keeping prisoners occupied. But not everyone was an artist. At one time, gardening and growing flowers and vegetables outside in the polytunnels had been a popular pastime. However, cutbacks and risk meant this activity was not a high priority.

One of my colleagues regularly visited a young man. He had mental health problems and was pale, timid, and undernourished. He was a pleasant soul. He suffered from depression and his cell was a bit of a mess. Adding to the mess, he had started scraping up dirt from the yard. Like a scene from The Great Escape, he would scrape up a little more dirt every day from the borders of the exercise yard. He put the dirt in plastic cups and anything else he could find to make plant pots. The plant pots were lined up and proudly displayed on his window ledge. With ingenuity, he also planted some apple seeds and some other weeds in the little makeshift pots.

In all innocence, my friend bought some seeds for him. They were just regular little plant seeds. He took great pride in talking to my colleague about the progress of his seeds. My colleague, a wonderful caring chaplain, bought him some gardening books. His intentions were good, and our friend had shown real progress with his new hobby. They were just seeds growing in gritty, yet nourishing earth; he watered them and watched them grow; he had something to think about other than himself. They were of no harm to anyone; it wasn't marijuana or anything illegal, just a few saplings. However, a particularly grumpy senior noticed the pots and saplings; he came into the cell and demanded that they be removed. They were thrown in the bin; my colleague was admonished, and the little garden plot was no more. The young man didn't react; he just accepted the outcome. He was just so sad and so were we!

Prisoners would plead and beg for radios. They were rare, like rocking horse poo! If they managed to obtain one, usually after someone had left, they guarded it with their life. One day, a man came down to the chapel. We had a discussion in my office about his future and whether we could work together to find him somewhere to live when he was released. He didn't want to live alone as he needed support and company. Shelter and Through the Gate had exhausted all options. So, we chatted for ages about the possibility of a Christian rehab. He left after some time, happy that there was hope.

We had an old radio with a wonky aerial in the Chaplaincy office and we just about managed to tune into Zoe Ball each morning, after moving it around the department to get decent reception. The radio had been left in the corridor for some reason, and it was just too much of a temptation. The radio was shouting out, "Take me, I'm yours!" and when the man I had been chatting to left, he stuffed it up his jumper and took off. Minutes later, I noticed that the old silver radio with wonky arial had gone. He had been the only visitor that morning. I asked security to look on camera and, sure enough, there he was, quickly marching up Main Street with a bulging stomach! Security wanted to punish him, but I asked them to give him a chance. I was furious and disappointed that I had spent time trying to help this man. I did my usual quick march up the corridor, boots on grates, found his cell and addressed him. After my interrogation, he still denied that he had taken it. We all knew he had. So, I gave him a last chance. "Ok, this is your last chance. I am asking you to return my radio. You have an hour. You can walk back down to the chapel and hand it in. I will leave the decision with you."

Within the next ten minutes, he returned. The wires had been pulled out and the arial bent. He had taken the wires out of the plug to try to fix it to the mains because his plug socket was broken. He handed it back to me and I thanked him. In desperation and in an environment of getting what you can at any given opportunity, he admitted to taking it. He just wanted a meagre battered radio. I wanted to give it back to him, but I didn't. He left prison soon after that; we couldn't find him any accommodation. I never saw him again.

The demand on the Chaplaincy team was relentless. Sometimes, I would have to gather all my strength, pray, and then launch myself into the day's work. Sometimes, I was just so tired of listening to problems and sadness. But the truth is that the prisoners needed us, but it was hard. My conscience was pricked once by a young man. He had severe mental health problems. I visited him regularly and, every time I visited the wing to see another prisoner, he would shout out, "Miss, don't forget me!" He would want a blessing and another set of rosary beads. Once, I was really shattered and it was nearing the end of the day. I visited someone on the same wing. I knew where his cell was so, when I passed by, I crouched down under his window so he couldn't see me. As I ducked down and passed his cell, his weak voice called out, "Miss, I know you're there. Stop hiding. Please come and see me." Caught out, I called in, put my hand on his bowed shaved head, said a prayer and left. He had no one in the world, and I tried to deny him a moment of my time because I was tired. I never did that again!

On rounds, the chaplains would carry stacks of small Gideon bibles to hand out. They were like hotcakes; everyone wanted one. Even people without faith or of other traditions took them. Sometimes, I would open a cell door, after knocking of course, and I would find a man propped up in bed reading the little book. It filled me with hope. A guard laughed at me one day and told me not to bother giving them out, "They don't read those, you know; they use the pages to roll up tobacco or weed." It was true; the pages were paper thin just like cigarette papers, but they would rather smoke their way through Matthew, Mark, Luke, and John than steal or get in debt for real Rizlas. His comments only encouraged me to distribute more! Even if they didn't read a word, they could still "inhale" hope.

And this is what we tried to share, hope. If nothing else, we showed kindness, gave our time, and worked hard to try to make a difference in the lives of almost 1,500 men.

The Chaplaincy team was and still is amazing. I still see them and when we get together, we have a very special bond, one that can only be understood by a team that supported one another through adversity. We looked out for one another through good times and bad. I miss them, and I admire them for all they did and continue to do.

Wagtail

Chapter 11
A house in not a home
"Home is where one starts from."
T. S. Eliot

Resettlement took up a lot of my time. I had an interest in homelessness and had previously volunteered with a Manchester charity back in the early 90s called Barnabas. Homelessness is an ongoing problem in the city, and we worked tirelessly with Shelter and Through the Gate to try and find suitable accommodation for prisoners on release. If we were fortunate, we had time to meet and discuss needs and liaise with homeless charities. There is a huge lack of suitable accommodation facilitated by Shelter, and so we begged and pleaded with others to help. If Shelter had not managed to find accommodation, the Through the Gate team would visit me and we would team up for the task.

There was a notice on the Chaplaincy board that said, "A house is not a home." I looked at this every day and I agreed with the sentiment. Just handing someone a set of keys on release is not enough to heal a broken soul. They were often lonely and bored and inevitably would find themselves back in prison in a few weeks or months. Alongside the poster were other leaflets and posters about rehabs and alternative 'homes' to Shelter. Sometimes but not often, we managed to rehome the men in suitable accommodation. Some would cope with a new home, but many would not. They were lonely and chaotic and didn't have a clue how to survive in the world.

Many of the Christian charities expected the men to be off drugs and medication and this presented more complications. If they were withdrawing from heroin and were on methadone prescriptions, they had to be reduced to none. Drug and substance misuse is difficult to manage and monitor and the hope of a new home with some care and company was often dashed by the speed of release date. There wasn't enough time to withdraw and so the men would leave homeless and helpless. If Shelter could not accommodate them, then that was it: back into a cycle of crime to finance their addiction, and back through the revolving door.

There were occasional happy endings. It wasn't all gloomy, but it is a failing of the State that we don't have enough places to house ex-offenders on their release. Even if there are enough houses or flats available, for many this is not going to help their situation. A house would not heal the pain and loneliness they suffered and a broken heart cannot be patched up with a roof and an Elastoplast.

Gate fever is a common phenomenon in the countdown to release. Although many will run like a bat out of hell when the gates open, some are more reluctant. The days and weeks prior to leaving can be stress-inducing.

Phoebe Willets describes this as one who suffered this herself. During her time in custody, she noticed a woman crying. She enquired with compassion, only to find out that the woman was due to be released the following week. Instead of being elated, this woman was terrified at the prospect. She writes,

"It was just gate fever, that queer, inexplicable incredible disease that was to come to all of us one day, the fear of life, like the fear of death; the fear of the unknown and the half-remembered world outside."
Phoebe Willets: Invisible Bars: 1965

The Through the Gate team was fabulous, and I made good friends with a couple of the young women there. Hannah and Olivia were super colleagues. Hannah was the nicest, and most compassionate person. She went the extra mile to help people. She arrived at my office in the Chaplaincy one day in floods of tears and told me this sad story. I stayed in touch with Hannah, and it is with her permission that I have shared this. Hannah's role at the prison was to help and prepare people for their upcoming release. In October/November 2019, she was allocated a Service User, who we will call John.

John was an older prisoner in his 60s, but due to his illnesses, he seemed much older. He was quite frail but made up for it verbally. Although John could be verbally abusive to other prisoners and staff, it was clear to her that this was a defence mechanism to cope with this time in custody. And coping, he was not.

John was getting bullied on the wing, his tea and coffee packs were stolen, and he didn't have many clothes. John often missed his medication time slot which also caused him some distress. When she (Hannah)arrived at his wing to speak to him, he rolled his eyes and pretty much dismissed me on the spot. It was a facial expression she had seen many times. She could almost hear the thoughts running through his head. "Who the hell is this young girl and why is she bothering me when I am trying to sleep? She looks like she's at the bottom of the hierarchy, she won't be able to do anything for me." Dismissed but not deterred, John muttered a few words to her where she was first able to hear his accent. Geordie. Fantastic, she thought. Her partner was born in Newcastle, she had picked up a bit of slang and culture from the Northeast. She knew the Geordie dialect, deciding not to discuss anything about his rehabilitation, but to ask him about Newcastle and his favourite parts. She told him she liked the Minchello Ice Cream at South Shields, but only with "monkeys bloody" (raspberry sauce) on it. She told him she liked Pease pudding, but it never filled her up so she would always get a bacon sandwich as well. Of course, she kept the conversation professional but casual and kept the details of how she had experienced Newcastle private.

She was slowly breaking down the initial stroppy barrier and building a rapport with John. She had a few more chats about the Northeast and then got onto why he had ended up in custody. The first thing she did for John was sort him out a proper cup of tea. It really took minimal effort to replace his stolen tea and coffee pack, but it meant a lot to him. Although she isn't a tea or coffee drinker, she knew it was something simple like that which could provide so much comfort to someone. So, in all honesty, that's all it took. A chat about Newcastle, a cup of tea, and some time to listen to

John's concerns. Over time, John became more comfortable talking to her. She ensured that he did not miss any more medication and moved him down to the lower level of the wing, as his mobility was poor. Hannah worked with him for 3 months to try and better his communication skills and challenge some racial ideologies he had. She said, "I will never know if I got through to him on the racial side of things, but I saw the communication skills enhance. He went from the grumpy old Geordie to the less grumpy old Geordie with a bit of banter, who greeted me politely."

John was released on 28 November 2019. The day was freezing, and he had quite the journey ahead of him. John had to present to Chester Le Street Probation in the Northeast that day, or risk getting recalled. For someone who has just been released from custody, who is old, quite unwell and in the middle of winter, Hannah thought this would be a challenge. She spoke to her manager who agreed that she could physically put John in her car and take him to the station. He wanted a cigarette desperately upon release and explained, "I was concerned he would look for a local shop first, get lost, not find the correct bus, and end up missing his train. I did not want this to happen."

So, with a male colleague, Hannah waited for John to be released from custody and took him to the station. He had a travel warrant, which was provided by HMP. We requested this to ensure his journey was paid for as he was completely out of the area. At the station, we gave John some of my partner's old walking boots, which were in great condition, and he was thrilled with those. The Chaplaincy provided a coat for John and some other clothes which he was also happy with, as well as a rucksack with extra items in. Hannah had made John a packed lunch, so he had no excuse to go to a shop (after the purchase of cigarettes) and miss the train. She had covered all bases.

They arrived at the Station and noticed the travel warrant was incorrect. "No bother," she thought, "I have a pen. I will just amend it, as it's handwritten anyway." This was a disaster and was not accepted by the extremely rude and obnoxious train customer service lady. She explained the situation, showed her prison ID, and pointed to John nearby. It was clear he had just been released, he looked homeless. The lady showed absolutely zero sympathy for the situation and deemed the travel warrant completely invalid. So, Hannah paid for John's ticket with her own money. Luckily, it was payday; if it had been a day earlier, the transaction wouldn't have gone through, ha! It's safe to say she made a formal complaint about the lady.

The most important thing for Hannah at the time was to ensure John was physically on the train to Chester Le Street, or all our hard work would be for nothing. The probation officer he was working with was great, he had ensured the keys to John's house were readily available at probation, and everything seemed in place. They argued their way through the barriers to make sure we physically put John on the train. In the end, he was very grateful for the help. She explained, "He could see I was quite flustered towards the end as time was ticking to purchase a new ticket and get the correct train, so he was very sweet and thanked me, in what I took as a very genuine way."

Hannah followed up with John's probation officer who informed me that he had made it on time, and he was now settled back in his house. We were really pleased with this news, it felt like it was a job well done. That was until 13 January 2020, when Hannah was contacted and told that John had died. Hannah was extremely upset as she knew he had no family and would have died in the house alone.

Although not a religious person, Hannah described herself as an Agnostic but wanted to talk to someone about this sad story.

"I went to the Chaplaincy to speak with Rev Annie about this news. The particularly sad thing about this case for me, was did John die alone? After overcoming his time in custody, finally being released, and getting home, he ended up passing away. Annie and I lit a candle in his memory and nice words were said to remember him and offer me some peace. I have thought about John several times since. This was a sad case for me, I was very upset when I heard the news. I can only hope that John felt that I showed him some kindness in a difficult part of his life. Thank you for taking the time to read his story."

Wagtail

Chapter 12
Oops, I did it again
"Mistakes are part of the dues one pays for a full life."
Sophia Loren

Of my own volition, I can honestly say I can be quite dippy. Trusting me with a set of keys was, quite frankly, hilarious. The number of times I lose my phone and my keys in a day is in another league. Being slightly older, post-menopause, and falsely blonde, I forget where I am going, am always late and cannot, for the life of me, remember people's names.

This was always an issue when I was a vicar. Before a wedding or a funeral, I had to rehearse names again and again. One sunny Saturday, I conducted the most beautiful wedding. One of the bridesmaids was the ex of the groom. As soon as the wedding party told me at rehearsal, I had images running through my mind of saying the ex-girlfriend's name instead of the bride's. Why had they told me? A forgone disaster! I rehearsed out loud again and again. The bride's name, the groom's name, trying to bury the ex-girlfriend's name in the depths of my grey matter. I think we can all identify with this: inappropriate laughing and giggling when we shouldn't be. I tried and I tried, but yes, you got it. On the day of the wedding, in front of a packed church, I called the bride by the ex-girlfriend's name. Fortunately, they thought it quite hysterical and took it with good humour, but I lived with this ridiculous scenario for weeks after.

It is a vicar's worst nightmare to get a name wrong at a wedding or funeral! I was tired and inexperienced, nervous at the prospect of conducting a funeral service followed by an interment at the graveside. The church service had gone without a hitch, and we arrived at the cemetery. The grave sides were covered with false green matting and planks were laid on top to rest the coffin. I took my position at the foot of the plot. The wind blew, and it started to rain, and I was caught up in my own thoughts about what I had to say next. I was fumbling with the soggy notes, trying to stop the rain from washing the words away. I called the family closer to stand around the empty grave. Once everyone had gathered, I began to recite the liturgy for the next part of the service. I lifted my head up and glanced over at the funeral cortege, smiled, and glanced at the hearse still holding the coffin. I Had forgotten the dear soul we were burying. My heart sank, I felt sick, and I wanted to throw up and jump into the deep hole and be covered by the wet clay! No, no, no! I had to rustle up some sense of decorum very quickly as the funeral director waved at me. I paused and then made up some prayers about us all preparing to receive the dear family member who was still lying in the ornate coffin in the black funeral car. I prayed a makeshift preparation prayer and bluffed out a few reassuring words. I looked up again and the funeral directors nodded, somewhat bemused, to tell me they were ready to bring the coffin over. I was mortified but relieved that no one, not even the super-efficient, professional funeral directors realised that I was about to bury a beloved and dearly departed soul without them being present.

When I am nervous, my mind runs amok. Sometimes, when I'm bored or feel detached from what is going on around me. It is in these situations that I start to think the most ridiculous thoughts. In long silences, I often crack jokes or jibber relentlessly. My brain goes into overdrive, and my mouth starts moving on its own, and without a brain-mouth connection, I waffle or say things I later regret.

I was once at a meeting with the then Suffragan Bishop of Stockport. The Bishop and I were like chalk and cheese. I was quite in awe of him. He had an ethereal presence; he was cool, calm, and holy. I felt he could read my mind, and I felt naked in his presence. Now, he is a wonderful man and later, as I got to know him, I found him quite a comfort. In fact, I always cried when I was with him as he touched my heart with his kind words. It was like being in the presence of God himself. I had been to a meeting with him and was sitting in his beautiful lodge, surrounded by row upon row of theological books. There were postcards everywhere and artefacts from his travels. He is a highly educated man and had at one time been a monk. I had received a poor education at a secondary school and was not an academic achiever. A girl who just about scraped through school with three O levels, then two AS levels at college, the minimal entry qualifications for general nurse training. I hadn't and still don't have a very broad understanding of the English language; I didn't understand half of the words he shared in the meeting. Memorising and hanging on to this word or that word, I thought, "That sounds very intelligent, I need to check my thesaurus." I listened for a while at the meeting and then found myself drifting off, glancing around at the bookshelves. Has he really read all these books? Lovely colour scheme. I wonder if he has any friends or family. Oh, the grey matter was working overtime. I passed by his kitchen going to the loo. It was reminiscent of a stately home, gorgeous and very posh, yet there was I, three 'O' Levels to my name. At the end of the meeting, we all got up to leave. As we approached the door, I thought, "I wonder if he has a cook or a housekeeper like Father Ted." Mouth, foot here we go!

"What are you having for your tea?" I asked, much to the bemusement of the other learned clergy leaving by the huge panelled oak door. "Err, I haven't really thought about it, my dear." I dug myself deeper and asked, "Do you make your own tea? Do you have a cook?" Oh no, please throw me in that grave again and cover me with clay. He tipped his head sideways, "Yes, of course I cook," he replied with a contrite grin. How stupid of me, I was just saying something, anything to contribute and make up for my lack of enthusiasm at the meeting.

On another occasion, while working as an emergency nurse at Manchester Airport. I had another embarrassing encounter. A very famous sporting celebrity was sitting in the executive lounge. We were called to see a passenger who had become unwell. Tending to the patient, I glanced over to notice a famous footballer. Unfortunately, he had been in the media quite recently. His drug issues and problems had made the headlines. After tending to the patient, I thought it might be a good idea to tiptoe over to him and have a chat. I plonked myself next to him. The verbal diarrhoea just spilled out between my very nervous, dry lips.

"Hello," I said. He stared at me, not friendly at all. Humph! "I'm so sorry to hear about your drug issues. I will pray for you to get the help you need." I sat and smiled whilst his eyes grew larger, and he wiggled about. I sat waiting for a response, hands clasped on my knees. My colleague was mortified and so was I. What was I doing? Oops, it just happened again! He said nothing and so I stood, straightened my uniform, said goodbye, and walked away, running once I was out of his sight. I should have just asked for his autograph like any other normal star-struck member of the public.

I often dreamed of being friends with a celebrity. I would be such a good companion and confidante. There is a scene in Notting Hill, which is my second favourite film, after The Sound of Music. In the hilarious scene, Honey meets the actress Anna Scott at a dinner party and reassures Anna that she would be the most amazing best friend. She stutters and blushes and comes out with the precious idea that Julia needs a best friend just like her. Well, if any scene can portray me, this is it. I must add here, and this is my claim to fame, that I really did meet Anna, (Julia Roberts). In the mid-1980s, I was working in Los Angeles. She was a patient in the private hospital where I worked on Venice Drive. We really got on well. She was lovely, and she really did ask me to meet up with her on Venice Beach. Ah, can you imagine? I never took her up on her offer. Then guess what? She rose to fame, and I missed my chance. What a good friend I could have been!

Now, I laugh at the many mistakes and crazy encounters I have had in my life. The reason I share these now is to paint a picture of me, my personality, and the potential for "*booberations.*"

And so, back to the real world and, on a serious note. Mistakes, a wrong word, or a misinterpretation, can take on an entirely different meaning and potentially have devastating outcomes in prison. And yes, I made them and quite a few. In the first few weeks of employment, you join all the other newbies in "prison craft," as the then-lead chaplain used to call it. You learn about prison regimes, the assessment and care process, the intricacies of communication, social conditioning, coercive behaviour, and never to bring in a mobile phone or anything else that might cause you to end up jobless and possibly on a stretch! We are reminded of the consequences of offering to post letters for prisoners and remaining on red alert for inappropriate or dangerous intent. We are also taught the wonderful skill of how to manage keys and open cell doors. I can't even begin to explain the weirdness of holding keys and the skill needed to flick open a cell door. It might sound simple, but it's not. You must close your mind and not think too much when you put a key in a lock and manoeuvre it in the right direction. This technique must appear second nature; you just can't appear nervous or inexperienced. One wrong move and the keys are stuck. Time spent fiddling with locks, letting keys drop and swing on chains or worse still getting them stuck can be incompetent and unsafe.

Holding a huge set of keys filled me with dread. Not only do I constantly lose my own keys, and I was very conscious of the power they held, but the keys made me feel awkward. It always reminded me that there was them, and there was us. Keys felt like a chasm between me and the prisoners I worked with. We had to hold keys to be able to move around the prison and to be able to open cell doors without having to drag an officer around with us, so whether I struggled with them or not they were a necessary hindrance.

In the second week of holding keys, I thought I had mastered the skill of the quick turn in an anticlockwise direction. No matter how many times I had done this before, I was about to receive a stark reminder of the complexities of getting a key well and truly wedged in a lock. After calling the resident's name through the door and receiving a pleasant, "Hello Miss, thanks for coming," I reached for my keys and, balancing my clipboard and a handful of New Testaments, I put the key in the lock and successfully turned it, first the right way and the door opened, but then I turned it the opposite way. The door was ajar, but the key was jammed. I juggled, wriggled, pulled, and wrenched to no avail. It was stuck. There were two men in the cell who very graciously, with cheeky smiles, offered me tips and hints but no matter how much I tried, I could not remove my key. There were other prisoners on the floor, and they started to gather around to watch this amusing spectacle. Then the officers, with bemused yet jovial looks, came over to see why I had attracted so much unwanted attention. A quick-thinking officer went into automatic pilot and took control. He ordered the prisoners who were working on the floor to step away, he had a wiggle of the key, tried to bang it with his fist, pulled it and twisted it unsuccessfully. "It's stuck," he said with a smile on his face. "Yes, thank you," I replied with terrible embarrassment.

I realised this, and I felt such a twit. So, the cell door was open, two men sat inside, and I was attached by my keychain. As prison craft skills require, you cannot release yourself from the chain. If I unhooked myself from the metal chain that was attached to my key pouch, I would be vulnerable and so would everyone else. There could have been a major incident, and my other keys could have been taken, which included the keys to the wing and corridor gates. There was the potential for "A Great Escape." I was mortified. The two prisoners had to be moved to another cell whilst I remained attached to the lock. A very kind man bought me a blue plastic chair to sit on and offered me a cup of tea which I graciously declined. All I needed was a grimy cup of tea with additives!

The officers called for the works department to rescue me, and I sat down and waited, much to the amusement of staff and prisoners. Whilst I sat twiddling my key chain and staring at the ground, a few of the wing cleaners gathered around. The officer was in view, so I felt ok. They started asking me about being a vicar. Some said they had never met a female chaplain before. The men were pleasant as they pulled up the plastic chairs to sit and wait with me. We talked about a lot of things. I gave out New Testaments with one hand, thumbed through the tissue-thin pages and explained the best way to read the contents. One of the officers laughed and told me that usually the prisoners ripped out the bible pages to smoke roll-ups. This was the first time I had been enlightened about the smoking of Matthew, Mark, Luke and John! It was all quite funny really. I was asked if female vicars were allowed to be married if they were allowed to have sex, if I had conceived any children through immaculate conception, and what they called me, Father or Mother. None, thank you, just Rev Annie.

Eventually, the tool-clad heroes arrived and, with a swift tap of a hammer, released my key. Everything was okay, and I returned to the chapel to the team, whom I thought would be none the wiser, until I did the same thing again the week after. I became the talk of the prison and a source of entertainment, and then my boss found out. I received a quick admonishment and, thankfully, it never happened again.

No amount of training can equip you for the strange experiences and encounters you have working in this environment. You really do have to learn on the job, quickly gain wisdom and, like an owl, have eyes and a 360° cervical spine, swivelling and aware of your surroundings. The prisoners were adept at doing this day and night. They were wary and cautious, mistrusting and sometimes devious. I wasn't quite as obsessive, and most of the time, I felt safe, and the prisoners treated me mostly with respect.

Some of my mistakes were purely out of naivety or just hormonal omissions, but a few could have had serious consequences. I was walking down the main corridor on my way to visit someone on the wings. Two prisoners stood outside the yard gate. They had a broom each and a plastic bin liner. They were very cheery and then came a request. They said, "Hiya Miss, you couldn't just let us in the yard, Miss, we've been told to sweep up the rubbish?" "Yes, of course," I answered in all innocence. I hesitated just a moment and asked, "Are you on your own?" To which they replied, "Yes, the officers let us off the wing and they will come to get us when we have cleaned up the yard."

It seemed innocent enough, so I unlocked the gate and let them into the litter-strewn yard. I thought nothing more of it, carried out my visits and went back to the chapel. I was working until 6 p.m., so everyone had gone home. Packing up and getting ready to leave, the phone rang. It was one of the very kind senior officers. He asked if I had a good day, and I replied, "Yes, thank you." "Where have you been today?" they inquired. What a strange question! They then asked if I could pop up to security on my way out! I didn't think anything of their invitation; it was just a friendly gesture. Perhaps they wanted to catch up with me.

I made my way up to the offices, and waiting for me with lovely, endearing smiles were two senior staff; thankfully, nice officers that I got on with. There was a cup of hot chocolate in a paper cup waiting on the desk and they asked me to sit down. Has someone died? Did they have some information about a prisoner? Did they need my help? They asked me if I had passed the yards today. "Yes," I replied. "What time did you go past the yard? Was it about 3pm?"

They then continued to unravel, minute by minute, the spectacle that the security team had watched. They told me about two prisoners who had been let off the wing after spinning a yarn to a junior officer. Then someone, namely Rev Annie, had been observed in full view, on CCTV, opening the gates and letting the prisoners into the yard. The prisoners had bin liners and brushes and had proceeded to sweep up parcels containing drugs that had been thrown over the wall. The Big Brother cameras had watched them and fortunately intervened with the two prisoners being tackled and removed to the Segregation unit.

That was it. It was my fault; I was party to a calculated and carefully planned incident. I had allowed the prisoners to carry out this ingenious plot. Make my cell up right away, that was it, I was done for. After swigging down the insipid powdery hot chocolate and with tears in my eyes, I blubbered out how sorry I was. They were lovely, they knew me well, they were aware of my somewhat dizzy reputation and unpredictable actions. They were understanding but told me this would have to be reported and investigated. I left with my head held low, even after their jokes. I left work, drove home, downed a large glass of wine, and had to survive a week without sleep. The prisoners were punished, a few days in Segregation, no serious harm had been done and I was forgiven, yet again!

You just can't write it, and although I am attempting to do so, nothing can prepare you for the crafty moves and ingenious plots made by some. The chancers and wingers are everywhere, and I just had to increase my awareness and never make this or any other mistake again - until!

I came into work one morning, laughing and smiling, through the main entrance, bag searched, me searched and then to pat down. My rucksack was flapping open as usual and everything - my hairbrush, lipstick (and brown eyeliner) - in full view. I stepped forward for the search and then out of the front pocket in tremendous slow-motion tumbled my mobile phone, tipping out of the unzipped pocket and onto the floor in full view of everyone. The very stern patting officer threw me a death stare. I babbled some excuse, took on the persona of a guilty passenger and scrambled to pick up my phone. She promptly leaned forward and removed it from my hand. I was in a line of waiting staff, they giggled at the guilty Reverend, taking their turn to be patted down, relieved that this time it wasn't them.

I was marched up two flights of stairs, spared the handcuffs but straight to the deputy Governor's office, thankfully another compassionate female. I sat down and she read me the riot act through a gentle smirk. My phone was taken; I provided my password, and the entire contents were checked. I don't know what was worse: photos of me make-up-free, in hair rollers, a selection of very unflattering holiday pics or the fact that I had been caught red-handed! Of course, this was a genuine mistake; the initial security check and X Ray missed the phone in my rucksack, only to be discovered by Ms Super Security. She never looked at me quite the same again and I think she was extremely unhappy that I wasn't marched off the premises there and then!

Once again, I found myself sitting in the naughty chair whilst my lovely boss explained the consequences of what could have been. He then kindly told me that it wasn't the first time, and no doubt would be the last that someone had accidentally walked through security with a mobile phone.

All these *Oops's* were completely unintentional and, once investigated, I was released without charge. The reality, however, is that actions can have disastrous consequences in a place like this, and I was thankful for the senior's compassion and trust that, "It was all a terrible misunderstanding, Miss!" These were genuine mistakes, and I was remorseful. We are all human, and we all have bad days. The next incidents, however, are not so much an error but more the result of frustration, tiredness, and simply having a tough day.

The young child of a prisoner was critically ill and required a transplant. The father and baby's Mum were no longer together. However, the hospital caring for the child was trying to match the baby for a transplant donor. You can imagine how complex this can be when one parent is in prison.

The necessity for blood tests to find a match and trying to keep Dad updated with his child's progress was a time-consuming and frustrating task. If you have a genuine emergency and, after proving a genuine request, prisoners are given emergency phone credit. However, getting a hospital telephone number on to your Personal ID Number, is almost impossible. This is where we stepped in. The Chaplaincy team was able to keep in touch with the hospital consultant and relay messages back and forth. The carrier pigeon race was on. Because I am a nurse, I had some understanding, and I took a special interest in this child's welfare and that of dad. The fear and worry that this young dad experienced were tangible. I spent hours speedily walking back and forth to deliver news. I had to liaise with the Healthcare team and, eventually, they managed to obtain blood samples from the dad. As the weeks went by, he was becoming increasingly impatient, anxious and concerned that his baby would die.

This situation was not helped by the fact that his potty cell mate decided that he was going to act as an advocate and solicitor for his pal. On one occasion, I arrived for the umpteenth time with an update. At this point, the defendant's Counsel decided to start keeping a diary of our conversations. He kept butting in, asking questions and telling me that I was incompetent and that if I didn't shape up, I was at risk of getting sued. He stood and lauded his notepad over me, taking notes with his broken biro. He was going on and on, and I lost my patience. My accompanying officer stood at the cell door, when I shamefully lost it and shouted at the defence Counsel, "Shut up, you little shit!"

Much to the amusement of the officer and the shock of both men, I then told him to get out of the cell and take his notepad with him. I think I was elevated in the eyes of the Officer who, after that, treated me with great respect. He told me he had never seen me lose my temper and he thought I was just a soft chaplain. Little did he know that I was exhausted, frustrated and fed up with prison politics and rules that didn't allow this man to talk to the hospital. Oops, yes, I swore, and yes, I did apologise again. The note writer retired after that, discarding his notepad, and finding something else to occupy his bored mind.

On another occasion, I was strolling down a connecting corridor on the way to the recovery wings, clipboard in hand, smiling to myself, confident that I had almost achieved the day's tasks. It was lock up, just after lunch. The grey, dreary yards were empty and so I scuttled on my way to see a man on the recovery wings. From an indistinguishable high landing window, a voice shouted, and they must have been shouting at me because I couldn't see another soul.

"Hey, you fat bitch, I'm going to stick my……up your …….!"

I will leave this to the reader's imagination but both expletives began with a C, and I can't bring myself to write it. I was startled and looked around. Fat bitch? I glanced down at the slight gathering of fat around my midriff! I need to stop eating prison chips. I looked around again, fat! You cheeky so and so. I was angry and offended, how dare someone call me fat! How dare they touch that nerve! Well, that was it. I gained speed, and with my face set like flint, I was determined to seek out the perpetrator. I ascended two stairs at a time onto the wing facing the yard. It was staff lunch time, and all the prisoners were in their cells. I announced my arrival and told the lovely officers, both ex-forces, what had happened. I then proceeded to knock on every door, opened every window hatch and asked, "Was that you?"

One by one, the prisoners came to the windows, listening to me ask the same question, "Was that you that shouted through the window at me?" Of course, by the time I had knocked on 20 windows, the prisoners were aware that I was very cross and insulted. Indeed, to be honest, I was hurt and humiliated. No one owned up and, by the time I got to the last cell, I was laughing at myself, and they were smiling and laughing with me. I returned to the officers; they were smiling too! I asked with a heavy heart, "Am I fat?" I plonked myself down in the office and they laughed and told me how impressed they were with me. Indeed, I was human, they had never seen me lose it before! They never answered my question! Some days, insults just fly right over your head, and some days, depending on the position of the stars, they just don't. Insults and bad language are all part of the prison scene. You would think I was used to it, but I still have feelings, and I am not totally desensitised! On this occasion, I reacted. Time to diet, I think!

Sometimes I thought I was being helpful. On first meeting prisoners, they can tell you what they like to do, apart from the obvious getting up to no good. Many have pastimes and hobbies. And so, I met Mr Tambourine. He was completely eccentric. He shouted constantly and was driving everyone potty. He was up all-night singing and talking and being a pest. The officers were getting increasingly impatient, and disaster was looming, so I took it upon myself to try to help. I talked to the chap, and he told me that he liked to play the tambourine. What entered my head at this point was what can only be described as a forgone disaster, something I foolishly imagined would keep him occupied and keep him quiet. In the chapel, we had a selection of instruments, including a nice leather and wooden tambourine. I'll let him borrow it! He can use it during the day, and it will keep him busy. So back I went with the tambourine. He was delighted, to say the least. Good job done Reverend, top marks.

The next morning, I came into work as usual, 08:05, I took my seat at the office desk and then glanced over, only to see the remnants of a battered tambourine on the desk. My boss told me that one of the seniors had kindly returned it to the office. She later popped in to admonish me. "What on earth were you thinking?" she said as I bowed my head in shame. He shook it, played it, and sang even louder all day and night until it had to be physically removed. The sad, battered tambourine sat there, a cruel reminder of yet another *oops*!

Clothes are donated to the prison. The prisoners mostly wear prison grey tracksuits. However, those who can afford their own clothes can wear them. There is a prison rule, only T-shirts, no offensive print or images, just plain, short-sleeved T-shirts. One man who was a regular at church and I have to say who we were very fond of, mentioned in passing that he had no clothes. He always looked unkempt. I rummaged in my bag of donated second-hand clothes and found him some lovely smart shirts. Unaware of the rules I gave him several Marks and Spencer best shirts. He looked much better and was so happy with the gift.

A couple of days later, I found the donated shirts back in my office. My friend had been parading up and down Main Street in shirt and trousers, looking like a member of the management team or, even better, the governor himself. Once again, head in hand, I was mortified and embarrassed.

There is much about prison life that you can only learn from your mistakes. Just as we learn through our own lives, the dos and don'ts, the whys and wherefores.

Here the simplest of actions can result in something quite dangerous or risky. Thankfully my mistakes never escalated into anything more than great entertainment and a dented pride. You must take it, learn, and move on. There is no time to dwell on errors made. You just learn very quickly and on the job. This is a place of ingenuity, of risk, of scheming. Every day was a huge learning curve for me and, thankfully, my name never ended up on the neon sign. Although humiliated by my own dippy mistakes, I had been spared.

When I first worked in the prison, I thought I had all the answers. I went with the intent of sharing my knowledge and improving lives. The truth is that the prisoners taught me so much about my predispositions and my own judgement. Sometimes, I was criticised, quite rightly for my comments or behaviour.

I once cracked a joke with a young man. I had gotten to know him well. He was a regular attendee in the chapel; he had found faith and was trying hard to change. He had a chaotic relationship with SPICE. He broke his leg when he was in prison. I cracked what I thought was a joke one day. "Well, you won't need to keep using SPICE now you're on strong painkillers." The words just tumbled thoughtlessly out of my mouth.

"You're out of order, Miss" was his reply, "I'm trying really hard. You shouldn't take the piss. You're a priest." I was embarrassed and humbled.

Prisoners are often very observant, they read you and notice all sorts of things. They notice a new haircut, if you have a suntan, if you're looking tired and they don't hold back with their observations, be they negative or positive.

I have a habit of picking the skin around my thumbs and biting it. I was chatting to a man at the cell door once, thumb in mouth, and he said, "Miss, stop doing that, it's self-harm." I quickly pulled out my thumb and said, "Yes, you're right!"

I still do it occasionally but not as much because every time I do this, usually when I'm a bit stressed, I hear those words resounding. Words, they say, have the power of life and death. It's funny how I remember these incidents; they are reminders of how we are not perfect specimens, we don't have all the answers, and we cannot judge. When one finger points, three will point back.

Chapter 13
"Tails" of the Riverbank

"Oh, Badger," cried the Rat, "let us in, please. It's me, Rat, and my friend Mole, and we've lost our way in the snow."

Wind in the Willows: Kenneth Graham

I don't have many fears or phobias, but rats are up there. They are everywhere, or so rumour has it. Never more than six feet away from a rat, as my beautiful stepdaughter, Niamh, reminded me, as a cat-sized rat dashed from under a rubbish bin right in front of us during a holiday in Rome! I would occasionally spot massive water rats on the bank of the winding river when I was walking through Jurassic Park.

Huge rats and mice took up residence in the prison. They were sometimes seen scuttling across the yards in search of discarded chicken, white plastic bread crusts and bruised rotting apple cores, all thrown from cell windows. One prison I worked in briefly as a nurse, employed feral cats to kill their squatting rodents. But here, free from lurching cats, they could thrive and set up home in the warm stony crevices. They had hiding places that no one would ever find, safely nested so they could spy out.

Wagtail

I have no idea where my fear of rats comes from, I have been wary of them for as long as I can remember. When I was a child, we kept guineapigs and, at one time, I had tiny little mice living on my bedroom windowsill in a square wooden cigar box. That was until they gnawed a hole in the box and then nibbled at my curtains. They were then banished to the shed. The mice and guinea pigs were essentially rats without ringed tails - but I didn't fear them. I held them and felt nothing but affection.

I had never been up close and personal with a pure ratty rat until an encounter back in the Autumn of 1980. I lived in Israel for a couple of months on a Kibbutz. During Shabbat, Friday afternoons until Saturday evening, we had precious leave from picking oranges. Time off was spent thumbing lifts off the non-Jewish citizens of Israel. I was exploring with my kibbutz pals. My dear friend, Jane B, was with me and another girl from the Kibbutz Neve Ur. Janey B and I still recall this story and giggle at our escapades. Existing on supplies of boiled eggs, oranges and water and sleeping on the beach experiencing the whole traveller thing. At that time, back in the early 80s, Eilat beaches were free from plush 5-star hotels and infinity pools. It was a hippie's hangout and a welcome and warm place to hang out for the poor kibbutz volunteers and Israeli soldiers to rest. One night as the sun went down and after a few glasses of Arak at the Peace Cafe, we settled down for a night on the sandy beach. Bleary-eyed under the palm trees, tucked up and fully dressed in Kibbutz volunteer clothes, in sleeping bags. Just as I was about to nod off, there was a scuttle, and a huge, nuclear-sized rat ran behind my head, touching the base of my neck and hair. I let out an almighty scream and several very handsome soldiers came to my rescue. I refused to sleep on the beach again and thereafter took shelter in a hostel.

Poor rats, they get such a bad name. For me, it is the tail. The little rings around the tail give me the jibbers. They make me feel vilified. I don't know much about rats except that they are vermin, carry diseases and should be avoided. I have never had a desire to learn more about them, their life cycle, the evolution of rats, or anything else. I don't really want to know about something, I fear.

I don't like to think of them being murdered in traps, but I still shudder at the thoughts of them being near me, in my house or within six metres as the legend goes. Rats have made several appearances since, not quite as close but nearly.

Wagtail

I was once sitting in a car in the petrol station forecourt, while my partner popped into the kiosk to pay for diesel. He turned to me and mouthed, "Do you want anything?" I glanced up and replied, "Chocolate, please." I watched him walk in the kiosk; I looked over at the huge industrial waste bins. Climbing up the bin was a huge rat. Underneath the bin were the babies, whiskered noses sniffing the air, patiently waiting to see what Mum (or Dad) could retrieve from inside the metal waste container. The rat climbed back and forth, delivered the morsels, and then returned to the precarious journey, doing what was necessary to provide for her babies. It was quite a treat to watch; they were far enough away. I thought about their need to survive, just like all of us, caring for their young. I told my partner who knew people at the council. He would tell the Rat Man. I had just sentenced a whole family of survivors to death.

As a newly ordained curate, I lived in a church property. The vicarage was a large house next to a railway line. I had two cats and a dog and a big cat flap big enough to let in the cats and, evidently, the rats. My cats were old and fragile, and I don't think they could have seen a rat let alone catch one. It was winter and I came home late at night. I was in my bedroom getting my pyjamas on when I was distracted by a little squeak, a furry little twitching nose, and great long whiskers, sticking out behind my bed. A rat! After a second glance through the slits in my eyes, making sure I wasn't hallucinating, I leapt onto the bed and screamed. The house was empty, it was just me, two ancient skeletal cats, a dog and it! I jumped from the bed toward the landing and slammed the door. Then, screaming for help and in a state of hysteria, I called upon the older, sensible churchwardens, who were in their 80s but very nimble. I waited well away from the enclosure after stuffing a towel to block the gap under the door. Clad with rubber gloves and wellingtons, my heroes arrived. With me outside the door panting, they managed to catch it. It had wriggled behind my blue plastic ironing basket, tipped the basket over, and then dropped dead with fear. The kindly warden scooped this poor defenceless creature up and laid it on tissue paper and placed it in a shoebox. I felt awful, poor thing; I had killed it, probably by jumping up and down on the bed and then being squashed by my un-ironed pile of clothes. I looked at the rat in the box. It had a cute little face, quite sweet, almost pretty. I didn't sleep well.

Rats are now more of a fear than a phobia. Accidental exposure therapy has extinguished some of the shivers. I realise that they are more frightened of me than I am of them and that helps. Sometimes phobias around spiders, creatures, or situations, fill us with fear. Frightening news, people in power, people who are better educated than us, those we envy, those who have better grammar, those people whose lifestyles cause us to reluctantly wriggle out of our comfort zone. Just like the comfortable church nestled in the trees; the congregation resistant to change; and me with my rats - we all live in fear of something.

Maybe fear is due to ignorance or simply to changes. Ignorance may be about other cultures, covered faces, different customs, or different beliefs. We live in a world fuelled by fear which is also caused by what we watch and what we read and, of course, the media. It's about situations that are out of our control; a pandemic, a war, a crashing economy, all too close for comfort. Fear; do we flee or face it?

Before working in the prison, I had a friend who worked with sex offenders. I would go visit my friend and her husband would talk about his work with people who genuinely frightened me. I too considered them to be on the bottom rung of the ladder! How could my super-intelligent friend possibly have any empathy with these people? Men and women who had offended and harmed. Sex offenders who had committed the most indescribable crimes against children and adults.

I grew up in a very ordinary Manchester Suburb. We played out for hours on end. I don't think my parents had a clue where we were at any time of the day. The only glimpse they would have of us was after school and when we came in for dinner. We walked to school, went on buses, were left alone for a few hours here and there, and had sleepovers at friends' houses, amongst other daring exploits. My parents never talked about sex, babies, periods, the birds or the bees. Such conversations were best left to human biology teachers. Apart from the odd rude or suggestive line from the Benny Hill show, these topics were mortifyingly embarrassing. I didn't know much about periods until the dreaded day it happened to me, and I thought I was dying! Anything that was ever mentioned of a sexual or reproductive nature was always muted and dubbed as if my Mum had lost the ability to say hysterectomy or period without dubbing the first few letters and saying them down her nose.

The muting and dubbing appeared again when we inherited a "flasher" In our neighbourhood. Me and my middle sister, "Our Jayne", were warned not to go onto the waste ground that stretched behind the railway track behind our house. He had been seen riding a bike and flashing his bits to passers-by. Well, I can't remember exactly how long it took us to eventually track this man down, maybe weeks of stalking out, but eventually we saw him. He pulled up on his bike above the railway bridge, stabilised his bike, pulled down his trousers and, in broad daylight, flashed us from the waist down. We screamed and ran; we never told a soul, and the memory is forever etched on my mind.

I can never recall hearing about sex offences when I was young. I can't recall any late conversations that I was party to through cracks in doors. There were TV comedy programmes that were sexist, seedy and smutty, misogynistic suggestive jokes on the television comedy 'Are you being served' were quite the norm. I have no knowledge of anyone, apart from the bridge flasher, who harmed in this way or who was harmed. Back then, there was no internet, no dark web, no glamorising abuse. There were, of course, offences of this type taking place, it just wasn't headlining news when I was growing up. Times have changed, and sex is everywhere. Sexual images, like partially clad men and women, adorn the pages of magazines, Netflix, and TV dramas. You don't have to look very far if you want a quick glimpse of nudity or sexual scenes.

When I was growing up and well before, sex was a well-kept secret. It wasn't talked about. There was a lot of shame attached to sex before marriage and children born outside wedlock. My sex education amounted to my mum asking me if we had Human Biology lessons at school. We did have sex education and just roared with laughter and giggled with embarrassment at the illustrations of human anatomy and how babies were made. There were however scandals and sometimes novels written that caused outrage.

Lady Chatterley's lover, by D H Lawrence, was banned because of its explicit sexual scenes. Way back in the early 1900s it caused outrage. We can read it now; if we so choose, we can read Shades of Gray or Jackie Collins novels; we can trawl the internet looking at soft pornography or purchase top-shelf magazines that make DH Lawrence's story look like a fairytale, never to be read by children, of course.

The flip side of the sex talk is, I suppose, a more positive one. We talk more openly today about 'bad men' (or women). We warn our children and tell them they must tell us if anyone is ever inappropriate with them. Cybercrime and the dark web can now be infiltrated thanks to cyber-crime police officers. Those responsible for purchasing extreme pornography tracked down. If people try to pay to look at images of young people and children, they can be caught. It seems like a double-edged sword. It is out there; we talk about it, and we expose the dangers, but how did we ever become a society that allows such easy access to this disturbing material?

The flippant recollection of my childhood experience is not to undermine sex offences. It's just to recall how time and our attitude to anything sexual has changed. How sex is portrayed and how easy it is to slip down this dark chasm of online pornography, sexually explicit material, watershed films and dramas.

In this chapter, I discuss phobias and fears, including my fear of rats. I do not suggest that the people I met are in any way being likened to rats, but I use them to compare my preconceptions of a community that I knew so little about. Fear often causes anger; ignorance can trigger violence; not only here but also in racism, homophobia, xenophobia, and much more. Fear isn't just a fear of what we can or can't see; fear can be fuelled by events or facts that we have no control over, no knowledge of and no idea how to deal with.

Sex offences are an everyday headline today. Some sex offences are unforgivable, horrific, and too awful to contemplate. Sex offences can be the lasting result of young children having witnessed or being the victim of abusive relationships. Sex offences can be the outcome of revenge or sometimes especially on the internet out of a dark curiosity. Sexual offences can be committed by parents, children, siblings, spouses. It's indiscriminate, this dark problem is like cancer, it is not a respecter of persons. It can potentially affect any of us at any time, in any place. This is such a controversial and painful subject. The reason I want to share this is more to point out my past predisposition. My own prejudice, my own ignorance. It is not in any way to demean or underestimate the devastation it causes. Neither is it to glorify or justify. It is just the stark truth. A truth that we hope will never darken our lives and that of our families and those we love.

I had neither met nor ever listened to people who had been abused or who were, in fact, the abuser. I was in no position to judge. People who are deemed to be vermin. Like the dead rat in my bedroom, I had never looked closely at their faces, never seen the pain, never listened to their stories. Yet, some (not all) - and this may be hard to read - changed my heart. They educated me and shifted my prejudice from viewing them as the worst of the worst offenders to seeing them as broken human beings.

Chapter 14
Bromide

"The word <u>bromide</u> comes from the chemical compound made of the element bromine and another metal. This kind of bromide was historically used as a sedative, a medicine that dulls your senses..."
https://www.vocabulary.com/dictionary/bromide (AKA Something you put in tea to stop sexual arousal)

Visiting Michael, offered a glimpse of life behind bars. My allocated hour with him was spent in a small visiting room with pale blue walls, in the chapel. I was made welcome, given a cup of prison tea in a paper cup, ("slutch," as my dad would call it). The door to the room was unlocked. The walls displayed a framed picture with various symbols of faith. I stared at it pretending to be interested in the decor! I sat perched on the edge of a blue fabric-covered chair with brown stained rings. I waited for what seemed like an eternity for the guards to bring him down. I paced a while and looked through the small window. The chapel garden was lush and green, there were a few memorial stones and a huge monkey tree. If I stood on the chair, I could just see a small, neglected pond and a decaying park bench that was screwed to the ground. The atmosphere here was so much better than the conditions I was to later experience. Now, Michael was not a sex offender, or On Protection, and visiting him didn't involve complex manoeuvres and covert operations. His misdemeanour was more of a nuisance to the police than a serious crime. The visit was short and sweet; we found plenty to talk about, we laughed, we prayed, and then he was escorted back to his temporary home, his room, his bed, and his duvet.

In the first few weeks, I dreaded hearing the words "Annie, can you go to the Vulnerable Prisoner wing?" referring to the sex offender and On Protection unit. I had dodged going but it was my turn. It was my time to face my fears, time to test my calling to love my neighbour, and time to come face to face with what? Monsters or normal, intelligent, polite, respectful, broken human beings hiding the darkest secrets and memories. Time to meet the prisoners who had raped and abused.

I do not say this flippantly, but I hope that sharing some of the real accounts of these prisoners will foster a deeper understanding of sex offences - not to excuse them and certainly not to add to anyone's pain. For those who have been abused and have not yet found the strength to speak out, or for those who need support, I encourage you to reach out to the support groups listed at the end of this book.

I live in Greater Manchester. I had very little knowledge of crime statistics before my new endeavour. Obviously, I was aware that there would be sex offenders in the prison and so would at some time have to meet them. I had been kindly reminded by my son that I was crazy to even consider going to work in this environment with all "those blokes." He was anxious and shouted at me, "What happens if you get attacked, Mum?" My family was used to my sometimes-alternative adventures or career paths. My parents had both died when I started working in prison. I think they would have been proud of me - maybe concerned, but proud. My sisters just wanted to know the ins and outs, but I rarely spoke about my work, so they didn't really know what my job involved. They didn't know then, but they will know now.

When I told my dear friends about my new job, despite all my previous soap opera swerves and curves, they were all somewhat aghast. They had just gotten accustomed to seeing me do the whole vicar thing in the comfort of a red-carpeted, ancient, listed building. I had rarely discussed how I spent my time as Vicar. Very few of them knew about my friendship with Michael, the dead bodies I had climbed over to give last rites, my relationship with drug addicts, alcoholics and the local 'Nar do wells'. I kept the risky side of my job to myself. They were unaware that I had travelled to London in search of Michael. They were unaware of my friendship with a lovely, local homeless man. They were unaware that I went alone, tramping across long grassy fields to find his latest hideout, leaving food and messages. All I allowed them to witness was Rev Annie, the reformed disco queen, conducting Remembrance, Easter and Christmas services which they would dip their toe in and attend.

I am blessed to have super friends and a wonderful family. I am an open book and so they know all about me, my vulnerabilities, my passions, and my interests. They all came to my Priesting, and we celebrated this rather auspicious occasion at the Cathedral together, exactly how I wanted it with all the people I loved. I suspect many of my friends and family, watching me kneeling at the altar in my Sound of Music cameo, had flashing memories of drunken nights out, my battle with breast cancer, and my sometimes heart-wrenching tears at the end of many relationships. My friend's Mum, with gentle judgement, said to me straight and without flinching, "I find it strange to watch Anne Woodcock (as I was), knowing you as a child, up there preaching and praying. I can't take you seriously."

Good Northern honesty, not a hindrance but a reminder that I was indeed a fish in a bowl, and everyone was watching me swim round and round, waiting perhaps for me to go belly up! Thankfully, most soon adapted to me turning up for a brew in my dog collar, finding some comfort and some kind of amusement that their buddy was now a priest! The one person who was delighted was my Mum. She made me go everywhere with her, even to her 80th party in my dog collar. She reminded me by saying, "It's who you are."

Despite her disappointment in not being a Methodist, she was proud that her daughter had maintained her faith and had made her proud. I hope that she could see me as I conducted her funeral, the last thing I ever did for my Mum.

However, moving into Prison Chaplaincy presented lots of negative comments from some, including one from my son who was convinced I would be gang raped. My partner didn't voice his concerns at the time but later told me he hated me working there with all those men, something I sadly regret. Had I shared the real experiences of being a prison chaplain, I expect I would have been rugby-tackled on the way out and forced to leave.

In 2018, Greater Manchester statistics recorded 3671 rapes and other sexual offences. I was now working with some of the prisoners who made up those numbers, I may have passed them on the street or in Asda! Although officers were regularly assaulted, there were no accounts of incidents of staff being raped in the prison. During induction, we were briefed on the possibility of hostage-taking. If we were taken hostage, the cell door would be locked, and we would be a prisoner of the prisoner. Even if we were attacked or raped the attending officers would have to watch on and would only intervene if they deemed it safe, even if our lives were at risk! That was a terrifying thought. However, I was, according to statistics, more likely to be raped walking to the local shop at dusk by someone who knew me. The only sex stories were of staff having illicit rendezvous, and I certainly didn't intend to join those ranks! Although I was working with some statistically dangerous men, I felt safe and so I stepped out, with trepidation but determination that I could, perhaps, make a difference - no matter how miniscule.

We no longer prescribe bromide and so the prisoners were normal, fit, and active. Here, healthy sex drives are quite evident as I encountered on several occasions. I learned this quickly after one very super-duper embarrassing incident. On my rounds to a general wing, I speedily turned the key with record-breaking efficiency and opened a young man's cell. Without considering his privacy, I burst in with a cheery greeting: "Good morning!" only to be greeted by the vision of a young, naked man lying prone on his pale blue sheets in the throes of a private sexual encounter. Hand on his bits, he let out an almighty scream, "For f**k's sake Miss, you should knock! This is my bedroom!" I was embarrassed and mumbled, "Oh, my goodness, I am so sorry."

Forget any pleasantries, I was, for once, lost for words. A silent witness to a young man passing his time with sexual relief. Please remember that I have been a nurse for many years and have seen more naked bits in various anatomical presentations but not quite like this. He wasn't unwell; he was very much alive, functioning quite well, and I was mortified. I scuttled back to the office and sat perplexed with the officers to recount my experience. They were all highly amused and reminded me that perhaps I should knock before entering. I didn't tell anyone at home! Private DIY sexual activity is not an offence within these walls unless it poses a threat or causes distress.

On another occasion, I visited a man in Segregation. After taking the printed sheet with prisoners' names from the tough Seg officers, I was warned about one man who might be a problem. The officers laughed and said in no uncertain terms he was naked and had a sex problem. Sometimes, I took heed of the warnings, but usually the steel door between me and them would be a safety shield. I approached the door and called through the hatch, "Good morning, it's the chaplain!" His face appeared at the small Perspex window set in the grimy frame. His face and bare tattooed shoulders were visible, but I couldn't see the rest of him. I asked how he was, if there was anything he needed, the usual banal conversation on a dreary winter's day. I smiled, battered red clipboard in hand. A Bible maybe? His arm moved down and then started moving furiously. Oh, my goodness, was he doing what I thought he was doing? I took a sharp intake of breath and smiled. He then proceeded to tell me that he had a problem and asked if I could help. Probably not. He told me he suffered from permanent erection syndrome; he couldn't help it, and no one was taking any notice. I was trying to keep a straight face and act completely shockproof. Ok, quick thinking, do not change your facial expression, no raised eyebrows. Without even the faint hint of a blush, I explained that I couldn't really help but I thought the doctor might be able to, and I would put in a request for immediate attention. I took a step back whilst he turned his back on me. I shut the metal flap very tightly and walked away bemused down the Segregation corridor.

Once again, it was another *Oops*, but one worthy of singular recollection. I sat with the officers, who laughed and told me, "It was a load of bollocks (literally)." And so, once again, I made a quick retreat. Time for a cup of tea.

So, self-administered sexual activity is quite the norm in the male estate. I have heard, and I recollect from the drama Within These Walls, that female prisoners often form same-sex relationships with fellow prisoners; my friend will share an account of this later. However, it is highly unlikely in this testosterone-fuelled establishment that men would be forming sexual relationships with other men, not least amongst the general population. This may have happened occasionally and on the QT, but not acutely evident. I had heard rumours that some prisoners were suspected of inappropriate sexual activity but very rarely. In a male prison, you are taking a huge risk by sexually exploiting other prisoners. This kind of behaviour opens prisoners up to verbal and sometimes physical abuse and, if caught, would result in a fierce beating, probable isolation, and an extended sentence.

The On-Protection cohort consists of those prisoners who are at risk of being harmed or threatened by other prisoners. Some of the prisoners are in debt to gangs or drug cartels, others because they may have harmed or killed the friend of a rival gang member. Unfortunately, and because of their high-risk status, they are housed with vulnerable residents, mainly sentenced or on remand. There is no separate facility apart from Segregation, so they are locked up for 23 hours a day with separate regimes on the same wings for their own safety.

Prisoners who are isolated but who are not sex offenders are often prolific criminals yet hold their own judgments and ideologies about the men who share their living spaces. You may have murdered your wife or owe thousands in drug debt, yet you are in no way at the level of depravity of men who would have underage sex, purchase child pornography or indeed have taken steps to engage with underage young people to engage in inappropriate sexual activity. They were 'nonces' and didn't even make it to the lowest rung of the ladder. They were and are seen as a marker to grade other offences by prisoners and, dare I say, most of society.

My fears about working with this category of offenders were influenced by the media, films I had watched, and books I had read. Yet here I stood, clipboard in hand, armed with books on forgiveness, New Testaments and "Rosemary's beads," ready to enter a dark world of previous detestable activity. Was I prepared? Simple answer, no! Did I have any preconceptions? Yes! I opened the steel gates and the blue, rattling wooden doors. I was in. Let's hope gang rape didn't happen today!

"Morning Miss." The first greeting. "Wow, he looks normal." This was followed by a flurry of friendly faces. Some were sweeping the debris off the floors, and some were playing cards. Painting the rungs of the flaking metal staircase was a common sight and it kept minds occupied. There were groups of young men lingering, some on their own reading, some chatting to friendly officers. They didn't have signs tattooed on their foreheads "I am a rapist," and there was no tangible evidence of dark dingy conspirators, no sunken heads, just very normal-looking blokes. They could have been my neighbour, my friend, my teacher, my childhood idol, or a family member. Some were educated men with responsibilities. There were teachers, police officers, church leaders and the general proletariat. We are always horrified when a person in authority is suspected or convicted of a sexual offence. How could the very people that society look to for protection be just as vulnerable and tempted as the rest of the population?

The Vulnerable Prisoners didn't look drastically different from anyone else. I had seen *them* walking to work en masse and observed them with a sense of morbid curiosity. Admittedly, I had some preconceived notions - that they would all appear creepy, seedy, suspicious, or otherwise suspect. Yet here I was, standing among a group of seemingly ordinary prisoners of all ages. Some were even strikingly good-looking and physically fit. The prisoners ranged in age from as young as 18 to, I would estimate, well into their 80s. Some had been found guilty and were resigned to serving out their sentences, while others awaited their court cases, clinging to the hope of a not-guilty verdict and the chance to return home.

There was almost a tangible peace about these units. Maybe the prisoners had come to terms with their crime and had stopped hiding. They were accepting of the punishment. Some were remorseful, some confused, some indifferent but they were in it together. Here they were amongst their own, no one can judge you here because most have done the same thing. Here there was minimal threat. The residents were happy to see me. Maybe a chaplain would be the one non-judgmental person they could talk to. Maybe I was the one person they could share their guilt with. If only they could read my mind, if only they knew I had been just the same as the rest of humanity, putting them at the bottom of the pile, presuming the worst. I wasn't quite sure where to start to bring them up at least one rung on that ladder of condemnation.

The routine was the same here as on any other wing. I purposely didn't look at any of the histories before I visited. Sometimes officers would fill me in on gruesome details if they had taken a particular dislike to someone. Mostly the officers conducted their duties the same way here as they would anywhere else. There were prisoners on assessment books and a daily or weekly visit was necessary.

Wagtail

It was during the pandemic when my colleague and I dashed through the prison trying to offer some hope. We were determined to deliver sweet cones to every single prisoner including the sex offender and On Protection prisoners. As we were tirelessly dashing with our Santa's sleigh, we had a call from security.

Late on Christmas Eve, the word was out (we had sought permission) that we were delivering sweets and short Christian tracts about the hope of Christmas. We were just about to go onto the Vulnerable Prisoner wings when we were stopped by security. The small booklets had an image of baby Jesus in a crib bare from the chest up. We were told to remove every page with the image before we gave them out to the Vulnerable Prisoners. There was a concern that the prisoners might masturbate over the pictures! With some sickness, sadness, and disdain towards our instructors, we threw off our Elves' hats and sat on a cold landing for an hour, piling up the single pages of a baby's shoulders and tummy. We discarded them into bins alongside all the old newspapers and magazines with other barely clad images that were somehow allowed. Who was in fear here? Who struggled with an act of kindness? Who had inherent guilt and unresolved fear?

Occasionally, but rarely, prisoners would voluntarily share details of their offences; sometimes, they would want prayers and want to come to the chapel services. The residents here were restricted from main activities due to the risk of mixing with the general population. The courses we ran on faith and forgiveness in the chapel were only for main prisoners and so we delivered teaching materials to them, catching up to see how they were getting on. We tried to educate, support, and encourage just as we did with everyone else.

I was surprised at the number of young men on the wing. Clad in Under Armour sportswear, they could have been running alongside me at the gym, attending college, working as baristas, or in trendy clothes shops. Several of them shared with me quite openly the situations they had found themselves in. There was quite a common thread, one that made me thankful that I had never been the parent of a young man in this horrendous yet guilty scenario.

Imagine this if you will. Your son is 17. He is at college, doing well, has a part-time job in a pub, has lots of friends, is a football fanatic, loves the gym, and loves his Mum. He has an almost 16-year-old girlfriend. The girl goes to the same pub, underage, but what's new?

With banter over the bar, they arrange to meet up after work. Your son strikes up a friendship with this stunning beauty. They fall in love and have a passionate, youthful relationship for a few months. Then your son meets someone new at college. They have the same interests; they love the same music and then he decides he would rather be with the other girl. And so, beauty number one gets ditched! She is 15 years and 11 months old; he is 17 and almost 18. The problem here is that she told him she was 16 when she met him; he later found out her real age, but she had, according to him, consented to a sexual relationship. The age factor never even entered his head until the relationship ended. The young, rejected beauty is distraught. She throws a drink over him in the pub; there is a brawl with the girl's brother and all hell breaks loose. The police are called. She then screams at him and tells him she is going to tell her Mum that he made her have sex with him! The rest they say…

An embittered mother trying to deal with a broken teenage girl reports him to the police. Of course, she has every right to do this, and I am not suggesting this is wrong. However, there are two parties here. One underage female, drinking and having sex at the age of 15 and one 17-year-old male nonchalantly in a sexual relationship with a minor! Fast forward 18 months; he is one year into a prison sentence and a criminal record that will change his life forever. A sex offender, a nonce on the bottom rung of the ladder just like those he had read about, had judged and laughed about in youthful ignorance.

He was one of so many. Sex offences are everywhere, every Friday and Saturday night, often fuelled by alcohol by handsome young men and beautiful girls in skin-tight bodysuits. Someone, please tell me what we can do to stop this. I have no idea. But prison wings have a population of offenders guilty of a bottom-rung crime. This is one young man's story, yet there are so many, enough to fill volumes.

Online sex offences and entrapment have resulted in the arrest of some criminals. We hear stories from victims of historical sex offences in schools, churches, and government offices - it is everywhere.

Another man was timid and quiet; his English was broken, but he got by. He got on well with everybody, he worked and minded his own business doing his time. But the time for his sentencing drew near. He attended the Roman Catholic services, and we never heard a peep from him; he was lost in his fear. He was taken to court, found guilty and came back to prison. In the quiet of the night, he sliced open a main artery, bled out and died. This was the ultimate price of shame; for him, there was no other way.

There were so many different situations and stories. Just as with the rest of the prison population, I rarely delved into the crimes of these prisoners unless it was offered or deemed necessary for safety reasons. I didn't want to prejudge, I needed to protect my mind, mental health, and the privacy of the human soul.

Rape is rape, and there must be justice and accountability for sexual crimes. However, perhaps there are cases where another perspective is worth considering - situations where intent may not have been present. I witnessed firsthand that some of these young men were simply doing what many others their age were doing; the difference was, they had been caught.

Chapter 15
And Then Came COVID
"The New Normal"

"We are in this together and we will get through this together."
UN Secretary, Antonio Guterres: United Nations

Prison is far from normal. Although being locked in was "normal" for those who worked and lived in prison, a new, new normal was about to strike.

March 2020 and the frenzied hunt for toilet roll! Toilet roll, pasta and hand sanitiser were in short supply as the public stashed supplies at home, wary that we might run out of these super essential items.

I was on holiday in Spain with some girlfriends in March 2020. The news was overrun with outbreaks of COVID all over the world. Countries were declaring national states of lockdown. It hadn't happened to us yet but the possibility lingered. And then it came. We were sitting having breakfast after a week of sunshine and relaxation. Our hotel, its staff and guests went into a frenzy. All the holidaymakers were glued to the televisions, texting home and waiting for instructions. It was utter chaos as we waited to hear from our tour operators, who didn't have a clue what to do. There were older men and women without mobile phones walking around the hotel frightened and dazed, as others packed up and hired taxis to the airport only to be told to return to their hotels and wait for instructions.

Hotel shutters went down and restaurants closed as the Spanish were also told that they were going into lockdown, and they could do nothing to help us. We were then herded like cattle to an older, dilapidated hotel while we waited. We were banished to our rooms and we watched from the balcony as the swimming pool was taped off and sun loungers stacked. My friend, Fiona, updated us hourly as her husband sent photographs of the rapidly diminishing supplies of food on UK supermarket shelves. We were petrified! I phoned home and demanded that a hospital wing be set up in the spare bedroom just in case and that everyone had to go out and buy as much hand sanitiser, paracetamol and dried pasta as they could get their hands on.

Eventually, we were all placed on rescue flights home and, on landing back in the UK, transported in rickety old coaches back to Manchester. The crisis was no longer a distant drama - it was upon us. We were in lockdown, and our lives were suddenly at risk.

By the end of March, the number of people in the UK with coronavirus had spiked. The virus had taken hold and the only potential way of slowing down the spread was by taking away our liberties, requesting that we work at home and stop all face-to-face contact with the rest of the human race. We all donned face masks and were allowed one hour of exercise a day. Pubs closed, restaurants closed, and the world became a very lonely place. As the pans banged out on Thursday evenings for the 999 heroes of the NHS, my colleagues and I continued to work - we were "essential workers." I returned to my job but it was an entirely different environment, a new regime, and a new common enemy.

The NHS was overwhelmed, and we were overwhelmed, yet prisons never got a mention; we were out of sight, trying our utmost to keep everyone safe in this confined space which held 1,500 prisoners and hundreds of staff. Sure enough, as time went by, staff sickness increased, and the prison was in crisis. Social distancing, handwashing, and wearing masks all day at work became normal. At first, Personal Protective Equipment was scarce, and risks were abound. The prison population, it seemed, was initially well down on the nation's priority list.

It was Week Six of the virus, and up to 30,000 deaths had been recorded in the UK. Prison wings went into total lockdown as suspected cases were isolated. The prisoners spent 23.5 hours in their cells. There was no movement, no jobs, no Gym, no visits. We all expected mayhem, but this was not the case with the prisoners. Officers, however, were slack as they gathered at close distance in offices to chat because they had nothing else to do. Some staff were very laissez-faire until, of course, the virus affected them.

As staff sickness levels increased, so did that of the prisoners. The only way they were going to contract the virus was from us or from new prisoners coming in. The treatment of Reception prisoners was inhumane. They were in total isolation for the first two weeks of their stay with nothing but a wash pack and a tiny, stained sink to wash in.

On one occasion, nurses donned white Bio-Hazmat suits visited the wings that were riddled with COVID. The prisoners were terrified, we visited but only those in crisis or to deliver more bad news. Donned in a Personal Protective Equipment suit, like something from an Armageddon movie, I appeared to talk to a prisoner.

"Are we all going to die?" he asked with tears flowing. "No, we're not," I replied. This was a lie. I had no idea who would be ill or even die; I was just as frightened. "If the world is going to end, will you come and let us out?" "Of course, I will." I already had a plan. We would take shelter in the forest; it was all in hand!

You would expect tempers to flair but, in all honesty, I have never seen such self-discipline. Apart from the detritus squeezed through the gaps in the windows (due to the fact bins weren't emptied), the behaviour of the prisoners was exemplary. The rats behaved accordingly and rummaged amongst the rubbish in the yards below. The prisoners put the rest of us to shame; they were amazing. I can't say the same about all of us. One member of staff came into work and, after working for a few hours, let slip that she had COVID. The management soon had her removed and then the pressure was on to ensure everyone was tested. The prisoners found out that this member of staff had put everyone at risk but apart from a few choice words, the incident was forgotten.

Eventually, we were supplied with test kits, and Industry was kitted out and became a swabbing centre. The camaraderie was good; in general, we all looked out for one another. Fortunately, we didn't have to break out and live in the forest. It wasn't the end of the world, but for families, staff, and residents, it was a real test of resilience and faith. Prison days were never the same, under normal circumstances, but now confusion and fear reached tumultuous heights and it was exhausting keeping up with daily changes.

During COVID, the chapel became "ground zero." Every morning, the senior staff would arrive mask-clad and socially distanced to listen to reports and updates on the latest cases of violence, self-harm and COVID statistics. We were made aware of the rapidly increasing numbers of COVID, staff sickness and wings that were shut down to try to contain the spread. The Chaplaincy manager or I would usually attend these meetings. They became a bit of a chore but were necessary to cascade vital information. If we were forewarned, we could take all the necessary safety precautions.

COVID was a test for us all, and while the nation's 999 services were pan-clapped, we carried on forgotten and unrecognised, yet COVID had a huge impact on prison life. Later, we experienced the first COVID Christmas. Once again, the kind and jolly officers dragged the plastic trees out of the storerooms. They were adorned with broken lights and a few tattered decorations. We were given donations of new decorations and paper garlands that we shared with the wing staff. My fabulous Elf and I then set to work to make sure that this Christmas, with all the other added stresses of lockdown, was going to be the one to beat, despite the restrictions that were upon us.

We took over a small office in the Chaplaincy and started begging for donations. It was quite a feat but, eventually, donations came in thick and fast from the Mothers Union and the local Deanery. The chapel orderly, a young Muslim man, and I and anyone else who was sitting for more than a minute began the huge and laborious task of decorating 2,000 paper prison paper cups with Christmas paper. Our colleague, who was shielding at home, helped us create gift cups by the hundred. We decorated them and added small handles so we could hang them on cell doors. Boxes of sweets and chocolate started to stack up and the room resembled Santa's grotto. We were given greeting cards and short tracts about the Christmas story. The Education department helped us create Santa's sleigh. It was incredible. With a bit of motivation and the kindness of those who remembered us, we achieved the impossible.

Wagtail

The magical Eve arrived, and we were ready. There were no services because of the dreaded lurgy, and the prisoners couldn't come to us, so we would go to them. Dressed as Elves with face masks and hand sanitiser, my friend from education in his brightly adorned Christmas suit, and we set off! We knocked on every door and opened as many cell doors as we could. We had blisters from turning keys. All day and into the evening, we did a trolley dash to every wing in the prison giving out these meagre gifts and cards.

You would think we were handing out gold bullion. For the most part, the prisoners and staff were delighted - grateful that someone cared, that someone remembered them. However, a few couldn't handle this small act of kindness and refused the gift. For some, it seemed too much to accept, perhaps evoking suspicion or serving as a painful reminder of something lost.

The little battered CD player blasted out "White Christmas" and "Jingle Bells", fading rapidly as the day progressed and the batteries ran out. Staff helped us distribute the gifts and, after ten hours, we accomplished our task. Santa's sleigh had lost its wheels, the sat nav was broken and we had sore feet and hands.

There was a last dash to the Vulnerable Prisoner wing and we know what happened there.

We left that night cold and hungry, with blisters on our hands and sore feet. As the real Santa flew through the skies, we were tired but happy. Then home for our own Christmas in a bubble.

Wagtail

Chapter 16
Friends

*"Don't walk in front of me …I may not follow
Don't walk behind me…I may not lead
Walk beside me…Just be my friend."*
Albert Camus

My son spent his younger and adolescent years (and still today) watching the iconic American sitcom, Friends. I love it too. "How you doin'?" is Joey's memorable catchphrase. This series follows the lives of six reckless and hedonistic adults as they indulge in the adventures of life both happy and troublesome. It would always make me smile when I could hear my son from his bedroom, howling with laughter at one of the epic misdemeanours or dry humour that made him chortle. The fantasy image of friendship and belonging was one I craved as a child and later as an adult. I think my son did too. He longed for a "friendship utopia." He eventually found it and has kept those friends for years.

I can't pinpoint exactly when I realised how lonely I was. I don't think we recognise insecurity and loneliness when we're young. However, I believe that, at some stage in our development - especially if we struggle with confidence - we begin to feel and acknowledge the pain of inadequacy and loneliness. I was a lonely child and I grew to be a lonely adult. I wasn't left to fend for myself as a child, I wasn't living in an abusive or unhealthy environment, and I was rarely physically alone. I was cared for, and my needs were met. As a family, we sat around the table every morning for breakfast and every evening for dinner. My Dad would set the table for breakfast the night before, and we would all sit together in the morning. My sister Jayne used to cry at mealtimes. I remember her crying at the table and watching herself in the reflection of the silver teapot. It amused all of us.

My middle sister was born when we lived in South Africa. I vaguely remember her coming home from the hospital and being the centre of attention. She was a very pretty child, with blonde curly hair and chubby cheeks. Looking back, I can't remember feeling jealous of her or resenting her.

I really don't know why or how I became so sad and lonely. On the outside, I was a gregarious and imaginative child, but inside, I was hurting. Insecurely clinging to friends was about loneliness, filling a gap, and getting that extra attention I craved.

As the parish vicar, I used to take assemblies at two primary schools. One of them, I must confess, was my favourite. I would often sit with the Head, a beautiful, calm, and compassionate teacher whose life was committed to these children. The school was on a social housing estate and, as most of the children lived a stone's throw away from the vicarage, they would hang off my garden gate. They would knock on my door late in the evening asking for help with homework or asking if I could photocopy or print something off the internet to help with projects. A large percentage of the children were pupil premium_students, in other words free school dinners, that would indicate struggling families. I loved those children and the community, but life was hard for them.

At the beginning of every assembly, the children sat in rows, cross-legged on the buffed hall floor. Miss would say: "Good morning, friends." She would refer to the children as her friend or our friend. Now at first, I observed this with some bewilderment. Should she be calling pupils "friends?"

I can't recall my giant of a headmaster ever referring to me as a friend. I was tiny and he was a Big Friendly Giant, or so it seemed at the time. There was never mention of me being his friend; for me, he was a terrifying, statuesque figure of authority. Eventually, I understood. I learned how this endearing phrase impacted the children. Here, they would learn the true meaning of friendship which meant love and respect. They were reminded about the impact of bullying and behaviour that was unkind, something that many may well have experienced at home. In my opinion (never mind Ofsted), the school was outstanding and, for some, a super pastoral and enabling experience. Miss just wanted them to feel special; and during this formative time in their lives, she was their friend. After assembly, the Head and I would sit in her office, and we would chat, and she would share her concerns about some of the pupils. Little lives traumatised by abuse, poverty, and chaos. She would often say: "That one will end up in prison." This made me shudder, I try to avoid making negative statements or declaring negativity over such young lives, but it was true, and she was right. Statistically, some of these children were destined for one thing, and one thing only in the next few years and beyond. They were destined to be my new friends, and I would be their new "Miss".

Now being a friend here in prison has no comparison to the friendship that Joey, Phoebe, Rachel,

Monica, Ross, and Chandler experienced in their suburban New York apartment or in Perk Café. Friendship here in prison is unique. But however unique, the men were still friends. Albeit for a short time, I would walk with them just like the quote says: *"Not in front they may not follow, not behind they may not lead but beside."* These were friends with boundaries and limits, but friends, nonetheless.

Only recently, in my job as a hospital chaplain, I walked onto a busy medical ward. I was visiting an elderly patient on a Sunday. Suddenly, from a hospital bed in the corner bay, a voice called out, "Miss Annie!" Now, when you are referred to as Miss, it can only mean one thing. Not only am I now 61 but I am also not a woman that society would refer to as a Miss. Hearing the name "Miss" being called out fills me with delight; they remember me, we have crossed paths before. I turned around, and there, hooked up to a drip, was my friend.

My friend had been in the prison where I worked, and he remembered me. To be honest, at first, I couldn't pick him out from the thousands of my incarcerated friends. I smiled, said hello, drew up a plastic chair and we re-established our friendship. I sat beside him, not in front, not behind but beside him. Another plastic chair but in a different institution. My friend explained that he was recently released from prison. He then continued to recall his sad, broken life and how he had tried to continue with his faith and had the support of his local church. However, his life was far from mended. He had suffered the loss of his child, and his own childhood was a myriad of horrific events. Yet here, he was my friend, alive, hooked up to a drip and on the out. We talked, we laughed, and he cried. He explained he had taken a massive overdose and that he just wanted to die. He was so lonely and broken; in fact, he was so lonely that "doing bird" again wasn't such a bad option, and if he didn't get his way and get a psychiatric bed, he would do something to get himself back inside. Despite pleading for help, despite having the choice to exist outside prison he just couldn't cope. He was homeless and had been sofa surfing (sleeping on friend's couches).

I visited him every day and enlisted the help of the Chaplaincy team. He was my friend but a friend with strict boundaries. I was unable to offer more than time, empathy, and Agape love. When I saw him for the last time, he reached out to shake my hand. I reached back and said, "Why are you shaking my hand?" "Because you are my friend," he replied. I don't know what became of him. Until this happened...

I was going for an evening walk recently. I walked to think about my day, to clear my head from the events of the day. I was walking alongside a river and listening to the birds, throwing a ball for my dog. I leaned over to pick up the ball when a voice shouted, "Annie is that you?" I looked up and initially didn't recognise the voice or the face. "It's me," he said and reminded me of his name. "I was in prison and the hospital; you looked after me."

After he recollected our previous encounters, and the story of his awful traumas I remembered. Of course I remembered, how could I forget. The was the same young man who I had formed a prison friendship with. He stood in front of me and tears fell down his cheeks. "I am okay," he said, "I have a partner, I have a dog, and I come to walk here to clear my head." He was with his friend, the one who had reached out to him and offered him a home and friendship. We chatted for a while, we reminisced and hugged each other. "Thank you," he said. "That's okay," I replied, "You are my friend."

After a tough day at work, my mood lifted and I grinned and laughed all the way around the park before making my way home.

Wagtail

Friendship in prison is brief and transient. You must not share what could be incriminating information such as where you live or anything about family or friends. Social media contact is an absolute no-go! You rarely discuss events in prison with your own social circle. I rarely asked about their offence; it is confidential and personal to them and to the judicial system. However, this is friendship; what else can it be? You are intrinsic and ever-present for a time, in the prison that is home to thousands of people.

My prison colleagues were my friends. We had nights out and we shared our lives quite openly. Mundane details about recent football triumphs, updates on our kids, holidays, dogs, and minor complaints about husbands and wives.

As a chaplain, you listen to the prisoners and are exposed to very personal and sometimes horrific details of abusive childhoods and continuing cycles of addiction, crime, fear, anger, and abject loneliness. These men were once sat in red sweaters, picking noses, yawning, in assemblies listening to a visiting vicar. Some may have had a lovely head teacher, who was for a time a friend, but the damage runs so deep that they end up in prison. The only present friends they have behind bars are staff and other prisoners who can identify with them because of similar life patterns and traits. I had to consider what it meant to be a friend here. Where the land lay and what the boundaries are.

I now have fabulous friends. A handful of funny, intelligent, and loyal friends who have walked beside me every step of my life. My very bestie is Fiona. She has been a staple in my life, we trained as nurses together and together we stand. She is Irish, bossy, outspoken but, all in all, fabulous. My perfecting of the Irish accent is all due to her. Our friendship will always be because we have been together on the roller-coaster of life. Second in line to God and my go-to spiritual friend is Mary. Mary is my other confidante, she has prayed with me, listened to me, and travelled the well-worn path with me, as I have her. I have other gorgeous and wonderful friends that I love and value.

Friendships in prison are different from my personal relationships; here, friendship, although in many ways the same, is re-written and presents itself in a different way. I would rarely discuss my hopes and aspirations with prisoners; they would never know about the tears shed, the cancer treatments, or the relationship breakdowns. This wasn't me -time. There are some things I did share but few. It was more like this. I could listen and advise; I could mediate and speak out; I could sit a while; I could contact friends and family; I could fetch and deliver books, paper, and pencils; I could complain and be an advocate, and I could pray. Friendship on the outside is two-way and to have a friend, you must be a friend, as my Mum would say. Healthy friendships are two-way, but here it was mostly one-sided. I learned so much from my prison friends; they helped me understand, inspired me and gave me hope. I was a friend to them, but there was little or (quite rightly) no reciprocation. We couldn't go out for coffee, we couldn't go for a walk, I couldn't share my dramas with them. When I left the gates, the friendship was as it was. The moment we left work, it stayed behind bars and would be taken back up the next day. I tried not to take them home in my head, but they were in my heart. When the men left prison, I heard very little about them, until perhaps they came back, and we took up where we had left off. It was, for all intents and purposes, a situationship rather than a friendship.

I realise that some may initially misinterpret my message, but I encourage you to consider the insight that I'm trying to share.

When I walked through the Jurassic Forest during COVID, I imagined how the world would look in Armageddon. What would happen if I couldn't leave and go home? Perhaps if I could get out and beyond the walls, I could survive in the forest with my friends. I used to consciously look for places of shelter and food to eat. However, most of the plants were probably poisonous here. If I let my friends out, we could build shelters and eat rats to survive! Silly, yes so silly, but now we would all have to be friends, deserted together with a few other remaining survivors. As COVID progressed and deaths increased, we were all scared, and that fear was tangible. Yes, we would all live and shelter under the Jurassic vegetation. We could boil water from the river; the ingenious antics of fire starters would be of great use. We had a common enemy that presented itself as a Pandemic. As I strolled back to the grey-clad walls, I would smile, yes indeed, we would be friends, and then, just as my imagination ran into the future of a Utopian community, I was reminded of a book, a book I had studied at school: Lord of the Flies. Like Piggie, I hurried back to terra firma, not from an island but ironically to the safety and the boundaries of the prison walls.

Wagtail

Chapter 17
Lord of the Flies
"Kill the pig. Cut her throat. Spill her blood."
William Goldring: Lord of the Flies: 1954

William Goldring's novel tells of a group of boys, not yet men, stranded on an island. The Island is deserted, they are alone, and there are no adults to care for them. They act on instinct. They elect a leader, Ralph, who determines the rules and tries to nurture a primaeval mechanism for survival. The nature/nurture instincts cause the boys to behave in cruel, barbaric and violent ways as they create this new order. With an instinct to follow rules and live in peace, they strive to survive in a vast and lonely place. Ralph struggles to maintain order as the younger boys just instinctively want to explore and play. Ralph insists on a fire being built to signal to passing vessels. Guards are down and the fire is left to fizzle out; Ralph is furious. The group is eventually divided, and they become enemies.

The story continues with brutal violence and fear as they hunt the wild sow. The character, cruelly named Piggy, is killed by a boulder which then rolls on to shatter the conch shell, the symbol of order.

Wagtail

Life in prison can pretty much mirror the behaviour of the boys on the Island. There are leaders, there are followers, there are weak and strong. There is conflict and tension. Here is a battle between emotional and rational, morality and immorality. The fight for survival is well and truly exposed as the prisoners arrive and try to find their place on this concrete island. Sometimes, there are great acts of kindness, but the truth is that most of these prisoners have nurtured a warped sense of morality, and here, unlike on the Island, it may be a while before they are rescued.

Viktor Frankl was an Austrian psychiatrist. During World War II, he spent three years in Auschwitz and Dachau. In the face of great suffering, he kept notes and observed the behaviours of men in the concentration camps where he was a prisoner of war. In his book *"Man's Search for Meaning,"* Viktor writes about the horrific conditions and the dark psychological behaviour of the camp guards and that of the prisoners. He tells stories about the pleasure of the guards taking away the basic needs and the smallest of resources from the prisoners. He suggests that some of them were sadists, carefully selected to enforce the tragic annihilation and holocaust. However, even amongst some of the most brainwashed, there was compassion. As the years dragged by, even the officers became weary and refused to participate in brutal measures taken against the men in the camp. They, too, were trying to survive; they were, by their actions, exposed to the darkest parts of their own souls.

In prison and facing the consequences of crime, be it murder, rape, fraud or even the most minor of crimes the prisoners had two choices. They could address head on and with vulnerability what they had done, or they could carry on regardless. Some didn't appear to have the ability to recognise the pain they had caused. Some were remorseful, some wanted to change. Being in prison was perhaps the one and only opportunity they would have to look at themselves, their lives, and even if they dared to have hopes and dreams.

The popular musical Les Miserable is set in 19th-century France. The lead character is Jean Valjean, an ex-convict. The transcendent themes of Les Mis resound the human condition of dignity, love, and resilience.

To set the scene, we find Jean at the mercy of the Bishop of Digne. The Bishop offers hospitality to the homeless and poverty-stricken Jean, but instead of being grateful he makes off with his host's silver. Jean is arrested and the police bring him back to face his victim. You would expect the Bishop to be angry and to determine his fate in prison. Instead, the Bishop tells the police that the silver was a gift for Valjean, and he is set free. This act of kindness lays Jean Valjean naked, exposed, and aware of his inner demons. He is changed by this man's act of kindness. The prisoner is now free and takes the opportunity to redeem himself.

How often do we face the consequences of our negative actions, the unkind words and behaviours that cause others pain? I would suggest many of us just sail through life without regarding unkind words or jokes. We can be oblivious to the pain we cause. The tongue has the power of life and death, and we are all guilty. If we are aware, then maybe we have the chance to apologise, to say sorry but so often we continue just to be hurt or hurt again.

I am not suggesting here that the chaplains were the only access to forgiveness and redemption. However, we were sometimes a catalyst for the prisoners in our care to stop and think of the harm they may have caused, and to face the music. It is not for us to judge lest we be judged. Here just listening and trying to empathise can allow hearts to be restored. A simple act of kindness, time and words of encouragement may offer a small step on the road to redemption.

Frankl says that human kindness can be found in all of us, even those that we would condemn. He recalls acts of kindness that were nothing less than a miracle from camp guards, yet at the same time prisoners betraying their own in order to survive. The contrast of the reaction from the heights of kindness and the unexpected to the lows of cruelty from within the ranks of survivors. The prison community was much the same. Always so thankful for a small act. Maybe a Polo Mint or a book, the offer of a phone call to a distressed Mum or some pencils and paper. The smallest act of kindness for a person who is deemed unworthy was so easy yet often so rare.

Survival in prison, for those facing the hardships of confinement, depends greatly on a delicate mental resilience - echoing through the walls as a distinction between those who endure and those who struggle deeply. While prison conditions differ vastly from the horrors of historical atrocities, the psychological battles faced by inmates are undeniable. Before they even enter the prison gates, approximately 75% of the men are already coping with varying levels of mental health challenges. These struggles, aggravated by the monotony of long, empty days and a persistent yearning for freedom, often spiral into worsening mental health.

Even though we were very limited in the field of psychiatry and psychology we could identify those who really struggled and those few who didn't. Those who could muster up the strength for the stretch and those who would just regress or stand still in time. Surviving the loss of liberty, facing the inner struggles and the situations they now found themselves in is a certain and painful journey. Sometimes, there was hope and sometimes, there was none.

We all experience difficulties in life and, if we have good mental health, we may seek help to overcome them. Here, the prisoners can get help but recognising their own pain is rare. Talking and asking for help can be seen as a weakness and it takes careful navigation to steer between suppressing feelings and honest vulnerability. It takes tremendous bravery and honesty to strive for a chance to release at least some of the pressure. Time inside can just create a combustible vessel. Those who had the strength to talk had hope, but those who didn't or wouldn't, held in their feelings, their fears, and their anger. This only creates a human time bomb. Feelings are often repressed and buried deep in the soul.

Emotions are suppressed and then, the moment they are released from prison, the lid blows off the bottle and there is an explosion. I witnessed this so many times. Men would be released, and, within days, they were back through the revolving door. No one really knows what a man or woman has experienced over the last two, ten or twenty years in prison. One night of release celebration. Fuelled with drink and drugs they would often return to the scene of the original crime. If they didn't go back to the same scene, then another situation would arise. A drunken pub brawl and back they come to start all over again.

In 2018, following a letter to the Archbishop of Canterbury drafted by Northwest Prison Chaplains, I was invited to facilitate a workshop at a mental health conference at Lambeth Palace. Dragging my small carry-on for an overnight stay in London, I arrived at the conference sweating with foreboding flu. Determined to deliver my message about the situation in the male estate I met with the higher echelons of Mental Health experts. I am not an expert in the field, just holding a certificate in minor mental health, yet armed with stories of mental ill health from my friends, I grasped the opportunity as an advocate for prisoners. I talked about the fight to survive; I gave examples of hope. I even delivered a pencil drawing from an artistic young man with Asperger's. I asked him if he could draw the Archbishop. The picture was an excellent resemblance of the weary Archbishop who confessed he had himself experienced some mental health issues. He, too, was vulnerable; this venerable and holy man could empathise with the worsening crisis. Shortly after the conference, we were plagued with COVID, so there hasn't been a follow-up. Note to self! Need to catch up with The Most Reverend Justin. Might have to if he reads this book with its plethora of swear words!

The nature-nurture instinct is very much a part of survival. Frankl would observe the same behaviours in prison as he did in the camps. Since time began, our inner thoughts have influenced our behaviours. The damage inflicted on the men often from being born paved the way for a life behind bars.

Sometimes, prisoners would tell me that they had been lying awake all night thinking about their lives. Staring up at the ceilings their souls would go over and over their childhoods, the abuse, the torment of poor choices. They needed to talk, but talking was seen as a weakness and it took some work to try to engage these souls in meaningful conversations. Most of the time it was the daily wants and demands that occupied their minds.

Some people do appear to have the skills to survive tragedy, illness, loss and pain. I have a friend named Lisa. Lisa is also my hairdresser and confidante. She is the most amazing woman, and she is an inspiration to many. Lisa has a plethora of swear words and has very few filters. She speaks the truth and never beats around the bush. You can tell her something and the next time you see her she has forgotten. She is beautiful, determined and strong. The reason I mention Lisa here is that, at the tender age of 39, she had a catastrophic brain haemorrhage and stroke. I was sitting in a bar in Spain when I got a call from her Mum asking me to pray for Lisa. I couldn't believe the news that my dear, funny, crazy, fun-loving friend was in critical condition. It was touch and go if she was going to make it. The first 24 hours, as we often hear, were critical.

Well, she did make it. From deep within she found great courage and resilience. Her guts and determination drove her to fight with every ounce of strength. She had months of intensive rehabilitation and, besides the plethora of unfiltered swear words, she is a testimony to inner strength and very positive thinking. Her body is not quite the same; she still struggles somewhat but her personality and her sense of humour keep us all in awe.

In prison, it is those who have hope, a purpose and a future that seem to make it through. There are those who have little hope but may see a glimpse of a different future. For those who suffer from abject loneliness, those who have never experienced love, who can't see beyond their next grey meal there seems to be no hope. They may as well stay in prison, life here is easier than having to rally up strength from an empty vessel.

Talking, confessing, and facing up to stealing the silver took guts and a determination to change. The meeting between the Bishop and Jean Viljoen was life-changing; as for the Chaplaincy team and some of the staff, we tried, God knows we tried.

Chapter 18
Family
"Goodnight John, Boy. Good night, Mary Ellen."
The Waltons TV series 1972-1981 written by Earl Hamner Jr

The Waltons was an American historical drama set in rural Virginia. It was broadcast from 1972 until June 1981, and I think I watched every single episode. It was set in the depression of war! It told the story of an idyllic farming family of 9; Ma, Pa and seven children. Hand-sewn pinafores, overalls, and pigtails. The family was hospitable; they shared meals together and they shared their cares and joys. At the end of every episode, just as they drifted off to sleep, they would all say goodnight to each other as the music faded. It was gorgeous, romantic and a portrayal of a perfect family life. A bit of escapism, just like my son and his Friends DVD set, I watched in awe and longed to wear a pinafore just like Mary Ellen.

Thankfully I don't remember being born. I certainly don't recall being forced down the birth canal and being hung upside down and my bottom smacked (as was common practice when I entered this world.) The only thing I know is that January 1963 was one of the coldest winters ever recorded. My Mum told me she came home with me from St Mary's Hospital to a sink full of dirty pots in frozen water. This was 1963 and although my dad was nurtured eventually into being a more domesticated man, at the time, he didn't think to wash the pots before collecting Mum on that Siberian day.

The other thing my Mum always said was that I was born the year President Kennedy was assassinated. Untold freezing weather, dirty pots and an assassination, the summary of my first year of life. My Mum used to often tell me, that when I was a baby, she would get up, get me fed, dressed, and washed and sit me outside in my Silver Cross pram, (just in front of the asbestos garage, available to be snatched), in my peaked, ear-knitted bonnet by 09:00 hours every morning. I have no doubt that my Mum loved me but, by her own admission, maternal instincts didn't come naturally.

I don't suppose it matters if our brain fails to store memories so early in life, I think it's probably a safety mechanism. Who wants to remember sitting outside in a pram alone, passing strangers talking to you and cooing, expecting a smile?

In the "Walton's world," idyllic memories are made with loving parents. Eating corn fritters around a big kitchen table with a checked tablecloth, rocking on a rope swing in the dapple light of an apple tree; the first step; the first trip to the zoo; the first seaside adventure; and the first tooth lost! These are all pleasant memories for parents and children. Some psychologists suggest that traumatic events can trigger feelings of fear or sadness even though we don't remember all the details. A child development expert, Chase Sheinbaum, says adventures and holidays start to find a place in our memories from the age of about two and a half.

Well, this is interesting because one of my earliest memories, and perhaps triggered by old black and white photos, are of me, Mum and Dad leaving the UK to go and live in South Africa. I don't recall leaving or sailing on the huge Edinburgh Castle passenger ship. I do, however, remember one thing. I remember, on our return, wandering around the passages of the ship, staring up at gigantic doors. I remember crying and being terrified. According to Mum, I had gotten out of bed and escaped when I should have been napping.

I can remember living in South Africa. I recall the parks we visited and our houseboy, Alfred, playing outside with my little friend Stephen. I can still recite the rude words the house boys taught me. I remember stopping at a roadside to give native children Easter eggs and I remember visiting Durban. It is a significant event that I remember in South Africa. I remember my sister Jayne being born and offering to give her my precious Teddy. These are all strong pleasant memories.

On the flip side, however, on holiday In Durban, I recollect going with Mum and Dad and staying with a family. Mum and Dad were dressed up. They were going to leave me with the family's nanny. They had put me to bed and told me they were going to fill the ship with oil, and they had to go out (a huge lie). I was absolutely traumatised; I cried. I begged them not to abandon me, not to leave me with the scary native nanny. But then, they left me. I remember quite distinctly thinking this is it. They had gone! I had to live with this new family, with a mean girl and a strange nanny! Of course, they hadn't abandoned me; they were partying on the ship before leaving and all was well, but this not-so-nice memory stayed with me.

I have lots of nice childhood memories, mostly family holidays, Sunday School pantomimes, putting on singing shows for the neighbours and playing out for hours on end. I have lovely memories of staying with a family friend in Yorkshire and the fantastic adventures she took us on. I remember scaling cliff tops and scraping moss off rocks with my sisters, (a family tradition). I remember having to balance on a stool in the back room, arms out like a scarecrow, while Mum, armed with sharp scissors, would cut out the arm holes of the dress she was making us. She used to stick pins in us and cut our armpits with the scissors (only kidding); it just felt like that at the time when we were desperate to play outside.

My Dad worked during the week and was always at the dinner table in the evening. I can recall a couple of special times I had with him on my own! He once took me to buy a new dress, (no pins or scissors). I can't imagine why I was on my own with him. I remember us going and buying the dress from a shop in the local shopping town. I remember walking with him and how holding his hand felt so special and different to my mother's hand. I can describe exactly what the dress was like. It was navy blue with no sleeves and a white trim, the fabric had a diamond pattern. It was a shop bought dress which made it so special.

Wagtail

I recall going with him on my own in his big yellow estate car to a wood yard. The smell of freshly cut timber stays with me! I remember him talking to the woodman and loading the wood into the boot, having to sit with my head tilted to prevent possible decapitation if the brakes were suddenly applied. Why do I remember these events so clearly? Well, I have a theory! Time spent with my dad, time alone just with him was rare and very precious. Day-to-day life was with my Mum and sisters and the only real time I spent other than this with my dad was on family holidays once or twice a year. It was only really in the latter years of my dad's life that I appreciated what a steady, reliable, and kind man he was and that he loved his daughters very much.

Nurture has given me mostly positive memories and a positive foundation on which to build my life. Of course, there are negative memories too, but I have managed to reason and filter those.

I am my mother's twin. I have a stash of unread books by my bed, I have a peg bag hanging on my washing line. I put my sheets out on the washing line in frosty weather to bleach them! All my mother's habits. Every time I step out into my garden, I hear my Mum say, "Don't forget to deadhead the flowers." Every morning without fail, before I venture to the loo, I peer through the blinds and say out loud to myself, "Let's see what the weather's doing." Now, that was my dad's morning routine before ablutions and I say it every day, and then just laugh.

These are my foundations, my memories, thankfully not tinged with much trauma or sadness. The reason I recall my childhood is because I became acutely aware of the memories and childhood traumas of almost all the men I ever worked with at the prison. Generations have passed since my childhood, and it appears that as generations continue many have lost out on the nurture and love of a nuclear family. I can only talk of my experience but can observe that positive parenting wasn't the main interest in the 60s, more like, "Just get on with it, love."

Positive parenting was a concept I rarely heard mentioned when prisoners shared stories of their childhoods. Often, the only positive and reliable figure in their lives was a grandparent - frequently a grandmother who took on the responsibility of raising the man-child. Mothers were often left to fend for themselves, sometimes with several children. Many were battling addiction or had been in prison themselves, while others endured abusive partners or husbands. The man-child had witnessed domestic abuse, violence and sometimes murder. Some of the prisoners had been victims of sexual abuse by one or both parents. Some had even been sold for sex to friends and family.

However, this was not always the case, some but few had wonderful families. Some of the men had usually "got in with the wrong crowd." Mums and Dads would ring the Chaplaincy and would offload about their disbelief that their precious child had wandered from the path. They couldn't believe that their sons, who had everything, would end up in prison. None of us are perfect parents, and life itself is far from perfect. However, I firmly believe that we are often shaped by our upbringing, the nurturing we receive, and the positive or negative foundations laid during our early years.

There are "ologists" and family experts who would debate and question my observations. Of course, men have been "missing" from family life since time immemorial. There have always been wars and rumours of wars. Men had to leave for months, sometimes years. They were enlisted and did not return for a long time if at all. This isn't a new phenomenon, only to say these are my personal observations of the present day. Few fathers have to go to war these days; few have to hunt for food; they are just missing.

It appears we live in what my friend would call "a fatherless nation." This isn't to put the onus on men and fathers, but rather to say we have thrown the baby out with the bath water, and we have forgotten or been dismissive of the role of men and particularly fathers. Men (not all, I'm not a female misogynist) seem to have been pushed aside, emasculated and left wondering what their role is in life. Now, these are my thoughts, and many will argue that children don't need a father; they just need love and acceptance.

I expect those children of my generation experienced similar situations. Dads were present and some, but not many, were adept at fatherhood and the precious role a dad plays in their child's life.

I believe society has increasingly devalued the role of the father, perhaps as a way to rationalise the brokenness of family life. We often place blame on men, but some of us - including myself - have contributed to this by emasculating them. As a result, many men struggle to understand where they belong or what their purpose is. I'm not sure when the role of the father seemed to fade; I guess it may have been post-World War 2. So many of them didn't return or, like my grandfather, were absent for years, leaving mothers to cope on their own. These are just my thoughts, and I haven't researched any deeper other than a couple of books I have read, and from my own experience. In the book, *"Father and Son,"* by Gordon Dalby, he says, *"As if to declaw the tiger, the world proclaims that fathers aren't that important after all."* He goes on to say, *"A man taught that a father is not important will act accordingly when he becomes a father himself."*

This may not be true for all men whose fathers are absent emotionally or physically but, when I look at the prison population, this would seem to be true. When I talked to the men about family, I often used the terms Mummy and Daddy. I don't know where this came from, but it struck a chord. The word "father" had notions of a disciplinarian. The image of a daddy brings us childlike memories, if we have any. These memories may be painful or there may be some glimpses of joy. The nice memories I have of my dad were when he was my daddy; those precious times we spent on our own when he held my small hand in his huge hand, and I felt close to him.

Mothers often want to protect their sons from violent or angry fathers, and this is understandable. However, in doing so, some women disparage all men and tar them all with the same brush. The reality is there are so many good men just as there are good women. I believe that to keep a child away from their father, apart from when there is a risk of physical, mental or emotional harm, may cause more harm than good. In the same book, *"Father and Son,"* Gordan Dalby quotes Robert Bly as saying this about positive father-child time, *"When a father and son do spend time together...we could say that a substance almost like food passes from the older body to the younger..."* This food, this nourishment, was missing from the lives of so many of the men that I met.

My Dad used to tell us a story about his childhood at a time when hundreds of fathers left a chasm in family life. He remembers back in 1939 standing at a bus stop in Manchester with his Mum and sister. They stood together waiting for a bus. The bus was to take his dad away for five years. Away to a war, away from his side, away from him during the most formative years of my dad's life. Now, my Grandad did return from war eventually, but he was gone for years. He, like many others, left his wife, my grandmother, to raise two children. No email, no mobile phones, just letters and the radio provided snippets of information about the distant war, a war that had taken Dad away. My Dad said he never really got on with his Mum because she was never happy; he never said much about his dad either except that: "He would drink beer out of a sweaty clog." Those were my dad's memories; this was his nurture experience; these were his beginnings. My Mum says she had a lovely Dad, but he literally went out to his allotment one day and dropped dead! My Mum must have been about 25 years of age.

When I listened to the prisoners recall their childhoods, they were so often tainted with negative experiences of family life. There had been little, or no attention paid to the nurturing of the prisoners when they were children. Mostly, (not all) the men would recall Dad, (occasionally Mum), being violent, in prison or just absent.

Generations of families have gone by since my dad was a boy but when I look around, I often hear discussions about the role of the contemporary man. I have heard women so often say, "I don't need a fella. I'll bring my baby up on my own." This baby doesn't need a dad; I'll be Mum and Dad." This may sound like a rash generalisation; however, it does seem to me that we are more and more living in a fatherless nation. Fathers have a huge impact on children. They have a role, and they should have a place, except in difficult or damaging circumstances, in the lives of their children. When divorce and separation are the only options, children should be the priority, and they need access to their Mums and Dads. Fathers bring something different; the essence of a good Dad is a gift. A Dad can form the way girls and then women view the male species. How we go on to choose life partners, and positive relationship choices. A good Dad and husband should enable and be an example for future generations. How to be a good husband, how to nurture and discipline our children in a healthy way.

Another interesting thing I want to share, not just in prison but from my friends. I have listened to some, (not all) men and women from my generation that did not have a positive experience with a father. Fathers appear to manage the role of a grandfather with much more ease. Maybe the media has helped, maybe because we are educated more about positive parenting. Subconsciously or consciously, they are aware that they were just not there for their own sons and daughters. Maybe our own parents recognised their omission and try to make up for this by being good grandparents. Our parents, now Grandparents have perhaps moved on from the Victorian concept that: 'children should be seen and not heard'. They have evolved into hands-on grandmas and grandpas, realising that maybe they didn't father their own children as well as they could, and so try to make amends with their children's children.

Today, so many children are raised in care, away from dysfunctional parents. On a Sunday in church, I sit and watch with admiration Debbie and Les, a couple who foster children. They are amazing and they love the children as their own. The discipline is given with love and the children experience stability and a sense of belonging. This family embraces others' children to make a difference, they are selfless and quite incredible.

There is a large percentage of men and women in prison who have been in care. I believe the care system has taken tumultuous steps to safeguard children. But even so, there seems to be a spiralling problem with families, incapable of providing a safe, loving, and nurturing home. Contrary to public belief, the men I met in prison are not "monsters." Most of them were broken and sad, and they were mostly sorry for the mistakes they had made. If the men I met, and many before, had been raised in different families with loving and positive parents, then I believe maybe, the world would be a different place, and we would have been out of a job.

Wagtail

Chapter 19
Somebody's Baby
"The child is the beauty of God, present in the world, that greatest gift to a family."
Mother Teresa

He was a difficult man. He was unkempt and he smelled bad. He wore the same prison-issue tracksuit that always had remnants of the last few meals spilt down his front. He came to church in his battered wheelchair smelling strongly of wee and disrupted the services with his requests to read the passage for the day. I really had to grit my teeth as he struggled to stand up and lean on the pulpit to read the chosen Bible passage. He had bulging eyes, and a mouth full of rotten teeth. He was loud and disruptive, and he really wound us all up.

I found it difficult to tolerate him. I loved him (with Agape love), but it was difficult to like him. As he was struggling to stand, spitting all over the Bible and trying to read the words before him, all I could think of to help me through this painful hour was 'He is somebody's baby. He really wanted to do this, and who was I to stop him? Once he sat down, I discretely wiped down my Bible and the lectern with a clinical wipe and carried on.

Wagtail

There would probably have been some short-lived element of joy as he entered the world. He would talk about his "mama" occasionally but not in great depth. He had a hard life and was mocked because of his disability and his bulging eyes. In prison, he was the object of others' jokes. Sometimes, he was completely inappropriate. He once asked me if he could stroke my knee-length boots! In his defence, they weren't on my legs. The boots were at the back of the chapel; they had been left there after I had dressed up as a crazy farmer, taken off my boots and donned wellies for the Christmas recital of the 12 days of Christmas. He had no filter, and he didn't care. I often wore knee-length boots before this incident; I quickly switched to prison issues. I didn't tell anyone; he was unaware that this weird request could have landed him a spell in Segregation. I gently reminded him that this wasn't right, and he just screwed up his face and wheeled away, disappointed at my rejection. Once a sweet baby, he was now a forlorn, weak man with very little to give him hope.

Another man, also somebody's baby, was very small. His head was always full of scratches and wounds that he picked at. He had mental health problems, and he was a bit of a pain. He had a distinctive, annoying voice that grated on everybody's nerves. He constantly bothered Officers and roamed around the wing making up stories about how he was being treated. He sent letters to Healthcare, the Governor and the Chaplaincy pleading his case. He knew how to work the system, and so when he wasn't getting his own way, he threatened to self-harm. He made superficial scratches on his arms, nothing life-threatening. There was no option but to put him on an assessment book. At least this way, he got to talk to staff every day about his ongoing concerns. He talked about his release and how he wanted to go to a mental health facility. He told us that he had been diagnosed with multiple mental health disorders. He was never deemed ill enough. So, he tried his utmost to invent mental illnesses, but they were never quite persuasive enough. He told us that he was hearing voices, that he was hearing threats being made against him. Try as he may, he was just the laughing stock of the staff. Everyone sighed at his attempts to gain attention.

Eventually, he was released back into the community. Weeks later he was back again, only this time with a longer sentence. We were the only people he had. A few years in prison would help his plea to try to get into the facility that he longed to live in. He was somebody's baby. I found it hard to like him but had to (Agape), love him; it was my job! All of us were once somebody's baby. Life is impossible without the gift of life from a mother and father.

There are so many unlovable characters in life. There are people who we find so hard to tolerate, let alone love. Of course, it would be impossible to like everyone we meet; there is, however, a difference between love and liking. There are also varying degrees and elements of love. The love we feel for a partner or husband is different from the love we feel for a child. Love is so powerful and, if we can overcome our prejudice and learn to love, we can have a huge impact. The kind of love I had for the prisoners was Agape love.

Agape love is described as a love other than romantic. It is love that requires a decision, it is an action. It requires giving of oneself with no expectation of anything in return. I loved the boot man with Agape love, he drove me potty, but I loved him for who he was, smelly with bulging eyes and spitting when he talked. I tried to imagine, tried to walk in the shoes of this very broken man. I loved the man with sores on his head with Agape love. He was small, unattractive and drove me crazy with his incessant talking, but he was the loneliest soul.

I was always drawn to those whom everyone had given up on, those for whom there seemed no answer. In the NHS, we used to call these patients "heart sinkers." I'm not sure if it was our hearts that sank with despair every time they walked through the door or that their hearts were unhealable. Prison is bulging at the walls with heart-sink people. So many of the prisoners had no hope, yet still, you can never deny that these men were all somebody's baby. Many of them still had contact with their biological parents but many didn't. Many of the prisoners were also fathers.

Prison comes with its own language - a whole new vocabulary to learn. You quickly become adept at understanding it, and it's often wiser to embrace it rather than dismiss it. One phrase I initially struggled with was the term prisoners used to describe the mothers of their children: "baby mamas." It was an entirely new concept to me. The men might or might not still be in a relationship with the mother of their child or children, yet she was always referred to as their "baby mama." With pride, the men would often show me photographs of their children - a whole gallery of beautiful faces stuck to the cell walls. I always made a point of looking with genuine enthusiasm. Then there would be a pin-up photo, and I'd ask, "Is this your girlfriend?" The response was always the same: "No, it's my baby mama!"

At visiting time, the men's mothers and baby mamas would line up and wait in anticipation to be checked in and patted down. Their loyalty to the men surprised me, no matter the brutality of the crime or the disruption they had caused. They were there week after week. I used to watch in amazement as the mothers and girls queued, babies in arms. The wives and partners, current or ex, are often beautifully made up with long lashes and skin-tight outfits.

One of the ways drugs were brought into prison was in nappies. They were also stashed in the legs of ripped jeans, which eventually became a no-enter rule. Partners and families are searched and sometimes caught trying to smuggle in a bit of weed, tobacco, or another illicit item. The astute officers would watch like hawks as the men embraced loved ones, watching for a quick exchange or a longer-than-usual hug.

Barely clad girlfriends and partners would be a tease for the men who had no chance of intimate contact. Loyal wives would sit with their husbands as the children would play with the family officers. There was a small shop where chocolate and sweets were bought as a small gesture for estranged children. It was a pleasure to watch the dads play with their kids, but it was tinged with sadness at the thoughts that would remain with the men and their families after this brief visit. The family team did what they could with limited time and resources to encourage bonding, and to reinforce the importance of Dads in the lives of their children. At the end of the visit, Mums, parents, and children would file out as the men turned back once more to catch a glimpse of the lives they had been removed from. It was a sad reality of the price of crime.

Sometimes, babies' mums would ring up and try to glean information about their babies' fathers. They may be in an estranged relationship. Often there would be a restraining order because of violence or threat. The girls would ask us to pass on messages and we had to refuse. There were women who had been sexually assaulted by the men or beaten, yet they tried to reach out through us to make contact. When men were released, sometimes partners or ex-partners would entice them with the promise of sex and, once they were entrapped, they would phone the police and "grass" on them. The men would be re-arrested and hauled back to prison to await another trial. If they had breached their conditions, they were back to square one. The pull for some men to go back to their partners or ex-partners was just too much; sometimes they would try to see their children or to beg for reconciliation; but these unhealthy tugs would mean another stretch.

Relationships fall apart for so many reasons. I heard time after time about men who were pulled back again and again into unhealthy relationships. Of course, this works both ways. The women were also pulled back into chaotic situations to the detriment of both parties. We can all be attracted to the wrong ones because of our own wounded hearts. What starts as an amazing electric relationship can soon become disastrous. Our own attachment styles and needs can draw us to people who are very much like us, or completely opposite.

The majority of the men did not have solid foundations. They could barely look after themselves let alone a girlfriend and maybe a baby. Their own wounds and poor coping skills in the face of a crisis had disastrous consequences. These mums were often left with a child, having to manage alone while the baby's father just carried on shunning responsibilities because they just couldn't cope. If there was hope for a relationship, this was tested to the utmost when the men were in prison again and again. It seems hopeless but some did manage to keep relationships alive. Unhealthy relationships are commonplace. The prison did offer courses in parenting, domestic violence and abuse which may have offered some hope for the future.

Prisoners' mothers pulled on my heartstrings. The phone in the chapel would ring off the hook with concerned Mums asking about their babies. These grown men were still somebody's baby. In a state of distress, some of the men would fill Mum's head with worry. The phone calls would be about their boy being bullied, and some were concerned for their mental health. Some calls could be quite abusive with Mums and Dads screaming down the phone. They had been passed from pillar to post and the Chaplaincy was the last desperate resort to get someone to listen. They would say, "I know he has done something terrible, but he's, my boy." How could we dismiss the desperation?

Once a Mum rang because she was concerned about her son, who was being held in Segregation at the time. We knew that he had caused trouble on the wing; we knew the details, but, of course, we couldn't tell Mum. She shouted and swore and told me that the prison was a joke. No one knew what they were doing, it was in the papers what a terrible place the prison was. If she didn't get some help, she was going to write to the Manchester evening News. This was quite a common threat, but we still listened. The young man concerned was unwell, he had serious mental ill health. His Mum ranted. Eventually, I asked if she would tell me a little bit about his life. As a young boy, this young man had witnessed his Mum's boyfriend kill his father. It was a savage attack. Although Mum had tried to raise him the best way she could, this devastating and horrific attack had scarred him deeply. I promised that I would go and visit him. I saw him daily and we got along well. He didn't talk about the incident, and I didn't push it. We just chatted and I listened and, with his permission, referred him to the mental health team.

I phoned Mum back after I had seen him. It was a small thing but all I could do to help, she thanked me and said all she wanted was for someone to listen. It's my boy! It cost me nothing.

Chapter 20
Prisoner Number E:31617414

A very compassionate member of the probation team contacted me and asked if I had time to go and visit a young man. She had visited him, and staff had raised concerns about his tendency to isolate. He rarely came out of his cell; he didn't mix with anyone else, and he lay in the dark all day and night. He refused to engage in any kind of therapy and just wanted to be left alone. I agreed to go and see him. I rang the wing to ask if he was in his cell. "Of course, where else would he be? He never comes out."

I had some idea about his history but not a great deal. I tended not to look at convictions; I preferred to deal with the person, not the crime they had committed. He was on the landing in a cell right at the end. I walked up the flight of stairs. At the top of the stairs, there was a group of my travelling friends. "Alright Miss, who have you come to see?" "None of your business," I replied and glanced over with a smile!

I knocked on the cell door, the small window was covered so I couldn't see inside. As we are all now aware, it isn't always the best idea to peer through a window before knocking. His door was slightly ajar. The lights were off. There was a bit of commotion amongst my friends on the landing. I turned; they were watching me. "Buzz off!" I shouted over the landing, with a Dublin twang. He got up off his bed, made his way to the door and spoke. "Hello, where are you from?" Despite the dog collar some people have never set eyes on clergy folk. Dog collars would mean nothing. He glanced down bleary-eyed at my collar and then said, "Oh, yeh, you're from the church."

My first impression was of a young black man, quite stocky, with a head of thick curly hair. He was wearing a black and grey prison issue tracksuit. He was a little unkempt. He looked down and he took a great big sigh. He rubbed his eyes; his cell was in total darkness, and I cracked a very unsuitable joke about him not coming out in the daylight. He shrugged his shoulders. He just was not motivated, he didn't care what I said, it just passed by him. I explained that I had been asked by the probation team to see him. I asked if he wanted to come out of his cell and onto the landing for a chat. There was some laughter and some jeering again from the little gathering. "They are f**king winding me up, day and night," he said.

The group of prisoners were just throwing looks and sneering, nothing derogatory but certainly enough to add fuel to his depression. "It's alright, had it all my life, usually from the cops." He was so fed up, and he couldn't, as he said, "be arsed with them. Just keeping my head down." He walked head down, body language silently shouting, "I just haven't got the energy." We sat next to the window on the ground floor. Most people were at work or at the gym. There were wing cleaners just pottering around with rag-head brushes. Apart from the group of Irish lads, it was quiet. I was quite shocked that he had agreed to sit down and chat with me, a middle-aged, white vicar. How could I understand where he was at or where he was coming from?

I instantly took a liking to him. He was so pleasant, we chatted for a while about trivia. Where was he from, what did he like to do, did he have family, friends, hobbies. I did all the asking. After a while, we had a little rapport. I only stayed with him for half an hour or so. I walked back to the landing with him. He had told me that he enjoyed writing, I told him I would get him some paper and pencils. I spoke to the Irish corner and told them to give him a break. "God sees everything, remember that." My parting words. It worked; they didn't bother him after that.

Wagtail

We met again the week after. I just checked in briefly; I did not want to crowd him. I told him I would be back. I left him with one task: to try to keep himself occupied during the day and sleep at night. When we met again, he seemed a little brighter. He looked fresher and he had some light coming into his room from the broken window. He had managed to get some books from the library. He had been trying to get a prison job but was rejected by a senior manager. He wanted to work off the wing, I can't remember what the job was, but as was his life experience, he was rejected. We sat down again. After he told me about the disappointment about his job, I said I would appeal for him to try and get some work.

Over several weeks our meetings were interesting. He started to share his life story. He told me that he had a difficult childhood. His family, well his grandmother, used to bag up and distribute drugs from the kitchen table. He was warned sternly that these were not for him to touch and the consequences of doing so. He was bright and enjoyed school. Eventually, he got a place at university. He started to study and was doing well. However, after a few misdemeanours, he explained that he started being hounded by the police. I have no idea if this was true, but I was aware that his crimes were only minor, but he was on their radar, and they just accumulated. He ended up in police custody. Every time he was out, the police allegedly followed him, or at least that was how it felt.

Eventually, he managed to get a fantastic job. He was gifted and had a great future. But under the watchful eye of the police, he was arrested again; this time, he was given a short sentence. No matter how hard he tried to move on, his past came back to haunt him. He had broken all family ties and was alone in the world. He had some mental health illness and a difficult history. He had tried to break free, but the world wouldn't let him forget.

He was very creative, good at writing and had some experience with the media. I told him I wanted to write a book, and he immediately offered to help me. He took the time to write a plan for me on bits of scraps of paper and some step-by-step notes on constructing a book. He gave me some ideas and websites that would help me. Once a week, we would sit on the broken plastic chairs by the huge window at the end of the wing. He began to trust me a little. I listened to his dreams and aspirations, and he listened to mine.

Eventually, he got a job as a wing cleaner, and things were looking brighter. But one of the officers appeared to dislike him. He had ignored a female officer's instruction to move out of the way. He was sacked immediately. In the following weeks, the incident was investigated, and no evidence was found. He had done nothing wrong; again, this was the consequence of an angry officer's lack of empathy and patience.

I continued to visit every week and encouraged him to write a poem for Prison Times (yes there is such a paper). He wrote the poem, and it was published. He got lots of praise from the Governor, staff and the Chaplaincy team. We boosted his confidence and I saw him smile for the first time.

The *Apple* poem reflects on life when we are young and the things we are taught - like being told, "an apple is red" (but is it really?). When someone says "apple," most of us imagine a shiny red one, yet apples come in so many shades. Often, it's the bright, shiny, and appealing apple that seems the most enticing but, as in *Snow White*, can prove to be the most poisonous. The poem's message was about nature and nurture - the way childhood lessons and experiences shape our lives. It's like watching your grandmother chop up weed while being sternly told never to touch it. Inevitably, you do.

He left the prison. I didn't see him again. I wanted to ask him If I could include his poem in this book, but I haven't been able to track him down. I don't think he would want me to track him down, he just wanted to get on, to be left alone with his creative mind. He was really worried he wouldn't be able to get a job, I hope he has.

He was, for a while, my friend.

Wagtail

Chapter 21
Prison number P:1412131513

He had been in prison for a long time. In fact, he had spent most of his life in prison. He was a tall man, dark rimmed glasses, the arm of the glasses held together with a bit of tape. He was always bobbing in for a new pair of glasses. Second-hand glasses were often donated, and he would take a pair if he could see through the lenses or not. He knew the system and worked the system, but he was never a real problem for anybody; he was just always there!

Prison became his home; he was comfortable inside. You could hear his laughter and deep, gruff voice from yards away; he was so very funny. His presence was always welcome. He brightened up a room with his joviality. He was a brave man in so many ways. He had suffered terribly as a child. He claimed to have been abused by a man in his community. I don't know if this was true. He didn't often talk about his past; he could live in the day, and he did. He was always up to mischief. There was always talk of him getting up to no good, but there was little evidence to prove this. He had suffered a stroke whilst in prison and had spent some time in hospital. Physically, he was reasonably okay, but his speech was slightly slurred and, having suffered a brain injury, he wasn't so quick off the mark.

He engaged in Chaplaincy activities and groups, and he really enjoyed spending time with us. He was one of my Oops moments. As I mentioned, he was delighted one day when I gave him some lovely, collared shirts. He paraded up and down in them until he was apprehended. We laughed secretly about my big mistake. So, he was very much part of our day; we saw him, heard him and enjoyed his company.

Eventually, he was released. We waited, as ever, in anticipation of his return and, after a few days, he was back. We were all so disappointed and upset to find out that he had assaulted someone. It was so hard to imagine many of the prisoners we knew committing such heinous crimes. Inside they were drug and alcohol-free, pleasant, and personable. However, as soon as they regain their freedom, they return to familiar territory. Same people, same habits, same routine; robbing to get drugs, committing crime to survive. He had a drug addiction and was prescribed methadone. However, once he was released from prison, methadone could only touch the edge of a lifetime of addiction.

Methadone is sold on the street and so the cycle starts again. And so, his cycle started over. Now, we weren't soft with him, we talked to him, and he gave us his account. He was remorseful. This does not take away the terrible pain he inflicted. His victim will never know him; never meet him and is left with the trauma and anxiety of the attack, which is an unforgivable situation. He was ashamed and he didn't think we would welcome the prodigal; but we did. This time he was in prison for a much longer stretch.

One day, he arrived at the chapel in a terrible state. He was distressed and in tears. I never knew if what he told was true; however, as always, we listened. He said that, during movement, he had seen the man who had raped him as a child. He was shaking and frightened as he recalled how, as a young man, he had been abused by this older man who lived nearby. We reported the situation but he declined any further investigation. However, he continued to cheer us all up with his jokes and his optimistic outlook. He stayed with us for a while, then he was moved to another prison. I haven't seen or heard about him since.

He was, for a while, my friend.

Wagtail

Chapter 22
Prison number P18381421

This man survived a near-death health experience while in prison. After this experience and a long stay in the hospital, he returned to the wing. I had the chance to get to know him. He reached out to us after his stay in the hospital. He wrote me a very long letter. The letter was shocking and difficult to read. The paper he wrote on smelled like prison, with the aroma of disinfectant and cooked cabbage.

I don't know if he had ever thought about the impact of his crime before this experience. I suspect he did; getting to know him offered an explanation. Not an explanation to make an excuse, but a story that led to why he ended up seeking sexual gratification from innocent victims. I am not in any way writing this to cover for him or to appease his behaviour. I write to try to help us all understand that there is often a reason for some behaviour. Not all sex offenders have a reason; some just live in very dark and secretive places. Some have had privileged lives, and I can't write about this because I personally never met any, I never met anyone without a sad story.

Let me share his thoughts. There is no vindication; he still had a choice. Let me return to the nurture and nature debate, to the power to make the right decisions, to the survival instinct. Let me demonstrate the possibility that how we treat others can have a greater impact on the community.

As a child, this man-boy was tormented for one simple reason. He had a rather large nose and wasn't particularly good-looking. He became the object of mockery and torment. He was isolated and had no friends. Eventually, he became withdrawn, living a very lonely life, and, with no chance of a relationship, he started the journey down a very dark path.

I didn't enquire about his crime; all I know is that it was sex related. The community suspected him and watched him; they persecuted him and, eventually, the prophecy became a reality for him and his family. He was arrested and sentenced, and his family were left to deal with the shame. They had disowned him but, as his Mum said, "I know he has done something very shameful, but he is my son." I can't tell you how many times I heard this from mothers, no matter how heinous the crime. In custody and in his cell one evening, he had a near death experience and then spent months in hospital.

After he returned to prison, he immediately wanted to engage with the Chaplaincy team. He recounted what he could remember about his near death experience, and he couldn't quite reconcile with the fact that he had survived, he didn't think he deserved a second chance. Back in prison, he started to talk about his offence; he attended church and hoped to change his behaviour. When help was available, he wanted to take it. He was a very unassuming and shy man, very quiet, very inoffensive. He wrote me a very long letter by way of saying "sorry." I won't share this letter here, but I will share something from another letter he wrote about his near-death experience.

He talked about going into a 'fake vision world' when he was critically ill. A lot of the letters didn't make sense to me. I have taken out some of the details. "In the fake vision world, I was to be punished; my right hand had sausages and meat tied to it…Two prison officers were brought in, one had two dogs, and they were to be set free to rip my hand off. One prison officer became a Nemesis; he was the one with the dogs…" This letter was bizarre, to say the least; the descriptions were more like dreams, or rather night horrors. I think, somehow, they reflected his fears, possibly a subconscious recognition of the crime for which he faced a long sentence.

I tried to imagine his mother's shame and pain. I tried to imagine if I was in his Mum's position. It doesn't bear thinking about, but he was her son; she gave birth to him and took care of him, and it was so hard for her to abandon him. I empathised, and it made me sad.

I didn't spend a great deal of time with him, but I liked the man, the person beyond the offence. He will be in prison for a while. I don't know what became of him.

He was, for a while, my friend.

Chapter 23
Prison number P147234

He was as pale as could be. There was always jail pale, but he was so pale he was almost green. I first met him at an assessment and review meeting. This man was withdrawn, isolated, and unwell. Due to the nature of his self-inflicted condition, he resided in healthcare. He was weary, head down, lethargic, yet obstinate.

He was monitored on a self-harm book and so a chaplain was required at his reviews. I was asked to attend. During the meeting the normal questions were asked by senior officers. We sat in the association area in healthcare. We sat on the usual plastic chairs around a large table. Several of us stared at him as we waited for responses to the questions. How was he feeling? Had he had any more thoughts of self-harm? I had only been in post a few months when I first met him. He was quite unlovable. He didn't respond, didn't lift his head. He looked quite intimidating and, when he did lift his head, his eyes were blank and dark.

He was in prison because he had been abusive to his partner. He had caused significant injury. He hadn't seen his children for years and he was slowly slipping away into the abyss. He didn't care about himself, let alone anybody else. He self-harmed by plucking the veins out of the crook in his elbows. The large pulsing veins would be plucked out using the plastic tube of a ballpoint pen or anything else he could get his hands on. He pulled out his veins, hacked at them and bled out. He had done this so many times that he was severely anaemic. Despite his visits to the hospital post-event, the anaemia did not resolve. He was exhausted. His eyes had dark rims, and he had no energy. He wasn't a priority for repeat hospital appointments until, of course, his blood tests were getting dangerously abnormal.

We sat around the table. Still no response. Eventually, I intervened. "Can I ask a question? What do you like to do, what are your interests?" With a shrug of the shoulders, he lifted his head and gave me a dark stare. "I would like to come back and talk to you some more; I would like to see if we can help you in some way. I can see you are an intelligent man." The team sat in silence, he eventually lifted his head and responded. "Yes, okay." And yes, okay was the beginning of an arduous "friendship." He was an outcast, no one cared about him, not really; he was a drain on resources, on time, and on patience. He was quite unlovable.

After this initial meeting, he was suddenly rushed back into the hospital to receive an urgent blood transfusion. His iron levels were so low he was at risk of dying. When he returned, he looked so much better. He had a pink tinge in his cheeks. And so, I started to work with him. I visited him every week. With permission, I supplied paper and pencils. The pencils were given to him and then taken back just in case they were used as a surgical instrument.

He started to journal to write down his feelings. We talked at length about his estranged family and how sorry he was for his actions. We started to think about a possible future, and we talked about his hopes and aspirations. He really hoped he would see his children again one day. I couldn't reassure him about this, I doubted he would ever be allowed near them.

I think he looked forward to our chats. Eventually, the self-harming stopped, and the physical wounds healed. He agreed to request some help. I suggested talking to our prison counsellor, but he had to agree. There were counsellors in the prison, but the waiting list was, as you can imagine, very long.

Wagtail

I returned to Healthcare one day to find that he had been transferred out. I never got to say goodbye. I don't know where or how he is. I was disappointed as I always was when the men just disappeared from our radar.

He was, for a while, my friend.

Chapter 24
The Hardest Word
"Unforgiveness is like drinking poison yourself and waiting for the other person to die."
Anonymous.

I really struggled as a teenager, but what teenager doesn't? In fact, I struggled most of my teens and early twenties with a plethora of painful issues. On the outside, I presented a creative, dramatic and funny girl. I was a people pleaser, and I longed to be liked. I was, as my Mum often reminded me, an attention seeker! Of the three sisters, I guess I was the one who caused the most angst for Mary and George.

The only thing "our Jayne" did wrong was getting caught with a packet of cigarettes. Even then, the only punishment she received was passive. Mum placed the offending cigarette packet on the mantelpiece. As we sat watching The Two Ronnies the cigarettes just stared at us. They said nothing, the silence and the tobacco spoke volumes.

Elizabeth, the youngest, was a perfect child until, of course, she discovered alcohol and had "parent away" parties at home with her school friends. I was quite rude and always needed to have the last word. I thought my parents knew nothing until I reached adulthood and realised, they were, in fact, quite knowledgeable.

Looking back, I was a child who craved attention. Yes, Mum was right; I was an attention seeker. Quite simply, I needed more and didn't know how to ask for it. Forming relationships wasn't easy for me. That said, I've always been blessed with two incredibly special friends: Helen and my mischievous partner-in-crime, Jane.

Some of my happiest childhood memories are with them—aside, of course, from shoplifting with Jane. Helen and I loved to put on shows in the asbestos garage for our neighbours. We hung makeshift curtains from Dad's dust sheets, secured with clothes pegs, and performed war songs, dancing for the whole avenue. Goodness knows how we learned the lyrics to *It's a Long Way to Tipperary*. When we weren't performing, we went door-to-door selling "perfume" made from rose petals or other homemade goods. We spent hours playing outside, returning only when it was time for dinner.

Those friendships went a long way in filling the gaps in my heart.

School was always a challenge—not because of the teachers; they were wonderful. In fact, I owe so much to the staff at West End Secondary School. They encouraged me to take leading roles in productions, speak at assemblies, and represent the school in cooking competitions. But being in the limelight came at a cost. To some classmates, I was the teacher's pet, which bred resentment.

Jane and I had known each other since primary school. She moved to Australia but returned in the second year of secondary school. Naturally, we stuck together. We were both a little geeky, from decent families, though not wealthy. We wore practical, untrendy shoes from Tommy Balls - a budget shoe outlet - which set us apart from many of the other kids. I was bullied for being different. I was skinny, flat-chested, and socially awkward, which made me a target. Jane, though well-behaved, also stood out with her Australian accent.

One unforgettable aspect of school was the playground fights. Lunchtimes often erupted with someone shouting, "Scrap! Scrap! Scrap!" A whirlwind of Tommy Ball shoes would signal the start of a vicious fight. Teachers in polyester flares and hacking jackets would sprint to break up the chaos, separating ringleaders and spectators. Once, two boys fighting in the yard were marched to the gym and ordered to continue in front of the entire school. The teachers meant to humiliate them, but can you imagine that happening today?

I didn't pass the entrance exam for a good high school, so I ended up at a secondary school with a poor reputation. Every morning, as Dad dropped me off in his yellow estate car, I prayed I wouldn't "get my head kicked in." Schools in the 70s were tough, at least in my experience. Resilience was a mask I wore to hide how deeply I was hurting.

I desperately wanted to be part of the "in crowd." Watching *Grease,* I related to Sandy - the geeky good girl longing for acceptance. She transforms to fit in with the Pink Ladies and wins over Danny, the school's bad boy. But I didn't have Pink Ladies to help me shape up. I had Helen and Jane, and while we occasionally smoked cigarettes in telephone boxes or met boys from the local estate, we were relatively well-behaved.

I was terrified of the other girls at school. They were physically mature, streetwise, and intimidating. Physical Education (PE) was a nightmare. The naughty girls excelled at sports, while I nursed bruised shins from hockey sticks hitting my thin, frozen legs. The showers after PE were even worse. All the other girls had bras and curves; I had a vest. Their mocking made me dread every weekday morning.

One Friday, after the school's Christmas Fair, our parents' gave Jane and I permission to take the bus home like other kids. The journey was supposed to be an adventure, a chance to walk in the dark past the park we had played when we were younger, and enjoy the independence. But as we crossed the park, a group of older kids from school surrounded us.

They mocked us and encouraged one girl to hit me. She lived in a children's home - someone Mum had warned me about, though I hadn't understood why at the time. She swung at me, and I slipped on the icy ground. What followed was a brutal attack. Kicks rained down on me, and finally, her monkey boot struck my face. Jane screamed as one older boy urged the group to stop. They fled, laughing and shouting. Bruised and battered, I spent time in the hospital with minor injuries and a fractured orbital bone. But while the physical wounds healed, the emotional scars lingered.

Wagtail

In their wisdom, my parents sent me back to the same school to face the bullies. Two of the pupils were expelled, namely the girl in care and one other boy. The ring leaders had been removed but that wasn't enough to arm me with the confidence I needed to go back and face the perpetrators. This was a sad event; it hurt me and battered my esteem and self-confidence.

There were no Pink Ladies to pick me up, no apologies, no advice, no trauma counselling, nothing. This event didn't shape me or equip me with anything more than fear. My Mum just pinched my cheeks to make them ruddy, hid the crying and told me to go back and face them. Nobody said sorry, and no one offered to be my friend. In fact, the other kids avoided me and were warned that if they went anywhere near me, they would be expelled, too.

There was no apology, request for forgiveness, or offer of reparation. I doubt any of the teachers, let alone the kids would know what reparation was then. I was a victim, they were the guilty, the event was swept under the carpet, and we were all expected to move on. Of course, I moved on eventually, but the fact that I remember every sight and smell of the event that happened in 1978 tells a tale of its own!

I hadn't expected to write about this incident, but it came to mind when I was thinking about this chapter. To forgive is a precious gift to ourselves. It was something I quickly came to realise when I became a Christian. I learned about the power of forgiveness, not for the benefit of the one who has harmed us but for the victim. Of course, you don't have to have faith to forgive but, for me, it was the strength and the words of Jesus on the cross, "Father, forgive them, for they know not what they do," that helped me choose the same attitude.

I have forgiven those young people who hurt me physically and mentally. I often think about them. I know one young man, who was a handsome, naughty boy, who died early in life from alcohol misuse. Apart from him, I don't know what became of the rest. I forgive them and I forgive anyone who has ever hurt me for whatever reason.

As many of us do, I have experienced unhealthy, painful relationships with human beings and had bitter words spoken about me by so-called "friends" and colleagues in the past. If I don't forgive, how can I expect my own behaviour and hurtful actions to be forgiven?

As the Elton John *"Sorry seems to be the hardest word"* goes, it truly is for so many of us. True repentance and a change of heart is such a painful process for those of us who have harmed or have been harmed. As *Joyce Meyer,* a famous American preacher says: *"Unless you change your heart, life will short-change you."*

Saying sorry is difficult, often tangled in a web of pride and feelings of entitlement. Uttering the words, "I am sorry" takes courage, but they pale in comparison to the challenge of saying, "I forgive you." This takes us into an entirely different arena - one that demands vulnerability, empathy, and strength. "I'm sorry. Will you forgive me?" These simple words hold immense power, yet they require a depth of humility and understanding that many struggle to embrace. Allow me to explain further.

Desmond Tutu said, *"Forgiveness is not weak. It takes courage to face and overcome powerful emotions."*

In a contrasting quote, C.S. Lewis wrote, *"Everyone says forgiveness is a lovely idea until they have something to forgive."*

How many of us truly forgive? Forgiveness is not easy, and I am no exception. Like many, I sometimes find myself bringing up the past, gently reminding someone, "But you did this to me; you said that to me." It's a deeply challenging concept, one that requires us to let go of hurt and resentment - a task that often feels insurmountable.

I cried when I wrote the story about the young Anne Caroline being beaten. I cried at the pain it had caused me, but I cried more when I thought about generation upon generation of men and women who don't have the tools to forgive; those who continue to live with the bitterness and resentment of harm caused. Many of the men in prison had suffered horrific trauma and loveless lives. They had also caused irreparable pain and damage. Nobody died in my drama; I wasn't left with life-changing injuries. I forgave them, I released them with all the others. If I had chosen not to, they would forever tinge my life with resentment and sadness. I have learned to love and respect myself too much for the power of another to rob me of my peace.

I really respected and had a high regard for Archbishop Desmond Tutu. The South African Archbishop was, among other great things, an activist for injustice, peace, and reconciliation. He was a leader and he led from experience. In 1986, he was elected Archbishop of Cape Town and was known as South Africa's moral conscience. After Nelson Mandela was elected in 1994, he led the Truth and Reconciliation Foundation to heal South Africa's fractured post-Apartheid state. He said, *"Without forgiveness, there can be no future for a relationship between individuals or within and between nations."*

After his work in Africa, he continued to share his experience and skill with post-conflict communities. I watched one of his conflict resolutions years ago. The meeting, facilitated by the Archbishop was televised by the BBC. It was a cross-table meeting held between members of the Irish Republican Army, and family members and victims who had suffered in the name of their cause. It remains with me as a powerful yet agonising discussion. It was painful, fuelled with anger and firm ideologies. The outcome didn't solve the issues of the untold pain, but it offered an alternative approach to healing.

South Africa may seem a world away from Manchester, but the lasting pain of conflict is universal and hard to comprehend. We don't need to look as far as South Africa or Northern Ireland to witness its devastation. Conflict can appear on our doorsteps, in our cities, in our homes, and even within our hearts. Its impact is catastrophic. Yet, we have a choice.

Being a victim of conflict doesn't always mean experiencing a tangible crime - it can stem from internal struggles. If we harbour resentment toward our families, endure pain inflicted by partners or friends, or carry bitterness in our hearts, we create an internal conflict. The poison we consume in our anger and hatred will never harm them; it will only destroy us. So, what can we do? The answer lies not in the "us," but in the "I." This journey toward healing and resolution is deeply personal - a one-man, one-woman path that each of us must walk alone.

There is an option, not an easy one, but one that takes a great deal of bravery, as *Archbishop Desmond Tutu* explains in *"The Book of Forgiving the Concept of Forgiveness."*

"What we must remember is that a correct conception of forgiveness does not require that we forgo punishment altogether or that we should, in forgiving, attempt to annul the existence of the wrong done.

Forgiveness does not remove the fact or even the wrongdoing but instead relies upon the recognition of wrong having been committed for the process of forgiveness to be made possible."

In the book, *"Exploring Forgiveness"*, the authors, *Enright & North* recount the story of a woman who was assaulted and robbed on her way home from work by a man. This man has no right to forgiveness. He is wicked, evil and violent. Yes, he is, his actions were all these things. He is in prison, but three years later, so Is she. She has not forgiven him; she looks over her shoulder all the time and she suffers with the memory. It has indeed ruined her life. She carries the memory every day and she has become a victim in all aspects of her life. The crime has bled into her work, her family, and her relationships.

Why should the perpetrator be forgiven?

When we have been hurt or harmed, we can live with the pain for years and years. We can be robbed of our peace, and we can go to the grave harbouring resentment and bitterness. We may hold onto secrets, trying to brush painful events under the carpet. But, like mould, anything kept in a warm, dark place will eventually fester. Inevitably, we become the ones afflicted, the disease infiltrating our hearts and minds. Unforgiveness is no different - it acts like a cancer, slowly robbing us of joy and peace.

Reconciliation and forgiveness may not often cross our minds; they are topics we rarely discuss. Yet, I believe they are among the most powerful tools for achieving freedom and release, offering us the chance to break free from the burdens we carry.

In *"The Book of Forgiving,"* Desmond Tutu says, *"Forgiveness is taking seriously the awfulness of what has happened when you are treated unfairly. It is opening the door for the other person to have a chance to begin again. Without forgiveness, resentment builds in us, a resentment that turns into hostility and anger. Hatred eats away at our well-being."*

The concept of forgiveness is an act, a decision and one that may require a great deal of contemplation. With understanding, if we consider this option, then we may have the tools to make that decision. How many of us give real thought to this notion? How many of us experience, or are guilty of, daily acts of unkindness? How many times are we the hosts for hurting others?

Are we all so innocent? Do we long to be forgiven too?

Many of the men I worked with in prison struggled to comprehend or even imagine the possibility of forgiveness - whether forgiving the harm done to them or being forgiven for the harm they had caused. They were raised in a culture steeped in revenge and retaliation, where forgiveness was rarely, if ever, part of the narrative. For so many of us, the idea of turning the other cheek is seen as a sign of weakness. Yet I believe it takes far greater strength to walk away from vengeance. Forgiveness is the hardest road to travel, and sadly, many of us choose not to take it. It's difficult to admit, but I think we have all hurt someone at some point in our lives. It might have been years ago or perhaps more recently. Let's hope that we, too, have been forgiven and are not lodged in the heart and mind of someone who finds it impossible to forget.

In the Bible, Jesus says we should forgive our enemies and treat people as we expect to be treated. Even if we are not people of faith, these words can help us to find our peace. They set a standard for society, one which, if built upon, would bring about harmony, understanding and a much faster position of reconciliation.

I once watched a documentary about World War Two pilots, one Japanese, one American. They had shot each other down and fortunately survived to tell the story. They met each other years later for reconciliation and to say: "I'm sorry;" two countries reconciling after disastrous conflict. Surely, if society embraced the concept of forgiveness before conflicts began, there would be no more war graves, young men and women would return home, and the world we live in would be profoundly different.

Is the act of forgiveness about the victim or the perpetrator? The answer, I think, can be both; it can take two sides. Sometimes the person who did harm may be out of sight, or dead. I believe that the saying "sticks and stones will hurt my bones, but words will never hurt me" is a lie, a misconception. Moreover, physical wounds heal but sometimes the heart remains broken forever.

Restorative Justice is one solution to work through the process of forgiveness and reparation. The concept has been around for years in different cultures. The principles of RJ are explained by *Zehr et al.* It is described as something that is not a new idea, but a historical and traditional one that can help understand the impact of wrongdoing. The Hebrew word Shalom describes the healing of wrongdoing, the Utopian dream of all of us living "in rightness and wholeness." This is described by the authors of, *The Big book of Restorative Justice*, an interconnection of society. When harm is done to one, it is done to all. Relationships are broken, and division in the community in turn demands a "putting right." Here there is an obligation which implies the need for healing. Compare this to one aspect of the traditional justice system which Zehr et al describe:

Criminal Justice	Restorative Justice
Crime is a violation of law and state	Crime is a violation of people and relationships

Outside prison, Restorative justice is used by the police force, in schools and in communities. It was used in prison to resolve disputes amongst prisoners, but it can also have a broader impact in the justice system.

Ray and Vi Donovan spearheaded restorative justice in prisons after their son was murdered. They used their pain to bring about peace of mind for victims and offenders. They wrote: *"Restorative Justice is a different way of tackling crime, based not on punishment but on healing the harm that has been caused."*

The process has been proven to reduce reoffending and can be used for serious, but more often for simpler 'lower level' crime. It takes courage from both sides and delicate facilitation.

Sycamore Tree is a restorative justice course offered to prisoners. The course is named after the tree that, in Israel, symbolises regeneration and transformation. Although based on a biblical story, it was offered to men of all faiths or none. The basis of the story is about a tax collector, small in stature and hated by everyone. Because he is small, he climbs up a sycamore tree, away from the jeering crowds to listen to the words of Jesus. He longed to change and be forgiven and risked all his earthly wealth to do so.

The principles of the faith-based course are the same as the secular approach, however in a slightly different style, but the men could sign up as part of progression and development, "a moving forward." Sometimes the probation team would refer men to the course. The participants were chosen with care. The course was facilitated by the Prison Fellowship. It was supported by volunteers, giving their time to champion and walk with the men through six weeks of what could be a painful and distressing reality. The course addresses the effects of crime in the community. The men each had a workbook to study and describe their thoughts, their actions, and their responsibilities.

At the end of the six weeks, senior staff were invited to listen to the men as they bravely stood and shared their pain, their reflections and sorrow about the harm they had caused.

Each man presented an act of reparation. They were not able to meet their victims, but in the safety of the chapel and with the people who encouraged them, they had a chance to say sorry. Some wrote poems, some made models and drew pictures, and some just stood and said, "I'm sorry." They just wanted to say it out loud and they wanted to be heard. We applauded their bravery and hoped this would be one step along the journey of forgiving themselves.

They had said sorry, the hardest word. We clapped and cheered, ate cake, and celebrated with them. It was powerful and emotional; it gave us all hope.

Chapter 25
Lizzie

"There are no bad boys. There is only bad environment, bad training, bad example, bad thinking."
Edward J. Flanagan

In 2018, I was invited to attend a meeting led by the Bishop for UK prisons. The meeting was held in a church in Greenwich. Chaplains from prisons across the UK attended, including a couple of us from the Northwest. Our time was productive, and it was helpful to know that the issues faced in the prison I worked in were not unique. During the meeting, the conversation addressed the difference in working in the male and female estates. My colleague from a female prison was quite animated and defensive when I was talking about my experience of supporting men in custody. She spoke strongly about men manipulating women and that most of the women she had met had been coerced, often abused, and frightened of their partners. There may be some truth about this, but we can't just put the blame on men. There are women who commit crimes with or without men in their lives. Women, just as men, are vulnerable, hurt and lost. They, too, may have been born into a prison. Life for some women has been a battle.

According to statistics, in 2022, there were 76,226 men and 3,216 women in custody. The number of males and females in prison has been increasing, the highest figure being 86,000 in 2012. There is a stark difference in the numbers of men and women in prison, which I think we would expect. I can't comment on the female estate. I haven't worked in a female prison, I wanted to assure readers that I had no bias between men and women, so I asked my friend who has been in a female prison if she was willing to share her experience.

The Church I attend is on the outskirts of Stockport. The Church, meaning the people, are welcoming, kind, empathetic and loving. They looked after me when I was struggling as a Vicar.

I refer to my church as the "hospital church." The people care for, love, and nurture the lost, the broken and the vulnerable. It is indeed a wonderful community of wonderful people. The church has a food bank, runs courses for those struggling with poverty, and has an amazing ministry to children, young people and the older generation. The leaders, Andy and Ruth, and all the volunteers are selfless and committed, they are indeed proper Christians with a real heart for service.

I have known Lizzie for a couple of years. We started chatting one Sunday. She was funny and open, and I instantly felt a close bond with her. As time went by, we talked, I listened, and I learned more about her and a little about her life. Lizzie has a story. She has given me permission to write/share it. Her story gives a female perspective of the justice system, prison and the consequences of her life that resulted in a stretch with HMP. My dear friend Lizzie worked so hard to share her thoughts, these are her words. With her permission I have changed them a little. She is brave, wonderful, and quite a character and this is her story.

Lizzie

"I was 17 years or thereabouts. I can't remember the exact year; my life was running at such a fast and chaotic pace. Since I was 13, I had been using heroin and committing crimes to fund my habit. The last few years had taken such a pace, no 17-year-old could have been prepared for a life fuelled with addiction. Looking back, I was never emotionally or mentally prepared for the world I had stepped into. I had always felt different, I couldn't and didn't connect the dots. There are so many of us in this world that have broken, traumatised childhoods and I was one of them. We try to find our

place and our way in life. We struggle and end up being dragged into dark places. These places do nothing to make us better, they break our hearts even more. When you are so lost, it seems attractive and there is a pull. If your self-esteem is so very low, we believe we are unredeemable. This myth and the judgement of others take us down a path with all the other lost souls.

"I remember the magistrates reeling off these sentences; 90 days for this, 90 days for that consecutively. I stood in the dock, vulnerable, weak and withdrawing from heroin. I looked at my solicitor for answers, and I searched his face for his expressions. He just put up his thumbs and winked. I thought it was a wink, everyone watching said it was a nervous twitch. Even if it was a nervous twitch, he was an amazing man. He loved to spend his time with us sinners. He fought for justice, but he didn't always get it right. The guidance and boundaries were blurred and bless his heart, he fought from his heart. He, too, ended up lost and in the dock.

"He looked at me and said, "Eight months, Liz." As if I should be buzzing as I was led out in handcuffs. I was loaded into the sweat box; the smell will never leave my mind or nostrils! I arrived at Low Newton Prison. I think

we arrived at about 6 pm. Some of the girls I had been friends with on the heroine journey were already in prison. When they herded us off the bus, I heard someone shout'. "Where's the van from Boss?" Then another female voice: "Is that you Liz?" I felt exposed, vulnerable, and extremely nervous. This was all so alien to me. My face was red, I was overwhelmed and felt like a broken child in an adult body. What the 'eff', am I going to do. I didn't reply to the voices coming from in the prison.

"Strip search" were the first words spoken to me. Two family members who have both been in prison had relayed the stories of the first few hours inside. Right, strip search. It wasn't my imagination, and the stories were true. This was really happening to me. The officers handed me a blue towelling dressing gown and told me to get undressed. I then had to drop and spin. This is to make sure I wasn't concealing anything in any orifice. They then said: "the baths run" and handed me a burgundy tracksuit. I was so young; I just saw them as teachers. They did have a good sense of humour but were scary. I was just a kid; I needed my sisters. 8 months, 8 months, that's all that I could think about. I didn't know where I was, no familiar surroundings, no sisters, no drugs, no shoplifting. I couldn't see my

nephew, nobody was there; I was so alone. The reality hit. I started shaking. I heard another voice. "Lizzy, Lizzy, is that you?" It was my sister's friend. She had been a heroin addict for years, since the 80s, nearly as long as I had been on this earth. She was gentle but always drawn in with the crowd. Now, years on, she had a big smile, but addiction had taken her top teeth. Addiction had stripped her of everything she had. Her Mum had died, and I felt so much empathy for her. There was no one to protect her when she was younger. She had faith, and she wore plastic rosary beads around her neck.

"I looked down at the track marks on my arms. I was freezing cold and withdrawing. The adrenaline in my body was rising, and I was anxious and frightened. I looked through the window and hoped to see a familiar face. She shouted, "Try to get in with me." I was 17 years old, and the officers were pretty understanding. My pageboy haircut, bonny round face, just a baby. I managed to get a cell with my friend. They handed me a green bed roll and I followed them. We went through locked gates, and the neon lights reflected off the buffed blue floor. We went to the wing; they took my cell card denoting my religion. I had a red card which meant I was Roman Catholic. I was ushered into the cell, and, to my relief, there she was my friend. A big smiling face,

someone familiar, I was so relieved. We caught up for the next two hours. She asked. "What was happening on the road?" The road, the outside world, our little broken world. We got our heads down; it was going to be a long night. I was withdrawing from heroin. I had told the reception nurse that I was on a methadone programme. This was a lie; I had heard that you should say this when you get in. I would need it, but this wasn't true. I wasn't on a programme, but I didn't care. The nurse told me I would get Methadone the day after. I held out for that methadone.

"The glaring lights woke me at 5 am. My friend started to fold her bed pack. I was really fed up watching her go through the routine of getting up and sweeping the floor. I was crushed and desperate. A call went out for medication, 'Yes', I couldn't wait, but I had to wait because I was on controlled meds. These were given out separately for safety reasons. I paced the floor with thoughts of how stupid I had been and how I was a useless grafter (meaning thief). I always get caught. No one will come and see you, no one cares, and you are unlovable and worthless. For the next 48 hours, I was stuck with revolving thoughts about what had happened.

"I was so excited about my fix that I felt my mood shift. A male officer opened my door and escorted us to the hospital wing. The two of us were being escorted by the officer. As we walked my friend told me the prison gossip. She told me about a woman who had murdered someone. I wasn't really listening; I couldn't give a shit; I was just fixed on getting my fix. They called my name, handed me the liquid in a small paper pot, and swigged it down quickly just in case they changed their minds. I had never used Methadone, so I didn't know how it would affect me. Down it went in a split second. Boom, I was back in the game!

"By noon the methadone had taken full effect. I was sitting in afternoon association, (time out of the cell), and I was gouching (partial loss of consciousness, nodding out), my head off. I reckon I was close to an overdose. She was nudging me. "Liz, Liz, wake up and go back to the cell." I took her advice and blearily made my way back to the cell. I slept and slept, which suited me. I just wanted to be out of it and away from reality.

"I prayed that God would help me. Would God help me? I wasn't sure. I wanted to know what He thought about me. Did He have empathy? Did He really love sinners?

"Four days later, I was found out. I had lied about Methadone. But they had given it to me on my word, nobody checked, and for a few days, I got away with it. They told me I could have overdosed or worse as the dose was way too high and dangerous. I did kick off; I was angry and withdrawing, now from Methadone. I was hauled in front of the Governor. I lost seven days' association. The same officers who had booked me were now sitting with me in the office. Back in survival mode, all those feelings of anxiety and fear swamped me. I had flipped a table, and officers had come running. Alarms were raised, and I was twisted up and taken to Segregation. I was strip-searched, all my clothes taken off me, and all I had was a blanket. Naked, with no human contact, at that moment, I would have chosen to die if I had the option. People talk about humiliation. After two days, I was oppressed and violated. I examined myself. Was there another way to get by? I realised I would have to behave differently to survive. I had to pull out my cheeky, funny self to get on the good side of the screws.

"After a week, I was shipped out to Styal Prison. The same bus, the same feelings, the same routine. I was rejected, even by a prison! I thought it was because of my behaviour. I hadn't realised at this point that this was

the process for sentenced prisoners, and I was one of them. No one explained; I just thought I was a troublesome prisoner needing to be controlled.

"When I arrived at Styal, I was taken to a Young Offender's House called Bronte. I presume it was named after Charlotte Bronte! Can't imagine why, she was a good girl! It was a hormone-fuelled house with 20 wild teenage girls running about. They were all broken. They were the product of broken and dysfunctional families, just like me. The girls had eating disorders, self-harmed, and had terrible mental ill health. The girls were medicated to keep them calm; they were drugged up with a plaster slapped on the deep invisible wounds they had. Some of the girls formed intimate relationships with each other, it was the only way to cope. I doubt the medical teams knew any of our real issues. We used to tell healthcare what we thought they wanted to hear; we were manipulative in the hope of getting a decent drug like Zopiclone. This drug just knocked you out and helped with the ordeal.

"So, there we were all broken, but somehow, we managed to help each other in the best way we knew how. Bullying was rife; I don't think we knew it was bullying. It was just sad and frightening. I would feel for

some of the girls as they were in a worse place than me. I would hug some of my fellow child prisoners and care for them.

"I had a plan and had recognised my previous behaviour had been fruitless. My soul was hurt, and I had lashed out. I hadn't responded to the want of my soul; I had just reacted in fear. I had a broken heart, but I hid my pain so deeply. I had a heart, but I didn't like myself. How can anyone with a heart behave in the way I had? I was full of self-hatred. My life carried on like this for 17 years, and for 17 years more. I became sadder, and the pain made me angry. I was angry at everyone and at the world. How can any of us get better in this system? I just didn't have the strength or the tools to change. I was stuck.

"I was born with a broken heart; I was born into dysfunction. I was the youngest of eight children from a travelling family. There was a 17-year gap between me and the first child, my brother. My brother worked with our stepdad on scrap metal. He later got a really good job out of the family business. He was kind and had a deep sense of family loyalty. My stepdad was brutally murdered one New Year's Eve, and our Mum, the Queen, was left alone. She did her very best to take care of us.

Wagtail

My Mum was beautiful, everyone loved her. We were highly protective of her, and we would have killed anyone who spoke negatively about her. I don't say 'killed' lightly, but it certainly felt like that.

"We loved our mum; she was a warm, empathetic soul, but she was troubled. All the local gangsters loved and respected her. But she was drawn into trouble. She would never 'grass' on anyone. The police used to enquire about criminal activity on the estate, but she never uttered a word. She was a bit like Robin Hood's wife, loyal, loving and caring, but it came with a price. We all learned from a very young age to be loyal to each other. My brother was very protective of his sisters, shouting at them for going out in short skirts. There was, in all this madness, a need for dignity for the girls and self-respect. One bit of bother and our brother was there, protecting us. This became a curse for him; he was well-known and respected, but people feared him. He could never step away from a situation, he couldn't work out his emotions, and he stayed the same. Our Catholic upbringing taught us a lot, but God's name was said with an overtone of fear and punishment. We interpreted 'love' as taking care of and being there for one another whatever the cost.

"As time passed, my three sisters and I became deeply entrenched in addiction. I thought love was providing us with drugs. I provided drugs when they were withdrawing, I thought I was helping. It upset me to watch them withdraw without their drugs. I would literally run out and steal a rack of clothes from Woolworths to save them. I was in survival mode for years, and it was exhausting. I was so sad but buried my feelings. Why would anyone cry for me? I was ashamed and just told myself I was unworthy and rubbish. I was rescuing and fixing everyone else but myself. I never imagined I would end up as the estate "Scagg" (heroin addict).

"I hadn't realised after taking heroin for the first time I would still be using it years after. The first experience was terrifying; I turned blue and sat in a derelict house; it was terrifying but not enough to stop me. I was 'panged' and scared of dying. I prayed to God to stop me, but He didn't help. Every part of my life was dysfunctional. Addiction had us all; how could any of us ever get out and see the light? No one helped me; no one talked to me or listened. Sadness, depression, and loneliness were my only values. I was never taught a different way to deal with my feelings and how to change my life.

Wagtail

"My family used to say we were like this because we were travellers. Of course, this is all we knew, and some of us loved it. We ran wild, finding ways to make money. Our father appreciated early learning skills, surviving, and contributing; it made us feel proud. Rightly or wrongly, the more you achieved, the more you were respected. The harder you were, the tougher you were, the more you were feared. Eventually we moved into a council house in York, and settling in was hard. Life was still chaotic and unnerving; we fought to survive. I am sure there were many angelic interventions at this time; we got into so many scrapes. We continued with our lifestyle of providing and pleasing, unaware and dismissive of authority. We tried to please no matter what that entailed; we just weren't our authentic selves, whatever that was supposed to be. We were lost souls, and we took addiction to another level.

"After years and years, I was beaten by life and addiction. I was giving up. Time and time again, I considered ending it all. Eventually, I agreed to go into rehab. It was the scariest experience I had ever had. More frightening than prison and living a chaotic life with no boundaries. No more selling drugs, no more chaos, I was safe but so very alone.

"I still can't believe I stuck with rehab. It was so difficult and painful. Eventually, extensive therapy and the 12-step programme turned my hectic life around. I started going to church and became a Christian. I can now love unconditionally; a church community supports me. My friendships are healthier, and I am growing every day. I love boundaries and protecting myself. I have learned to love myself. I don't need to fight and defend myself; I know I am loved. I have learned that I deserve forgiveness and that I can forgive others.

"I now work in drug and alcohol rehabilitation. I understand, and I can support other men and women who are going through the same emotional struggles as I had and sometimes still do. It's a long journey, but I am on the train.

"I am innately loyal; I love my family so much, but now with healthy boundaries. I had to look after myself until maybe I was strong enough to help them. I am far from perfect, but I now know I don't need to be."

Thank you for reading Lizzie's story; it hasn't been easy for her to write this for you. She is an incredible woman, and she gives me hope.

She is my friend.

Wagtail

Chapter 26
"Go free, little Wagtail"
"Our soul has escaped as a bird from the snare of the fowlers. The snare has broken, and we have escaped."
Psalm 124:7 King James Bible

In a place so grey and dreary, the little wagtails were a welcome sight. They gave us all a ray of hope, and of all the places they could explore and visit, they chose this one.

They visited throughout the seasons; sometimes, they were absent for months, and then they would return. These delicate little birds would swoop and fly down Main Street, flying in straight lines from one end of the corridor to the other. The Wagtail Olympics made us all smile. They were noisy, tweeting over one another to be heard.

When they weren't darting and dashing, we could watch them take off and land with precision on an evergreen that grew behind a steel fence on Main Street. I don't know if it was planted there when the prison was built or whether the roots had broken through the concrete. Its roots were deep, they had to be in this arid ground. It was sheltered in this little corner, and it survived the elements. Although its colour was rich and succulent and it looked inviting for the birds, the leaves were deadly. They were like thick Holly leaves, curled up ridges with a lethal pointy spike at the end of each leaf. The little tree had lots of tiny bugs living on the leaves. It provided food and shelter, and along with the hilarious activity of the little darting wagtails, it was always a pleasant spectacle.

If we clapped our hands when we walked past there would be an almighty gush and flurry as the birds took off and landed precariously on the curled barbed wire above the walls. They landed delicately between each spike. It was a wonderful site. At dusk, they would settle down; the odd one sat and kept watch on the turrets of the prison while the rest of the wagtails settled for the night. They slept when the men slept, they woke early in the morning and were sometimes an irritating alarm.

One day, it must have been early spring or winter because I remember my accomplice and rescue officer was wearing a blue prison-issue woollen hat. The morning activities were coming to an end. Movement had started, and the prisoners escorted by officers were returning to their wings for a head count before lunch. I was on my way back to the Chaplaincy office. Walking down the steel-fenced corridor and noticing lots of commotion and shouting, I walked toward a group of prisoners and an officer. They were all gathered around the evergreen enclosure. I couldn't really see what was going on. I presumed or thought there must be a parcel coming over, or they were shouting at someone in healthcare. The officer they were with smiled at me and rolled his eyes. I stood on my toes to peer over a shoulder. This was the reason for all the commotion. One of our tiny wagtail friends was caught and hanging upside down, its tiny body suspended in mid-air. It had somehow picked up a length of fine cotton which was tangled around his match-thin legs. Every few minutes, it would wriggle and shake, trying to break free. The other end of the string was wrapped around a branch. The prisoners were frantic and shouting at the officer to do something.

Now, imagine a dozen prisoners, tough, hench guys all shouting for help; it was quite distressing. The officer managed to move them on but as they did, they all shouted to me. "Miss, Miss, please free the bird. Miss, get in there and let it go, please Miss, please!"

I stood on my own, cold, with my clipboard in one hand, cardigan pulled around tight and a bag of Bibles in the other. The corridor emptied as the prisoners returned to the wings. I had no idea how I was going to do this. The friendly officer stayed with me, woolly hat, eyes down. "Hiya," I said, "You couldn't just give me a hand, could you?" His eyes darted about and then he looked at me. "Er, yes, ok, what is it, Miss?" We looked together at the hanging little bird. "I need to get in there!" I explained my plan. "Not really supposed to open this gate, Miss." I couldn't imagine why; it didn't go anywhere. There was just a tiny triangle of earth, an evergreen tree that was surrounded by steel. There was a narrow channel down the side of the Healthcare wing. The access was lined with rat traps and window detritus. I needed my accomplice; my keys didn't open this gate.

Time was running out, my little friend was flapping about and getting weaker. I placed my clipboard and bag of New Testaments on the floor. "Right then but hurry up." He opened the steel gate, I crept up to the leafy, scratchy tree. I pushed the larger branches away with my elbows and, at the same time, managed to cradle the little bird in my hand. I sheltered its little eyes, its long tail just fitting through the gap in my clenched hand. It was so very delicate; it weighed no more than an eggshell. I lifted it from its noose and held it for a moment to expose the dirty thread.

Now, obviously, I had nothing sharp on my person. I tried to cut through the string using my keys, but nothing worked. I asked the officer if he had anything I could use. He wasn't willing to get involved in this part of the mission. I tried to unravel the string from the branch and tried to snap the stem. The leaves scratched my hands, and my little friend was weary. I cradled its delicate face, its tiny legs dangling from the bottom of my cupped hand and did the only thing I could. I used my teeth and bit at the hanging thread. The officer must have thought I was absolutely nuts. It was lock up, the corridor was empty, and here we were, rescuing a tiny bird.

Wagtail

I gnawed a bit more, spitting out bits of the thread as it came away from the wagtail's claw. Eventually, the strand broke away from the tree, and I unravelled it from the bird's leg. I took a little look at its face, checked it over for injuries then lifted my hands high and let it go. The other wagtails watched on. They had retreated up high, some sat on the wire fence, some on the roof. They watched as their little friend was released back to them. At that moment the little bird was at my mercy. I opened my scratched hands; I let it go, and it flew back to its friends.

Every time I walked past the bush, I used to say, "Are you there, little friend?" I never heard an answer. I delivered the good news when the prisoners returned on their way back to work. They cheered and were delighted that today, this little soul had been rescued, had made it through its traumatic ordeal, and was free. The officer did a quick dart, hoping we hadn't been seen on the security cameras. I returned to the chapel office, and we carried on with our day, happy despite the odds, that our little wagtail had survived.

Chapter 27
The Final Chapter

Thank you for reading this book and for coming with me on this journey through the prison gates. I expected to be working for many years in prison, and I didn't really want to leave but personal circumstances dictated my future.

I am a "super empath". This means I carry others' pain; I feel their sorrow. I listened and, for hours, I tried to work out in my mind and imagine what life must have been like for many of the prisoners I worked with. It was difficult for me to forget. When I got back home after an 11-hour shift, I was exhausted. I couldn't speak and just wanted to sit alone to reflect. I rarely spoke about the day's events. I found solace in Netflix dramas to escape. Small talk became painfully boring, leaving me feeling like a social cul-de-sac.

I suppose I am writing this by way of contrition. I am so sorry I left the prison. I am sorry I left the team, the staff, and the prisoners. I am sorry I couldn't stay but I was exhausted and frustrated and going through a difficult time myself. It was time for me to move on. COVID 19 brought so many more challenges.

Wagtail

Sometimes, it felt so exasperating working in the prison. We were accustomed to limitations and restrictions, but this was in another league. When I told one of my officer colleagues that I was leaving, he was disappointed. However, he said he understood, "Your wings are clipped here." I think he got it.

When I told a senior staff member, I was abandoning ship, she said, "You can't leave; the men need people like you!" It wasn't me they needed; it was a mighty miracle. There are so many people who really care still working at the prison, but the prisoners need so much more. They need a dramatic change in the prison system, and some compassionate justice. They need the love of non-existent or distant families; they need healing; they need to know that they are precious and loved.

One day, while browsing the internet, a job popped up that combined my skills as a nurse and chaplain. The salary as a chaplain was meagre and this new opportunity would be a welcome provision when my home situation changed. I didn't think I would get the job, but I did. Within a week of the interview, I sat with my boss. He knew what I was going to say.

My lovely, gracious boss was sad, but he understood. The amazing Chaplaincy team was supportive of my decision to leave. After a lovely leaving lunch, gifts, and many words of encouragement from other staff members, I was ready to go. My boss told me to go home early, but I didn't really want to! I felt soft, invisible hands on my shoulders guiding me out of the Chaplaincy doors.

I took my final walk down Main Street. As I walked past the evergreen bush, home of the Wagtail, I clapped my hands one last time. I expected to see them flurry but they didn't. They had left the prison for a season and so had I.

Wagtail

Biblical References

1. **E21617414**
   E3:16,17,4:14,

   Ecclesiastes
   3:16: Moreover, I saw under the sun that in place of justice, wickedness was there, and in the place of righteousness wickedness was there as well.

   3:17: God will judge the righteous and the wicked, for he has appointed a time for every matter, and for every work.

   4:14: One can indeed come out of prison to reign, even though born poor in the kingdom.

2. **P1412131513**
   P14:12-13,15:13

   Proverbs
   14:12-13: There is a way that seems right to a person, but its end is the way to death. Even in laughter the heart is sad, and the end of joy is grief.

   15:13: A glad heart makes a cheerful countenance, but by sorrow of heart the spirit is broken.

3. **P18381421**
P18:3,8,14,21

Proverbs

18:3: When wickedness comes, contempt comes also; and with dishonour comes disgrace.

18:8: The words of a whisperer are like delicious morsels; they go down to the inner parts of the body.

18:14: The human spirit will endure sickness, but a broken spirit, who can bear?

18:21: Death and life are in the power of the tongue, and those who love it will eat its fruits.

4. **P147234**
P147:2,3,4

Psalm

147:2-3: He gathers the outcasts of Israel. He heals the broken hearted and binds up their wounds.

147:4: He counts the number of the stars; he gives to all of them their names.

Bibliography

Anglicised NRSV

The Holy Bible; New King James Version

The Power of Restorative Justice. Restored and forgiven: *Ray & Vi Donovan 2018*

The Book of Forgiving: *Desmond & MPHO Tutu. 2014*

Light through Prison Bars: *Jenny Cooke. 1995*

The Big Book of Restorative Justice: *Howard Zehr et al. 2015*

Glimpses of Grace: *Donald Stoesz. 2010*

Father and Son. The Wound, The Healing, The Call to Manhood: *Gordon Dalbey. 1992*

Christianity Rediscovered: *Vincent J Donovan. 1978*

The Prison Doctor: *Dr Amanda Brown. 2019*

Exploring Forgiveness: *Robert. D. Enright & Joanna North. 1998*

Working with Released Prisoners: *Stephen Dailly. 2019*

Long Walk to Freedom: *Nelson Mandela. 1994*

The Secret Prison Governor: *Anonymous. 2022*

A Bit of a Stretch. *Chris Atkins. 2020*

Prison. A Survival Guide: *Carl Cattermole. 2019*

Criminal: *Angela Kirwin. 2022*

Man's Search for Meaning: *Viktor E. Frankl. 1946*

Foundations: The Biblical Foundations of Prison Ministry. *Course offered by The Christian Leaders Institute. 1996*

Voices Unheard. A Study of Irish Travellers in Prison: *The Irish Chaplaincy in Britain. 2011*

Bromley Briefings Prison Fact file: *The Prison Reform Trust. 2024*

Invisible Bars: *Phoebe Willetts. 1965*

Useful Organisations

The Hope Foundation. Anfield, Liverpool
www.the-hope-foundation.co.uk

The Message Trust, Manchester
www.message.org.uk

The Prison Reform Trust
www.prisonreformtrust.org.uk

The Samaritans
www.samaritans.org

Action for Prisoners' and Offenders' Families
www.facebook.com/ActionPrisonersFamilies/

NACRO (A Social Justice charity)
www.nacro.org.uk

Out There: Supporting Families of Prisoners
www.outtherecharity.org

Back on Track
www.backontrackmanchester.org.uk

Street Support Network
www.streetsupport.net

Victim Support
www.victimsupport.org.uk

The Survivors Trust for Victims of Sexual Crime
www.thesurvivorstrust.org

Prison Advice and Care Trust
www.prisonadvice.org.uk

Christians against Poverty (CAP)
www.capuk.org

Acknowledgements

It is impossible here to mention everyone I am thankful for here. I have met many an inspirational person in my 60+ years on this planet.

I must start with my dear parents who gave me the gift of life and who nurtured me to be patient and kind, and to find excitement and interest in many aspects of life. My creativity and humour were inherited from mum, and my patience and kindness from dad. I miss them both.

For my sisters, Jane and Liz, and my brothers-in-law, Martin and Brian, who have always made sure I had a place to stay and access to a fridge full of food. They have accepted me and loved me through many a difficult time and, for that, I love them dearly. My nieces and nephews Ella, Jake and Huey, Molly, Emily and Katie who always make me laugh and give me hope as I watch them develop into wonderful human beings who are bright and compassionate and will all make a difference in this world.

For my amazing son, Joshua, who has grown into a beautiful man with a strong and determined nature, and a loving and empathetic spirit. Now, as a teacher, he is walking alongside young people to make a difference by sharing his knowledge of the Spanish language but, more importantly, his life experiences. He has been my greatest critic, always with love. I am so proud of him I could burst.

For all the teachers and tutors who put up with me always having the last word; for the staff at the prison I worked in, especially my manager who said I was unpredictable, but he knew that, and I quote, "All would be well when he wasn't there and I was holding the fort!"

For my church leaders, especially Andy and Ruth, and for my Christian family who love me with Agape and unconditional love.

For Christine, Brian, Steph and family - you really are quite amazing and thank you for allowing me to share Michael's story.

For my dear golden friends. We have travelled together, laughed together, cried together and, for that, I love you all. For Fiona, Mary, Karen, Julie, Dianne, Sue, Lisa, Louise, Angela, Lindsey, Martin, Helen, Jane - my Kibbutznik and Jane - my partner in crime - you have been rocks. We don't live in each other's pockets but you ground me and give me loving security and wisdom. For my nursing colleagues, and for new and old work friends - it is a privilege to have worked alongside some amazing people.

For my dear friend, Barbara J - my mum always said you would be a strength to me when she was gone, and you have been. For the Parkhurst family - for inviting me to be part of their family when my parents died.

For Charlie dog, who has been my faithful companion for 12.5 years and sat at my feet when I wrote this book. I miss you.

For The Soho Agency, especially Marc and Niamh who kick started this journey and gave me support in the beginning. For Julie Davies for encouraging me to write this book and giving me pointers.

For June Russell-Alexander, my Editor and Publisher. Thank you for having the patience and the insight to recognise how I work and for being such a fabulous editor on this, my first endeavour.

For Donna Laverty of Donna Laverty Design for my wonderful book cover and wagtail illustration; and for

Markus Marshall and his marketing team at Rane Digital; thank you for your patience in waiting for me to respond to emails!

For all the men and women that I worked with in the prison and for those who volunteer - this book is for you to hopefully make a difference to those going through similar situations. Thank you to the men I worked with - you inspired me and gave me hope in the darkest of times.

The biggest and most important shout out is to My Lord and Saviour, The Author and perfector of my faith who has held me, comforted me, been down in the valleys and up on the mountains with me. He who in His word writes:

"The Spirit of the Lord is on me, because he has anointed me to proclaim good news to the poor. He has sent me to proclaim freedom for the prisoners and recovery of sight to the blind, to set the oppressed free." Luke 4:18 NIV

About the Author

Since leaving her job as Prison Chaplain, Annie has worked for the NHS. Her first post was as a Hospital Chaplain Manager across Greater Manchester Hospitals.

She currently works for a Manchester Mental Health Trust as a Spiritual Health Care Chaplain.

Her passion and calling is to work with and walk with people who are often very unwell.

She still has a hope that the prison system will change for the better and that we will recognise that building yet more institutions will not change this ongoing crisis.

Printed in Great Britain
by Amazon